INTERPRETIVE APPROACHES
TO INTERPERSONAL COMMUNICATION

SUNY Series, Human Communication Processes
Donald P. Cushman and Ted J. Smith, III, editors

Interpretive Approaches to Interpersonal Communication

Edited by

Kathryn Carter
and
Mick Presnell

State University of New York Press

Published by
State University of New York Press, Albany

©1994 State University of New York

For information, address State University of New York Press,
State University Plaza, Albany, N.Y., 12246

Production by Marilyn P. Semerad
Marketing by Fran Keneston

Library of Congress Cataloging-in-Publication Data

Interpretative approaches to interpersonal communication / edited by
    Kathryn Carter and Mick Presnell.
        p.   cm. — (SUNY series, human communication processes)
    Includes bibliographical references and index.
    ISBN 0-7914-1847-2 (alk. paper). — ISBN 0-7914-1848-0 (pbk. :
alk. paper)
    1. Interpersonal communication.   I. Carter, Kathryn, 1954–   .
II. Presnell, Mick, 1950–   .   III. Series: SUNY series in human
communication processes.
BF637.N66I68   1994
153.6—dc20   93-7710
                                                                 CIP

10 9 8 7 6 5 4 3 2 1

NWST
1 AFL4795

Contents

Introduction

MICK PRESNELL AND KATHRYN CARTER

INTERPRETIVE APPROACHES TO RESEARCH are not new to the field of human communication studies. The study of rhetoric in the United States, dating from its beginnings in the first decade of this century, can be considered a rich history of one kind of interpretive scholarship. However, two recent developments indicate that a new direction of interpretive research in communication studies is underway. First, interpretive research is increasingly being articulated as a third perspective that links the humanities and social sciences, rather than identifying itself as a humanist opposition to scientific investigation. The field of communication experienced lively debates between the so-called Cornell and Midwest schools of speech in the discipline's formative years, representing, respectively, humanistic and scientific approaches to speech (Leff & Procario, 1985, pp. 8–12). The themes of these debates were revisited during the 1970s and early 1980s, a period of intense reflection on the basic theories and paradigms vying for dominance of the field.

No such hegemonic influence emerged. The late 1980s and early 1990s present us with a plurality of approaches to communication, and scholars debate over the advisability of even searching for a unifying perspective. Generally, the focus has shifted to exploring possible links between research interests rather than searching for a universal theoretical model or paradigm. Contemporary interpretive research represents a shift from its early identification with humanistic approaches to an acceptance of methodological and theoretical pluralism. It emphasizes a broader understanding of research as discourse, that is, research as a coordinated process of socially constructed meaning.

A second development that indicates a new direction is the expansion of interpretive research beyond the discipline of rhetoric to include many areas of communication studies, including mass communication, organizational communication, and most important for this volume, interpersonal communication. Many contemporary fields of study are experiencing what has been called an "interpretive turn" in their scholarship (Hiley, Bohman, & Shusterman, 1991). Interpretive approaches are being developed by philosophers, sociologists, anthropologists, and critics and theorists of the arts, as well as communication researchers.

Bochner (1985) describes three general approaches to interpersonal communication and categorizes research according to general goals rather than methods. According to Bochner, social scientific approaches seek to predict and control, critical perspectives seek to change social conditions, and interpretive approaches seek to enrich understanding. Each paradigm may require different methods or a combination of methods to meet its research goals. Thus, the qualitative and quantitative distinction of years past no longer serves to effectively describe the categories of possibilities for research design. Methods are no longer automatically associated with a single paradigm, and a variety of paradigms inhabit the field of communication studies, differentiated more by goals than by strategies of data collection. The interpretive paradigm can link the social scientific and critical paradigms, if understanding communication events and relationships is held to be prior to the prediction, control, or change of communication. Whether our understanding is implicit or explicit, we begin with an understanding of communication and then attempt to build causal models, develop strategies for uncovering ideologies, or promote the interests of oppressed groups. Interpretive research seeks to explore this prior understanding, and may employ a variety of methods to do so.

Even though interpretive research may be thought of as a means of investigating the discursive underpinnings of all research strategies and paradigms, it does not follow that the goals of interpretive research must be accomplished before other research goals can be fruitfully pursued. In fact, most interpretive researchers argue that understanding is an incommensurable process, although we are capable of distinguishing between more or less adequate interpretations. Thus, interpretive research is not reducible to either scientific or humanistic research, but constitutes a distinct problematic (a context that frames what questions are asked and what problems are considered pertinent).[1]

FROM RHETORIC THROUGH SCIENCE TO INTERPRETATION

The study of interpersonal communication has a diverse history regarding its content, methods, and theories. Interpersonal communication first became the theme of investigation for the communication discipline in the 1930s. The General Semantics of Alfred Korzybski promoted the therapeutic benefits of changing everyday language to reflect the dynamic and noncategorical nature of reality asserted by the new physics. Business schools were exploring gains in productivity that improvements in human relations could bring (Rawlins, 1985, p. 109). These research efforts shifted investigation of communication from public speaking grounded in rhetoric to the study of face-to-face interactions grounded in the social sciences.[2]

Inquiry into ordinary or everyday conversation began to blossom during the early 1950s. Elwood Murray coined the term *interpersonal communication* in 1953 (Pearce & Foss, 1986, p. 11). According to Murray, "speech should serve as a social integrator; as the tools which enable attention to be obtained, comprehending and understanding to result, [and] experience to be shared . . ." (quoted in Rawlins, 1985, p. 113). Interpersonal communication, according to Rawlins, was seen as a way to support the social order: "health was the stamp of the able communicator . . . but it was a normative, social conception" (p. 114).

During the 1960s scholars in interpersonal communication began to suggest that "good" communication involved something other than adaptation to social goals; instead interpersonal communication should be seen as the path to self-actualization. Pearce and Foss (1986) label this period of interpersonal communication scholarship, "humanistic celebration," stating that the goals of communication were to "improve human existence by reducing the effects of alienation, low self-esteem, competition, and manipulation" (p. 14).

During the late 1960s and early 1970s interpersonal communication shifted its focus again. Humanistic approaches were viewed by some communication scholars as too subjective and individualistic. Therefore, communication scholars began to investigate relational communication, grounding their inquiries within the pragmatic approach inspired by Gregory Bateson and a group of psychotherapists and family therapists known as the Palo Alto Group. This version of a pragmatic approach in interpersonal communication research relied heavily on systems theory and traditional social science methodologies. Social science approaches were evoked as a supposed cure for subjectivist approaches. Interpersonal communication research became dominated by social science methodologies, although interpersonal textbooks continued to reflect a humanist emphasis on experience, the self, alienation, and personal growth.

In 1975, during the Speech Communication Association Convention, the discipline engaged in the "great metatheoretical debate" (Pearce & Foss, 1986, p. 15) and began to discuss and critically evaluate research done within the discipline. Many communication scholars began to question the feasibility of using physical science methodologies to analyze human behavior. Scholars representing the humanistic tradition continued to draw distinctions between persons and objects and maintained the presence of fundamental differences between the two (Stewart, 1973). Humanists argued that human agents, unlike physical matter, are volitional, reflective, choice-making beings. The result of the paradigm debates of the 1960s and 1970s is a deeply entrenched pluralism of research approaches across the various content areas of communication studies. Some areas of study, like interpersonal communication, remained more methodologically homogenous than others. In the late 1980s and early 1990s scholars are looking for ways to integrate research findings and interests while generally accepting that the various paradigms each have something to offer.

Although humanist theorizing was becoming more sophisticated and increasing its impact on communication research in general, interpersonal communication research was less influenced by these developments than other areas of communication studies. One reason for this may be the association of humanist research with some of its more superficial applications during the 1960s and early 1970s. Interpersonal communication textbooks continued to use some of the exercises and rhetoric of humanist psychology. These techniques and views enliven the classroom experience but tend to reinforce the stereotype of humanist approaches as "touchy-feely," reflecting the worst examples of subjectivism and impressionism that social scientists sought to counter. However, the continued development of humanist research not only became more subtle and articulate in its own right, but eventually was able to contribute to the emerging interpretive paradigm.

The main source of inspiration for humanist and interpretive research in their continued development has been continental European philosophy. The impact of phenomenology, structuralism, semiotics, existentialism, hermeneutics, and deconstruction has been felt in a wide range of disciplines in the United States, including departments of communication and rhetoric. As the individualistic emphasis of existentialism waned in its influence after being introduced in the 1950s and 1960s, attention turned to philosophies that addressed the language and social underpinnings of experience. Subjectivist versions of phenomenology gave way to a focus on intersubjectivity, glorification of impressionistic interpretations were abandoned in favor of textual hermeneutics, and the phrase "meaning is in people, not in words" was rejected by structuralists, semioticians, and other social constructionists that saw the link between person and community as much more complex. Poststructuralists examined the nature of language and discourse, exposing theoretical contradictions and ironies in traditional conceptions of human communication.

Early contributors to the introduction of European approaches to the communication research community include Richard L. Lanigan (1979, 1982, 1988), John Stewart (1978, 1983), Joseph J. Pilotta (1982), Stanley A. Deetz (1973, 1977, 1978, 1992), Stanley Deetz and A. Kersten (1983), Leonard Hawes (1977, 1978), Michael Hyde (1980), and Michael Hyde and C. R. Smith (1979). Joint teaching efforts with philosophy programs have drawn communication and philosophy together in their exploration of language and discourse. Algis Mickunas at Ohio University and Calvin Schrag at Purdue are two philosophers who have had a particularly significant influence on the importation of these continental influences (Mickunas, 1982; Pilotta & Mickunas, 1990; Schrag, 1985). Some communication scholars have pursued postdoctorate education in philosophy or completed second Ph.D.s in philosophy, such an Lanigan, Pilotta, and the influential teacher and long-time director of graduate studies at Southern Illinois University, Carbondale, Thomas Pace. The philosopher Richard Rorty, a contemporary pragmatist, has contributed to the development of the rhetoric of inquiry, a project that has inspired many conference papers, articles, and several books regarding the rhetorical construction of knowledge (Nelson & Megill, 1986; Nelson, Megill, & McCloskey, 1987; Simons, 1989). *Recovering Pragmatism's Voice* takes up issues of contemporary pragmatic philosophy and their relation to communication (Smith & Langsdorf, in press). The collection of essays by communication scholars appearing in *Rhetoric and Philosophy* presents a range of philosophical perspectives that have influenced communication research (Cherwitz, 1990). The Foreword is by Henry W. Johnstone, founding editor of the journal *Philosophy and Rhetoric*, which began publication in 1968. The International Communication Association's Philosophy of Communication Division also supplies an outlet for interpretive scholarship. A recent publication, *The Critical Turn: Rhetoric and Philosophy in Postmodern Discourse*, is a collection of essays by some of the more influential interpretive researchers in communication studies (Angus & Langsdorf, 1993).

One major contributor to contemporary interpretive research that is predominantly indigenous to the United States is feminism (see, for example, Bowen & Wyatt, 1993; Foss & Foss, 1983; Carter & Spitzack, 1989). Although American feminists often rely upon various continental philosophies, women writers in the United States are the major source of feminist thought. Feminism contributes an appreciation of diversity, everyday examples of how meaning and perception are deeply shaped by social and cultural processes, and the vision of how enriched understanding can empower those who are excluded from mainstream discourses.

Another influence on interpretive approaches to other areas of communication that is beginning to be felt in the study of interpersonal communication is ideology criticism. Ideology criticism developed out of neo-Marxist thought and now enjoys a sizable audience through its influence on rhetorical and cultural criticism (see, for example, Burleson & Kline, 1979; Grossberg, 1979; Wander, 1983). The recent work of John Lannamann (1991), which calls for an investigation of the ideological dimensions of interpersonal communication theory, indicates a relatively new direction for inquiry. It is ironic that just as the long-held feminist tenet of "the personal is political" is being questioned as itself potentially oppressive to women (see, for instance, Baker and Benton, Chapter 9 in this volume), the field of interpersonal communication is beginning to raise the question of the political dimensions of how we understand face-to-face interaction. It remains to be seen how this promising area of research unfolds.

The essays in this volume provide the reader with a range of approaches to interpersonal communication that exemplify "interpretive research." Not all perspectives that can be considered interpretive are found in this volume, but most of the major interpretive approaches to interpersonal communication are treated in some fashion in the following pages. These perspectives include phenomenology, semiotics, hermeneutics, postmodern ethnography, deconstruction, social interactionism, feminism, and existentialism. Many of the essays include reflections on the ideological implications of interpersonal theory or research.

A number of the following essays develop or explore definitions of what constitutes interpretive research and apply these to interpersonal communication research issues. Some essays provide important contributions to forming a definition of interpretive research. Others are more concerned with working out particular problems within this paradigm. The purpose of this volume is not to specify what interpretive research *should* be, but rather to explore the diversity and richness of what interpretive research *can* be.

NOTES

1. One of the unique characteristics of the interpretive paradigm is its ability to investigate the grounding of both its own and other paradigmatic assumptions. *Grounding* here means "sufficiently clarified regarding the discursive underpinnings of what is studied and why" rather than "definitively founded in a priori principles or empirical realities."

2. For critical evaluations of interpersonal communication research, see Bochner, 1984; Rawlins, 1985; Hewes, Roloff, Planalp, & Siebold, 1990; and Wood, 1993.

REFERENCES

Angus, I., & Langsdorf, L. (Eds.). (1993). *The critical turn: Rhetoric and philosophy in postmodern discourse.* Carbondale: Southern Illinois University Press.

Bochner, A. (1984). The function of human communication in interpersonal bonding. In C. Arnold & J. Bowers (Eds.), *Handbook of rhetorical and communication theory* (pp. 544–621). Boston: Allyn and Bacon.

Bochner, A. (1985). Perspectives on inquiry: Representation, conversations, and reflection. In M. L. Knapp & G. R. Miller (Eds.), *Handbook of interpersonal communication* (pp. 27–58). Beverly Hills, CA: Sage Publications.

Bowen, S., & Wyatt, N. (Eds.). (1993). *Transforming visions: Feminist critiques in communication studies.* Cresskill, NJ: Hampton Press.

Burleson, B. R., & Kline, S. L. (1979). Habermas' theory of communication: A critical explication. *Quarterly Journal of Speech, 65,* 412–428.

Carter, K., & Spitzack, C. (Eds.). (1989). *Doing research on women's communication: Perspectives on theory and method.* Norwood, NJ: Ablex Publishing Corporation.

Cherwitz, R. A. (Ed.). (1990). *Rhetoric and philosophy.* Hillsdale, NJ: Lawrence Erlbaum Associates.

Deetz, S. (1973). An understanding of science and a hermeneutic science of understanding. *The Journal of Communication, 23,* 139–159.

Deetz, S. (1977). Interpretive research in communication: A hermeneutic foundation. *Journal of Communication Inquiry, 3,* 53–68.

Deetz, S. (1978). Conceptualizing human understanding: Gadamer's hermeneutics and American communication studies. *Communication Quarterly, 26,* 12–23.

Deetz, S. A. (1992). *Democracy in an age of corporate colonization: Developments in communication and the politics of everyday life.* Albany: State University of New York Press.

Deetz, S., & Kersten, A. (1983). Critical models of interpretive research. In L. L. Putman & M. E. Pacanowsky (Eds.), *Communication and organizations: An interpretive approach* (pp. 147–146). Newbury Park, CA: Sage Publications.

Foss, K. A., & Foss, S. K. (1983). The status of research on women and communication. *Communication Quarterly, 31,* 195–204.

Grossberg, L. (1979). Marxist dialectics and rhetorical criticism. *Quarterly Journal of Speech, 65*(3), 235–249.

Hawes, L. C. (1977). Toward a hermeneutic phenomenology of communication. *Communication Quarterly, 25,* 30–41.

Hawes, L. C. (1978). Language-use and being: A rejoinder. *Communication Quarterly, 26,* 65–70.

Hewes, D. E., Roloff, M. E., Planalp, S., & Seibold, D. R. (1990). Interpersonal communication: What should we know? In G. M. Phillips & J. T. Wood (Eds.), *Speech communication: Essays to commemorate the 75th anniversary of the speech communication association* (pp. 130–180). Carbondale: Southern Illinois University Press.

Hiley, D. R., Bohman, J. F., & Shusterman, R. (Eds.). (1991). *The interpretive turn: Philosophy, science, culture.* Ithaca, NY: Cornell University Press.

Hyde, M. J. (1980). The experience of anxiety: A phenomenological investigation. *Quarterly Journal of Speech, 66*(2), 140–154.

Hyde, M. J., & Smith, C. R. (1979). Hermeneutics and rhetoric: A seen but unobserved relationship. *Quarterly Journal of Speech, 65*(4), 347–363.

Lanigan, R. L. (1979). Communication models in philosophy. In D. Nimmo (Ed.), *Communication Yearbook 3.* New Brunswick, NJ: International Communication Association and Transaction Books.

Lanigan, R. L. (1982). Semiotic phenomenology: A theory of human communication praxis. *Journal of Applied Communication Research, 10,* 62–73.

Lanigan, R. L. (1988). *Phenomenology of communication.* Pittsburgh: Duquesne University Press.

Lannamann, J. W. (1991). Interpersonal communication research as ideological practice. *Communication Theory, 1*(3), 179–203.

Leff, M. C., & Procario, M. O. (1985). Rhetorical theory in speech communication. In T. Benson (Ed.), *Speech Communication in the 20th century* (pp. 109–129). Carbondale: Southern Illinois University Press.

Mickunas, A. (1982). The dialogical region. In J. J. Pilotta (Ed.), *Interpersonal communication: Essays in phenomenology and hermeneutics* (pp. 55–68). Washington, DC: Center for Advanced Research in Phenomenology and University Press of America.

Nelson, J. S., & Megill, A. (1986). Rhetoric of inquiry: Projects and prospects. *Quarterly Journal of Speech, 72*(1), 20–37.

Nelson, J. S., Megill, A., & McCloskey, D. N. (Eds). (1987). *The rhetoric of the human sciences: Language and argument in scholarship and public affairs.* Madison: University of Wisconsin Press.

Pearce, W. B., & Foss, K. A. (1986, November). *The future of interpersonal communication*. Paper presented at the Speech Communication Association Convention, Chicago.

Pilotta, J. J. (Ed.). (1982). *Interpersonal communication: Essays in phenomenology and hermeneutics*. Washington, DC: Center for Advanced Research in Phenomenology and University Press of America.

Pilotta, J. J., & Mickunas, A. (1990). *Science of communication: Its phenomenological foundation*. Hillside, NJ: Lawrence Erlbaum Associates.

Rawlins, W. K. (1985). Stalking interpersonal communication effectiveness: Social, individual, or situational integration? In T. Benson (Ed.), *Speech Communication in the 20th century* (pp. 109–129). Carbondale: Southern Illinois University Press.

Schrag, C. O. (1985). Rhetoric resituated at the end of philosophy. *Quarterly Journal of Speech, 71,* 164–174.

Simons, H. W. (Ed.). (1989). *Rhetoric in the human sciences*. Newbury Park, NJ: Sage Publications.

Smith, A., & Langsdorf, L. (in press). *Recovering pragmatism's voice*. Albany: State University of New York Press.

Stewart, J. (Ed). (1973). *Bridges not walls: A book about interpersonal communication*. New York: Random House.

Stewart, J. (1978). Foundations of dialogic communication. *Quarterly Journal of Speech, 64*(2), 183–201.

Stewart, J. (1983). Interpretive listening: An alternative to empathy. *Communication Education, 32,* 379–391.

Wander, P. (1983). The ideological turn in modern criticism. *Central States Speech Journal, 34,* 1–18.

Watzlawick, P., Bavelas Beavin, J., & Jackson, D. (1967). *The pragmatics of human communication*. New York: W. W. Norton.

Wood, J. T. (1993). Enlarging conceptual boundaries: A critique of research in interpersonal communication. In S. Perlmutter Bowen & N. Wyatt (Eds.), *Transforming visions: Feminist critiques in communication studies* (pp. 19–49). Cresskill, NJ: Hampton Press.

1

Postmodern Ethnography: From Representing the Other to Co-Producing a Text

MICK PRESNELL

ETHNOGRAPHIC RESEARCH METHODS are catching the attention of an increasingly wider audience of communication scholars. Researchers of organizational communication, performance studies, and rhetoric, as well as interpersonal and intercultural communication are gaining a deeper appreciation of the potential usefulness of ethnographic methods. This surge of recent interest is in part the result of a postmodern turn in research; that is, the turn to research methods that seem especially suited to the contemporary age of electronic media, increasing ethnic diversity, pluralistic views of social norms and values, and a sense of the fragmentation of meaning into localized contexts. Anthropologists, sociologists, and communication researchers have re-examined the practice of ethnography in light of the contributions of poststructuralism, deconstruction, semiotics, hermeneutics, and cultural criticism. These influences are inspiring a shift from modernist ethnography guided by traditional research goals to postmodernist ethnography guided by interpretive research tools.

I argue that this shift can be understood as a shift from qualitative methods indebted to a traditional research paradigm to methods conducted within an interpretive research paradigm. I review the development of ethnography from its modernist to its postmodernist versions and argue that postmodern ethnography can make unique and important contributions to the contemporary study of interpersonal communication. I propose a threefold typology of ethnographic practice viewed from realist, romantic hermeneutic, and postmodern perspectives. Finally, I expand on four themes of postmodern ethnography introduced by Dwight Conquergood to provide a more general understanding of postmodern issues important for the interpretive study of interpersonal communication.

The motivation behind the process called *ethnography* is the attempt to understand and write about, in some systematic yet openhanded way, the mystery, frustration, and excitement of encountering others. In earlier days of the practice of ethnography, this meant encountering and writing about others who were not only strange to the investigator, but who had no written account of their own culture. Today, the challenging endeavor of ethnography has been made even more complicated. For instance, the "natives," whether us or members of another culture, may have read or written works that inform ethnographers and provide the researcher with background material before he or she goes into "the field."[1] Also ethnography as a form of writing has come under scrutiny for how the chosen genre and style interact with the knowledge conveyed, and how writing represents the relationship between investigator and investigated. A third complication for ethnographic researchers is the heightened awareness of the effects and significance of colonialism, gender, race, class, and how ideological differences informs much of contemporary social science. There is an intensified suspicion of the potential arrogance of supposedly "capturing" in representations the meaning, beauty, and everyday nuances of someone else's everyday life experiences.

The basic impetus for doing ethnography, however, has hardly abated and perhaps has gained a certain urgency. The increased cultural diversity of society, accentuated by the development of rapid transportation and communication, is a feature of everyday life in the 1990s. The average person increasingly finds himself or herself in the role of amateur ethnographer. This cultural condition of the United States is not unique nor is it universal or timeless. It is a feature of our contemporary society and the context within which the professional development and practice of ethnography takes place.

Since the 1960s, social sciences have tended to focus on how cultural context informs gestures, thoughts, and emotions of individuals and local interactions. Combined with the Western European emphasis on liberal individualism, privacy, and family, cultural diversity has turned social scientists' attention to the local, interaction level of cultural expression. The social sciences struggle with an ironic juxtaposition of two contemporary beliefs: (1) knowledge is shaped if not determined by social and cultural experience, and (2) local communicative performance is inventive and potentially transformative. Both of these beliefs hinge on the assumption that meaning and action are significantly dependent on context for their understanding. Unfortunately, some social scientists respond to the challenge of "context" by treating it as the boundary of analysis rather than its expansion. Consequently, many social scientists, including interpersonal communication researchers, attempt to limit the scope of their inquiry within perimeters that can be handled by variable analytic analysis. The appreciation of the formative role of context has led to reductive "microanalyses" of individuals and face-to-face interaction. In short, our concern for the constitutive significance of the context of the individual has often led to a narrowing of the scope of inquiry and a devaluing of the inventive uniqueness of persons. Postmodern ethnography in particular explores the tension between social constraint and individual creativity, partly by placing the researcher-researched relationship in a social and political context.

WHY ETHNOGRAPHY?

At first glance, ethnography as a research methodology might seem an unlikely candidate for use in interpersonal communication research. The question can be raised: Why would we expect that generalizations about cultures and societies will be directly relevant for understanding particular interactions within these normative contexts? Communication scholars typically treat different communication contexts as evidencing characteristics unique to that context. Small groups are treated as having unique characteristics that are not reducible to a collection of individuals or two-person interactions. Organizations are investigated as more than just a collection of small groups. Developed primarily by anthropologists, ethnographic research seems geared to explore social and cultural dimensions of human experience, using data collected in face-to-face situations, to form generalizations about cultural values, norms, and practices. What seems most interesting about interpersonal communication is not how interactions reveal cultural norms, but how some communicators form situationally appropriate relational patterns that modify, break, or invent norms and expectations.

Traditional research programs have struggled with these issues. According to Knapp and Miller (1985), one challenge that interpersonal researchers have faced has been the reconciliation of two imperatives of experimental design: (1) the assumption that ongoing interactions cannot be understood as finite sets of stable variables, and (2) the need to identify constants (p. 14). If the variables that govern interpersonal communication are potentially invented or renegotiated in every dyadic encounter, how can experimental researchers hope to discover valid and reliable explanatory variables? Knapp and Miller suggest that turning to the investigation of naturally occurring interactions can help researchers discover some constants that can serve in the construction of "more realistic laboratory situations" (p. 14). This is one important function that a qualitative method such as participant observation by ethnographers can serve.

I propose that the ethnography of interpersonal communication can offer more than just the discovery of stable or cross-situational variables for traditional experimental research. When understood within the context of an interpretive paradigm of research, ethnography has its own research strategies and goals, yielding results that are unique to the interpretive paradigm. An assessment of the potential contribution of ethnographic research to interpersonal communication requires clearly distinguishing ethnography as a qualitative method from ethnography as an exemplar of interpretive research.

ETHNOGRAPHY: QUALITATIVE OR INTERPRETIVE?

Ethnography emerged as a systematic qualitative method of anthropologists in the 1920s and quickly became the dominant approach. It merged the distanced speculations of earlier university-bound researchers with the more informal observations and data collection of travelers, merchants, government officials, and amateur field anthropologists (Marcus & Fischer, 1986, p. 18). Historians often credit the British anthropologist Bronislaw Malinowski and the American Franz Boas for the introduction of ethnography as a method in the 1920s (Marcus & Fischer, 1986, p. 18; Van Maanen, 1988, p. 16).[2] However, anthropologists used the term for decades to designate all anthropological methods, including those of archeology and physical anthropology (Penniman, 1974, p. 17).

Some scholars attribute the development of the ethnography of communication to Dell Hymes in 1974 (e.g., Littlejohn, 1992, p. 227). This is over 50 years after Malinowski's contributions to ethnography in general, and the accumulation of massive numbers of studies. However, the attribution is understandable. Hymes, a sociolinguist, has made major contributions to the ethnography of communication stemming from his work on the ethnography of speaking (1962). Because the discipline's interest in sociolinguistics dates back at least to the early 1950s, communication researchers readily assimilate Hymes' work. And according to a recent bibliography, over 250 studies on the ethnography of communication have adapted his research strategies (Philipsen & Carbaugh, 1986).

The method of participant observation is often treated as virtually synonymous with ethnography, the ethnography of communication included. The experience of field research has become one of the key requirements for education as a cultural or social anthropologist.[3] Van Maanen remarks that

> In Anthropology, field work alone sets the discipline off from other social sciences. A lengthy stay in an exotic culture (exotic, that is, to the fieldworker) is the central rite of passage serving to initiate and anoint a newcomer to the discipline. (1988, p. 14)

Standard training in social anthropology typically includes a year or two of field work and the eventual production of a written text that reports and analyzes data collected in the field.[4]

As its name implies, the essence of ethnography is writing about experiences and observations of a cultural milieu. During the immersion within the investigated culture, field notes, photographs, film, and audio and video tapes may be employed to record events and processes. Research reports are then generated by the investigator, using the recorded data as a source. The result is a written representation of the investigated culture.

Interpretive research emerged during the 1960s in social anthropology and stood as a challenge to the qualitative methodologies of the previous 40 years. The traditional methods and styles of presentation of ethnography were criticized for their positivist underpinnings and complicity with imperialism and colonialism. Thus anthropologists, as well as researchers in some other fields, typically treat the choice between qualitative and quantitative research as a methodological choice, while a further distinction is made between positivist and interpretive qualitative research. In short, qualitative methods are not necessarily employed as expressions of the interpretive paradigm, and quantitative methods are not necessarily employed as expressions of the positivist paradigm.

Communication scholars and teachers, more often than cultural anthropologists, collapse the difference between quantitative and qualitative methods and the difference between positivist and interpretive paradigms.[5] For instance, Poole and McPhee (1985) call for an appreciation of a broad variety of theories and methods for interpersonal communication research. But because they confuse the methodological distinction of quantitative and qualitative with the paradigm distinction of positivist and interpretive research (p. 159) the authors criticize the results of qualitative research according to the goals of positivist science, without considering if it is being employed in the context of an

interpretive paradigm (p. 123).[6] Poole and McPhee (1985) are representative of the attitude of many communication researchers who use social science approaches when they remark that "The skepticism many
'traditional' researchers accord to qualitative research is well-founded:
Many current studies seem impressionistic and shallow. It is by working
out routines for validating and supporting observational conclusions
that these problems can be remedied" (p. 123).

These remarks might be appropriate if the authors developed a
context for understanding the difference between positivist research and
interpretive research so that questions of validity and support for conclusions could be raised that are relevant to the different research contexts. Instead, Poole and McPhee consistently rely only on positivist
assumptions about what counts as validity and what kinds of support
for conclusions are acceptable. These authors continue a long-standing
confusion by assuming that qualitative methods can be evaluated without regard to their metatheoretical context.

Philipsen (1992) reviews a number of qualitative research texts
and does briefly distinguish those that present methods within an interpretive framework from those that operate within an "objectivist and
variable-analytic" context that is "a positivistic kind of qualitative research" (p. 242). However Philipsen limits his definition of interpretive
to research that "argue[s] what the meaning of the incident is to those
who produced it" (p. 242). In response to a work that suggests that
interpretations "emerge," Philipsen remarks that such a view of qualitative research "is a great mistake, and is usually a signal that the author
is about to throw mush at the reader" (p. 242). Philipsen eventually is
made to feel comfortable with the qualitative approach he is reviewing
because the researchers include methods of coding data that are consistent with the goals of a positivist paradigm.[7]

Some qualitative studies may indeed be shallow and impressionistic attempts to accomplish positivist goals. Other qualitative studies
may be attempting to respond to a quite different problematic (context
of inquiry) and consequently require a very different sort of evaluation
than offered by Poole and McPhee, Philipsen (1992), or Bostrom and
Donohew (1992). This difference in metatheoretical context is what I
refer to as a shift in paradigm from positivism to interpretive research.

This confusion is more understandable in the field of communication than in anthropology. No wide spread use of qualitative methodologies occurred within academic social science research in communication until the 1980s with the incorporation of interpretive approaches to organizational communication (Putnam & Pacanowsky,
1983) and cultural studies (Hall, Hobson, Lowe, & Willis, 1981; Hall,
1985; Collins, 1986). The influence of phenomenology, semiotics, struc-

turalism, Frankfurt School Critical Theory, and poststructuralism tended to be confined to rhetorical theory and the philosophy of communication. The difference between the study of rhetoric and the social science investigation of human communication tended to be characterized according to Dilthey's distinction between the humanities (Geisteswissenshaften) and the sciences (Naturwissenschaften), each with its own goals (understanding and explanation) and object domains (subjective experience and objective facts). Research approaches also have been designated as either quantitative or non-quantitative, treating the difference as between the social science paradigm and all other modes of inquiry. Here, *non-quantitative* not only implies that the social science paradigm is the norm against which "alternative" views are judged, but it also obscures important differences among methodological and paradigmatic options.

Today, an argument can be made that social science is in part a synthesis of the aims of the humanities and physical sciences (Littlejohn, 1992). Some communication researchers argue that the sciences and humanities are distinguishable but symbiotically related (e.g., Bormann 1989, pp. 231–233). For instance, social science inquires about the meaning of social action, and it also treats meaningful action as objectively identifiable and measurable. Social science also accepts a degree of ambiguity in its findings by generating probability statements rather than laws (e.g., Littlejohn, 1992, pp. 10–11). Thus, communication researchers using social science approaches are able to embrace some features of interpretive research while retaining positivist strategies. Continued positivist inclinations within social science research include goals like quantification, the search for invariant causal relationships, the attempt to minimize ambiguity even though some degree of ambiguity is accepted as unavoidable, and the attempt to construct value-neutral objective research procedures and genres of report writing.

Bostrom and Donohew (1992) respond to an understandable frustration that some practitioners of "conventional science" feel. Overzealous humanist and interpretive researchers sometimes attack social science research as if contemporary research design simply mirrors the goals of early positivist philosophy and physical science. The most obvious mistake is assuming that all of the social sciences adopt the deductive-nomological methodologies designed to discover "covering laws." Most social science is inductive rather than deductive, and deductive-statistical approaches are subject to some but not all of the interpretivist objections to deductive-nomological theory construction (Bostrom & Donohew, 1992). Debates in the early 20th century between positivists and phenomenologists, humanists, and critical theorists tended to revolve around the merits of deductive objectivist assumptions, on the one hand, and early versions of what are now called *interpretive* approaches. If contemporary interpretivists focus on limitations of other paradigms, our efforts would be more useful if we account for how issues have been made more complicated by advances in social science research design and theory construction. Such an approach would be more likely to foster a dialogue with colleagues that work within different research traditions, rather than perpetuating stereotypes that foster a priori divisions. Likewise, traditional social scientists who wish to raise questions about interpretive research will be more persuasive with their interpretivist colleagues if they make the effort to appreciate the goals and issues of the interpretivist paradigm.

PARADIGMATIC PHASES OF ETHNOGRAPHIC RESEARCH

Some of the shifts in theories of ethnography have affected its methods, techniques, and focus more than others. The most radical shift can be characterized as the shift from the traditional attempt to represent the experiences of others, to postmodern ethnography as the collaborative production and interpretation of texts by researchers and persons investigated. Postmodern ethnography focuses inquiry on local interactions in a way that enhances ethnography's potential contribution to the interpretive study of interpersonal communication. Because there are several ethnographic approaches in addition to the postmodern that can be considered interpretive, I will briefly trace the shift from qualitative to interpretive ethnography.

By *interpretive* I mean, minimally, any approach that (1) accepts that knowledge is an inventive, reflexive, socially inscribed symbolic process and (2) seeks to elaborate and enrich understanding rather than establishing parsimonious, correspondence validity claims that serve as generalizations about prediction and control. Thus, interpretive paradigms make assumptions about both epistemology (sometimes by rejecting the traditional division between epistemology and ontology) and the goals of research. Interpretive approaches redefine rather than reject traditional concepts like validity, reliability, and explanation. They also reject categorical differences between subject and object, theory and fact, and representations and their meaning. The relationships between these conceptual pairs are considered dynamic and interdependent, requiring explication within their respective contexts of use.

Ethnographic research can be typified as having occurred in three phases, which I will call *realist, romantic hermeneutic,* and *postmodern.* The realist paradigm is an expression of positivist philosophy, whereas the romantic hermeneutic and postmodern are names I use for two expressions of the interpretive paradigm. Although the three phases do reflect the chronological development of arguments and research strategies, the changes cannot be characterized as evolutionary. Such a view would imply that the current approach has superseded the previous ones. Instead, the current phase, the "postmodern," incorporates rather than transcends earlier views, and realist and romantic hermeneutic approaches are still very much alive. In this sense, I am borrowing only part of the concept of paradigm as developed by Kuhn, taking the term to mean a related cluster of fundamental assumptions that underpin theory construction. In other words, the cluster forms a metatheoretical type that can be recognized by its distinctive epistemological and ontological ramifications.

I treat paradigms as a general characterization of a disciplinary discourse rather than a single set of abstract assumptions that axiomatically dominates an entire age (as in Kuhn's formulation). Consequently, the sharpness of boundaries between paradigms may vary according to the current state of a discipline. Thus, the coexistence of two or more paradigms does not necessarily imply that they are competing with one another. Viewing paradigms as competitive entails the belief that all discourses of inquiry must be understood as moving toward a single unitary metatheory. The goal of unifying all fields of knowledge has been held by positivists and their most faithful heirs, but not by all interpretive researchers.[8]

Realist Ethnography

An ethnography can be called *realist* insofar as the epistemology of positivism informs its goals and methods. These assumptions include Cartesian dualism and the assertion that phenomena ultimately can be explained by logically coherent causal propositions (see note 5 for my slightly more detailed definition of *positivism*). I call this paradigm *realist* both to refer to its epistemology of realism and because its descriptions of the experiences of the researcher traditionally have been accomplished through a style of writing similar to the realist literary genre (Atkinson, 1990; Marcus & Fischer, 1986, pp. 54–57; Van Maanen, 1988). Realist ethnography supposes that an objective narrative can more or less accurately represent the lives of the group studied.

Van Maanen, describing four genres of ethnographic writing, observes that "By far the most prominent, familiar, prevalent, popular, and recognized form of ethnographic writing is the realist account of a culture" (1988, p. 45). He suggests four characteristics of this genre that distinguishes it from other ethnographic approaches: (1) experiential author(ity) partly expressed through a third person narrative that avoids implicating the author in the telling of the story, (2) a documentary style that focuses on the details of everyday life, (3) the ethnographer's representation of the "natives'" point of view on the described events and surroundings, and (4) interpretive omnipotence. Van Maanen elaborates on the last characteristic as follows:

> Realist tales are not multivocal texts where an event is given meaning first one way, then another, and then still another. Rather a realist tale offers one reading and culls its facts carefully to support that reading. Little can be discovered in such texts that has not been put there by the fieldworker as a way of supporting a particular interpretation. (p. 53)

The techniques of writing that Van Maanen describe as realist are only one possibility for the support of this paradigm. They form a description of a prototypical example rather than a definitive and necessary set of features.

Van Maanen points out that there are a number of techniques that anthropologists and sociologists have devised "to shape the 'native's' point of view into something reportable" (1988, p. 50). He collapses all of these methods into this third characteristic of realist ethnography, the representation of the "native's" point of view. However, some of these methods mark a shift from a realist representation that implicitly accepts a positivist paradigm, to an interpretive paradigm. In particular, some versions of ethnomethodology clearly break with most of the other features of the realist genre. Their phenomenologically inspired theoretical orientation, combined with their interventionist techniques to disrupt and bring to the foreground the tacit assumption of social actors, are in tension with the detached objectivity typical of realist ethnography.[9]

The other genres that Van Maanen describes are the confessional, impressionist, and a fourth category that is a catch-all of approaches that do not fit the other three. Revealingly, Van Maanen lumps the contemporary strategies and methods of ethnography that most directly challenge positivist assumptions into this "other" category. These include critical methods and methods that emphasize "jointly told tales." Van Maanen explains his treatment of these perspectives: "Put candidly, these are residual categories of ethnographic writing (quasi ethnographies) formulated largely so that my house of ethnographic classification can be ritually swept clean" (p. 8). The shifts in the genres he describes do announce corresponding shifts in methodological focus. However Van Maanen's categories do not consistently distinguish between positivist and interpretive paradigms.

Romantic Hermeneutics

My choice of the terms *romantic hermeneutics* and *postmodernism* is prompted by a consideration of trends in both the history of ethnography and interpersonal communication. Postmodernism includes the postmodern hermeneutics of Heidegger and Gadamer as well as poststructuralism and cultural criticism inspired by the Centre for Contemporary Cultural Studies at the University of Birmingham.

George Stocking, Jr. (1991), describes both the positivist and humanist contributions to anthropology as "romantic." He notes that Boas, one of the founders of modern ethnography, considered the study of humanity to be guided by two modes of inquiry, exemplified most clearly by the physicist and the historian and corresponding to objective and subjective methods (p. 5). Boas's distinction between physicists and "cosmographers" parallels Dilthey's Naturwissenschaften and Geisteswissenschaften dualism. Stocking wants to interpret this duality as itself a romantic theme such that *romantic* names both a tradition in opposition to positivism and a pluralist view that includes both the sciences and humanities.

Stocking's motives are in part similar to mine: he wishes to emphasize that more is at stake in a paradigm shift than a choice of methods. However, Stocking ultimately asserts that the physical sciences are implicitly part of the romantic tradition because "both forms of inquiry were subjectively grounded" (p. 5). This move by Stocking potentially collapses the difference between the sciences and humanities by reducing science to a sub-discipline of the humanities. I prefer to treat the two modes of inquiry as different problematics that may overlap on given issues and consider the acceptance of this pluralism as one characteristic of a postmodern discourse. My use of *romantic hermeneutics* thus roughly corresponds to Boas's *cosmography* and Dilthey's *Geisteswissenschaften*. It has a narrower meaning than Stocking's *romantic anthropology*, which I take to misleadingly include interpretive approaches that break with fundamental tenets of early modern (romantic) hermeneutics.

There is also some ambiguity among interpersonal communication scholars about what is meant by *hermeneutic* approaches. For instance, in Bochner's (1985) discussion of the history of theoretical developments in the study of interpersonal communication, he discusses three types of goals for interpersonal communication research that guide inquiry, corresponding to three major perspectives (empiricism, hermeneutics, and critical theory). Bochner includes interpretation as the goal of hermeneutics. Although the book chapter has had some influence over the years, Bochner nonetheless equivocates regarding what he means by *interpretive* research.[10] At first he calls Dilthey's hermeneutics *interpretive* and seems to reject it in favor of pragmatism (p. 34). Later he calls pragmatism *interpretive* and *hermeneutic*. For instance, Bochner remarks that: "Pragmatists see a unity to science but it is not the same unity to which the logical empiricists pledged their loyalty. The unity is hermeneutical, not methodological" (p. 35). What I call *romantic hermeneutics* corresponds to what Bochner initially calls *interpretive*, and what I call *postmodernism* corresponds to what Bochner calls *pragmatism*.

The *romantic hermeneutic* paradigm cuts across Van Maanen's distinction between the confessional and impressionist genres. It emerges as a general trend of thought in the humanities, more specifically as the development of modern hermeneutics. Stewart and Philipsen (1984) remark that

> Kant's discovery of the crucial role of the knower in all processes of knowing supported the growing interest not just in texts but also in their authors. This new interest in both the artist and his [*sic*] work, which grew into Romanticism, created a challenge for hermeneutics. No longer could immanent textual analysis suffice; if a major part of the text's meaning were anchored in its author's psychological and spiritual experience, then the procedures for interpreting that meaning had to be modified to tap those depths. The task was a major one; romanticism altered the definition of what counts as accurate understanding. (p. 181)

Romantic hermeneutics seeks to discover the meaning of a text by examining how the individual consciousness of the author reflects and refracts the spirit of the age. The full expression of this version of hermeneutics would require a detailed exegesis of the relationships among the authors' personal experiences and their historical context. This would include psychological, biographical, social, and historical influences that might shed light on the meaning of the text. It assumes that texts have a discoverable coherence of meaning embedded within a matrix of intentional structures which serves as its semantic context.

The romantic ethnographic text is prototypically a first person narrative about the participant-observation experiences of the researcher. An interpretation of the account may be supplied by the author or may be left for the reader to accomplish. The validity of the interpretation is supported by a sort of triangulation of the different contextual influences that shape the author's intention.[11] Although the findings about the meaning of the text of the author are not generalizable to other texts, the process of interpretation reveals important features of the con-text (literally, those texts that are "with" the investigated text). This is part of the point of a romantic hermeneutics, and the relevant point for its use in ethnography: the text of the author serves as an entry point into the matrix of meaning that constitutes its social context. Unlike a semiotic or structural view that attempts to explain the meaning of the text as the product of its relations to other texts, romantic hermeneutics seeks to make explicit the implicit meanings of the author's intentions as an exemplar of an intersubjective field of experience.

Intention here does not refer to the psychological sense of consciously willing something, but rather refers to the notion as it has been developed within phenomenology. *Intentionality* in phenomenology is the name for the synthetic activity of subjectivity that "intends" or "points to" its objects. The psychological characteristics of a particular individual are only one feature or facet of his or her total subjective life. Subjectivity is conceived as a much more complex phenomenon than the learned dispositions and behaviors of each individual. It is informed by the person's "stock of knowledge" about socially relevant events, matters of conduct, and expectations (Berger & Luckmann, 1966), as well as their emotional, practical, and aesthetic sensibilities. These are shared meanings and are understandable only in relation to a social context of meaning. Intentionality is emergent with the person's "life-world"; that is, the full horizon of social and cultural experience of the person as a synchronically describable field. The life-world supplies the background upon which the foreground of conscious experience makes sense and is given a depth of meaning. The meaning, structured through the intending of a particular experience (text), serves as a touchstone for coherently understanding the context (the life-world of the individual).

Multiple studies of the same text, and of different texts from the same context, build a richness of understanding that functions somewhat like the accumulation of knowledge in the positivist paradigm. Because the web of meaning is held to be interdependent, subsequent historical findings may be the occasion for a refiguring of large portions of the context. A wide variety of means are available to determine how much influence newly discovered aspects of the context might have, including evidence of historical influence of an idea or person, arguments for the discovery of key metaphors that govern other aspects of the context through entailments and rhetorical force, or psychological theories that help explain motivation of key actors, especially the author. Thus, the romantic hermeneutic paradigm supports a range of explanatory theories, incorporates its version of validity tests, and allows for a sense of progress in the enrichment of understanding through the collective efforts of researchers.

One of the most celebrated and misunderstood features of hermeneutics is the so-called hermeneutic circle. This describes the reflexive character of hermeneutic methodology. This basic structure of reflexivity is found in a variety of approaches and can be considered one of the defining characteristics of all interpretive methodologies. The necessity of using a reflexive methodology is nowhere more evident than in ethnography. Faced at first with nearly incomprehensible expressions of an unknown culture, the ethnographer must move back and forth from expressions to cultural context to discover the means of expression. In a short monograph, entitled "What Is Ethnography?" Dell Hymes (1978) describes this reflexive process as it is practiced by the linguist, Kenneth Pike:

> In order to discover the system of sounds of a language one had to be trained to record the phenomena in question and one had to know what types of sound were in general found in languages. Accurate observations and recording of the sounds, however, would not disclose the system. One had to test the relations among sounds for their functional relevance within the system in question. The result of this analysis of the system might in turn modify the general framework for such inquiry, disclosing a new type of sound or relation. Pike generalized the endings of the linguistic terms "phonetic" and "phonemic" to obtain names for these three moments of inquiry. The general framework with which one begins analysis of a given case he calls "etic$_1$." The analysis of the actual system he called "emic." The reconsideration of the general framework in light of the analysis he called "etic$_2$." (p. 9)

Hymes says he is introducing this description to show the connections between ethnographic methods and the "general scientific method," but the description has more in common with the hermeneutic circle than with experimental or other positivist methodologies. One thing Pike's approach and the scientific method do have in common is that both are strategies to enhance the validity of findings. In hermeneutics, the reflexive movement of inquiry does not lead to the clarification of a finite object of analysis that is considered separate from the process of investigation. Instead, the hermeneutic circle could continue indefinitely, because each turn of the reflexive movement itself alters the context of meaning within which the objectified experience is found and subsequently (re)defined. In practice, the process is halted once the analysis sufficiently clarifies the part-whole relationship for the purposes of the particular inquiry. In other words, the sufficiency of the validity claims made by hermeneutics and the degree of elaboration of its findings is determined by the pragmatics of the research context.

Romantic hermeneutics, although a hermeneutics of subjectivity, provides criteria for objective claims of knowledge. Its immediate data are texts, analyzed and compared to reveal the sometimes conscious and sometimes unconscious intentions of their creators. Ultimately, it seeks to produce a text that represents the spirit of the age (Geisteswissenschaften). It is the paradigm that has underpinned centuries of literary, historical, and rhetorical scholarship, forming the core of what has been called the *humanities*.

In its worst form, romantic hermeneutics is reduced to the unhappy task of reconstructing the author's intention as the single determining moment of textual meaning. This avowedly subjective version of romantic hermeneutics supplied the philosophical rationale for the humanist psychology movement of the 1960s and early 1970s. The movement tended to collapse the study of human subjectivity into an exploration of the particular psychological character of the Western individual. The result was implicit and explicit claims of universality founded on narrow, culture-bound conceptions of the individual. Because there were few intradisciplinary checks against these glorifications of the Western psyche, humanist psychology eventually earned the label "narcissistic" (Lasch, 1979, 1984).[12]

Romantic hermeneutic ethnography clearly breaks with some aspects of the positivist paradigm. To the extent that a shift has occurred from the general goals of causal, objective explanation to the explication of historically and socially situated experience, romantic hermeneutics constitutes a paradigm shift. However, some important features of the positivist paradigm are retained. For instance, Cartesian dualism is retained, although a redefined concept of subjectivity rather than objectivity is the focus of analysis. Even the goal of objectivity is often retained as romantic hermeneuticists struggled to avoid relativism and solipsism. The search is for an objective study of subjectivity that could accomplish a revealing and enriching exegesis rather than prediction and control.

Postmodern Ethnography

The definition of *postmodernism* varies both across and within different fields of study (Arac, 1986; Featherstone, 1991; Foster, 1983; Lash, 1990; Lyotard, 1984; Presnell, 1989). Some general themes have emerged regarding postmodernism but a categorical, decontextual definition of the term would be counter to most of its tenets. I will reserve my remarks about postmodernism to summary remarks about one of its manifestations, namely, postmodern ethnography.

Postmodern ethnography is the product of critical reflections about the nature of culture as symbolic and how systems of representation not only reflect power interests but are themselves instances of power relations. One motivation for the development of postmodern ethnography is the intensified awareness of the role of the ethnographer as a conscious or unwitting partner in colonialism (Stocking, 1991). Another motivation is the contemporary experience of living in a fragmented, urban society in which images and symbols create their own reality. Facing the loss (or at least local disruption) of a coherent social context that might underpin a coherent sense of individual meaning, postmodern ethnography often seeks "to reassimilate, to reintegrate the self in society and to restructure the conduct of everyday life" (Tyler, 1986, p. 135). Therefore, it can be understood as in part an activist response to what Lannamann calls "the ideological context of interpersonal communication inquiry" (1992, p. 198), as well as a new development in ethnography.

Conquergood (1991) has described four themes of postmodern ethnography that emphasize the role ethnography can play as a critical methodology. They are common themes for most approaches that are considered postmodern today. These themes are (1) The Return of the Body, (2) Boundaries and Borderlands, (3) The Rise of Performance, and (4) Rhetorical Reflexivity. I will expand on Conquergood's themes to discuss trends in postmodern ethnography.

RETURN OF THE BODY   By the Return of the Body, Conquergood means a heightened emphasis on investigating communication from the perspective of the actual physical involvement of the researcher in the presence of the investigated persons and their co-presence within a particular setting. "Recognition of the bodily nature of fieldwork privileges the process of communication that constitutes the 'doing' of ethnography: speaking, listening, and acting together" (Conquergood, 1991, p. 181). Not only does the encounter of the researcher and researched become a focus of postmodern ethnography, so does the physical processes of data collection, recording, transcription, analysis, and dissemination (Nelson, 1989; Rose, 1990; Tyler, 1986).

The conception of the body in postmodern writings borrows extensively from poststructuralism, particularly the work of Lacan (1977) and Deleuze and Guattari (1977). The postmodern body is different from either the positivist accounts of behavior or the romantic hermeneutic body as a synthesizing wholeness. The postmodern body is the source of desires that are never quite contained by rationality. Instead, the experience of our bodies and bodily presence to others always remains a partial enigma. Embodied experience is both that which motivates our most intimate intentions (directedness to others and to ourselves as an object of our own reflection) and that which continually exceeds efforts to circumscribe it. Desire is the product of a biological need that comes to be socially constituted as a particular lack, that is, the symbolized absence of fulfillment. Lack, already only an incomplete representation of need, gives rise to a symbolically invested object of fulfillment. Hence, there is always a gap between the experience of biological need and the socially constituted object that promises to satisfy it. Objects of desire generate a frustrated sense of incompleteness at the very moment of our attempted appropriation of them. The result is that we are constantly reminded of the irreducibility of the dynamic non-rational bodily experience of the world and others. Desire and its attempted satisfaction constantly open upon horizons of meaning that cannot be contained and that therefore create the Other as an evocative enigma.[13]

The "Return of the Body" shifts our attention to the constantly off-balance dialectic of desire as part of everyday experience. The non-rational, non-appropriated bodily experiences appear as irrational excesses of meaning that disrupt our attempts to inscribe them within a coherent rationalization of either self or social meaning. This dynamic is made more problematic within postmodern culture, that is, within a culture that thrives on a symbolic exchange of imaginary desires with increasingly short "product lives." The hyperreality of postmodernism is not a world of symbols that are mistaken for reality, but rather a world in which the bodily experience of symbols is reality. Symbols cease to be representations of something. The language of postmodern culture is no longer semiotic in this sense (Baudrillard, 1983; Derrida, 1974; Stewart, 1986). Instead, the expressive materiality of symbols (symbols as signifiers) evoke rather than refer (Barthes, 1975; Tyler, 1986). The evocativeness of language is infinitely interpretable as in romantic hermeneutics, but not because language is an infinite self-contained system of meaning. Language throws us outside of ourselves, or evokes a response that could not entirely be anticipated. It does not *represent something else* so much as *present itself* as an ambivalent, self-contradictory, yet sensuous reality.[14]

Understanding speaking as evocative, embodied, and contradictory raises fundamental questions about interpersonal communication conceived as either the transfer of information or a dialogical movement toward an empathetic identity. Both conceptions assume that successful interpersonal communication depends on the coherent matching of speaker and listener perspectives. In the information model, listening is accomplished through accurately representing the meaning of the other's messages. In the empathetic model, the difference between self and other is erased, leaving communication with nothing to do. A postmodern understanding of interpersonal communication would not attempt to chart out the movement toward the coherence of meaning. But neither does a postmodern view of communication assume that communicators are locked into solipsistic subjectivities. The focus of a postmodern interpersonal communication is instead suggested by Conquergood's second theme of critical ethnography, Boundaries and Borderlands.

BOUNDARIES AND BORDERLANDS   The most revealing moments in communication are partial failures, misunderstandings, and awkward silences, in other words, the boundaries and borderlands formed through discourse. These moments reveal the self-other encounter as a communicative problematic; that is, a context within which our encounter raises questions about who we are and what we want. If we assume that members of a dialogue already have clear identities that they subsequently attempt to represent to the other, the inventive, critical, and liberating role of communication can be overshadowed by the reification of its past accomplishments. We might, for instance, fail to encounter living persons struggling to make sense of themselves as part of the process of making sense with us, by grasping onto previous role identities as definitive of the person. We might also fail to understand how the sedimented meanings of our encounter can be refigured to accommodate the circumstances and desires of our speaking together by assuming that previously successful communicative strategies continue to be appropriate. Attention to the nature of subjectivity as embodied helps to reveal the emergent boundaries and resulting borderlands of communication.

Conquergood describes two kinds of boundaries: (1) those between genres of writing, and (2) those between the geography of the investigator and investigated (p. 184). In a postmodern context, the diverse and fragmented context of meaning blurs both kinds of boundaries and the relationship between them. Encountering another embodied subjectivity requires being open to the co-production of the text of our communication. It is this co-produced text that evokes what understanding we manage to invent. In other words, the boundaries of meaning evoked by our co-produced text form the borderland between the geographies of our life-world.[15] The process involves two phases: (1) the co-production of a text, and (2) the collaborative interpretation of the text, emphasizing its evocative power rather than its supposed representational accuracy.

Postmodern ethnographers have recognized that the unilateral representation of one person by another is ethnocentric at best and at worst a formula for a colonialist strategy. Sharing a reality requires that we share the texts that evoke it. Because the evocative power of texts is not separate from the embodied, real activity of creating and using them, cooperation entails that we share in the production and use of our common texts. The postmodern ethnography of communication requires the collaborative effort of investigator and investigated to decide how their encounter will be embodied in a text, what genre of text is produced, and how those texts are used. The researcher typically has the goal of "bringing back" to the researcher's community the experiences of the other for the researcher's own use in the pursuit of knowledge. This appropriation is a goal among others that should be not only negotiated in the encounter, but also should be open to redefinition.[16] For the postmodern ethnographer, the use of *we* in the research report names the collaboratively established boundaries and borderlands of persons that experience their mutually recognized differences as well as similarities. Difference between researcher and researched is not erased but rather made a theme of cooperative effort. The enigma of the Other is evoked through collaboratively produced and interpreted texts. Thus, texts stand as an objective moment in our struggle for mutual understanding without becoming static representations that pretend to solve the mystery of Others. As mutually produced, texts are invested with the power to evoke a common understanding. *Successful interpersonal communication occurs when co-produced texts function as evocative sources of cooperative interpretation by participants.*

Some postmodernists, including Conquergood (pp. 188–191), caution that an overemphasis on texts can privilege a literary model of understanding that is restrictive of expression and ethnocentric in orientation (Goodall, 1990; Tyler, 1986). By *text* I mean the product of the tendency of human thought to distance ourselves from experience by objectifying it in some kind of expression. As Ricoeur argues, the structure of experience that makes the invention of writing possible is a general structure of consciousness. I retain the metaphor of text as appropriate for postmodern theorizing because one characteristic of postmodern communication is the treatment of texts as if they are expressions of an oral culture. The tension between the permanence and change of messages becomes a theme for postmodern accounts of invention. In this respect, postmodern culture is a "cold" rather than "hot" culture (McLuhan, 1964) and evidences a "new" or "secondary orality" (Ong, 1982). Textuality is not superseded nor does it monologically determine modes of expression and understanding. The postmodern text is always a cooperatively sustained text, not an objective entity that has an ontological status outside of communicative processes. Texts are always texts in performance. They are objectifications of experience in semantically rich expressions and are not distinguishable by any particular technical or material means of objectification. Postmodern texts are messages among other messages, sustained by communicators, and constantly subjected to new interpretations as performances unfold.

THE RISE OF PERFORMANCE   Both the postmodern emphasis on the body and the cooperatively located borderlands of understanding that serve as the hermeneutic space of investigation, turn our attention to the performative character of communication. Conquergood contrasts "the world as text" with "the world as performance" as modes of understanding (p. 190). As mentioned previously, Conquergood is concerned that communication scholars have fallen into the Western cultural tendency to privilege written documents as the primary object of investigation (pp. 188–191). It is indeed ironic that although the traditional focus of the discipline has been public speaking events, public address has focused predominantly on transcripts of speeches rather than their actual performance. Similarly, the study of interpersonal communication has stressed the investigation of the frequency and conditions of communicative behavior, patterns of interaction, and more recently, the cognitive underpinnings of behavior. Rarely have investigators reflected upon the richness and complexity of particular interactions as unique and interesting events in their own right.[17]

Conquergood emphasizes the work of Victor Turner as the foremost performance-oriented ethnographer (p. 187). According to Bruner (1986), Dilthey was a primary influence on Turner. This influence does link some of Turner's perspectives to what I have called *romantic hermeneutics*, because Dilthey is considered one of the primary architects of modern hermeneutics. However, Turner emphasized those aspects of Dilthey's thought that are more often associated with postmodernism. In particular, Turner emphasizes Dilthey's appreciation of the dialectical relationship between experience and its expression, rather than accentuating Dilthey's descriptions of the unity of "inner experience."

Turner interprets Dilthey through Dewey's theory of aesthetics as a dynamic tension between the experience of harmony and disturbance (Turner, 1986, p. 38). Turner articulated his convergence of Dilthey's and Dewey's thought through his performance theory of social drama. According to Turner, the social drama expresses the limenal or threshold experiences of everyday life. "The limen, or threshold, . . . is a no-man's-land betwixt and between the structural past and the structural future as anticipated by the society's normative control of biological development" (p. 41). He describes theater as in part a ritual that allows cultural experiences to be "replicated, dismembered, re-membered, refashioned, and mutely or vocally made meaningful" (p. 41).

Turner argues that the experience of theater and other limenal rituals have become fragmented and truncated in modern industrial societies, and have been replaced by "entertainment genres." He remarks that "there are signs today that the amputated specialized genres are seeking to rejoin" their ritual function within society (p. 42).

Turner's approach draws together a number of postmodern themes. His investigation of limenal experience can lead to a deeper, culturally rich understanding of the fragmentation, cultural juxtapositions, aesthetic ritualization of everyday life and normative pluralism that are often described as characteristics of postmodernism. Turner's concept of limenal experiences names a concern similar to Conquergood's concepts of Boundary and Borderland. The experience of performance provides social actors with an opportunity to make collective sense of their social milieu. In the postmodern condition of a society so saturated with symbolic meaning that the very distinction between symbol and referent begins to disappear, meaningful, coherent action increasingly finds expression as collective ritualized performance. However, postmodernists suggest that, contrary to Turner's expectations, performances might find expression through an "entertainment genre" as well as the telling of stories among community members.

The contemporary recognition of the pervasiveness of storytelling has led to the proposal that communication is fundamentally narrative in character (Fisher, 1987). The "narrative paradigm" can be understood as one response to postmodern conditions that draws attention to an important mode of communicative performance. But understanding the narrative paradigm within a postmodern ethnographic context can highlight some needed cautions about narrative models. First, narrative performances invent as well as express cultural norms. Consequently, the function of narratives cannot be "read" from their decontextualized structure. Interpreters must account for how performances creatively combine and juxtapose cultural expressions into local expressions that make sense for those participants. Broader structures of social meaning serve as parts that are redefined and recombined within performances as participants muddle through the task of making sense together. Second, everyday performers use a variety of modes of expressions, settings, props, and narrative devices to construct their performances. Understanding a narrative would be incomplete if it did not include the influences of "performance choices." In short, the performance metaphor reminds us that communication is more than a "script" and that the textuality of performance is not sufficiently understood by thinking of it as a written document.[18]

Recall that Bochner describes the pragmatic approach to interpersonal communication as one of its major paradigms. Placing pragmatism within the context of postmodernism can enrich the pragmatist's agenda. The Return of the Body reminds the pragmatist that local goals unfold through the actions of embodied subjectivities. Further, the desires that motivate persons in their inquiry are not pre-given functions of the situation, but rather emerge out of the tension between biological needs, symbolized desires, and emotionally invested objects of desire. Thus, postmodern pragmatism rejects functionalist versions of pragmatism that mirror status quo goals. Functionalist versions of pragmatism implicitly rely upon a positivist epistemology that undercut their potential as critical modes of investigation. Instead, the collaborative efforts of researcher and researched define goals of inquiry, rather than goals being defined through the application of axiomatic assumptions about systems and systemic functions. Although systems theory has made valuable contributions to our understanding of human communication, postmodernism suggests that the positivist assumptions of functionalist pragmatism that systems theory often incorporates, should be abandoned if pragmatism is to serve as a critical rather than an implicit ideological mode of investigation.[19] In addition, the postmodern understanding of desire articulates an understanding of goal seeking as an internally dynamic process rather than as a static pre-given teleological structure.[20] Desire is understood as richly evocative rather than just a motivation to satisfy specific ends.

RHETORICAL REFLEXIVITY   Reflexivity is a feature of virtually all interpretive approaches. Reflexivity is asserted as a characteristic of the threefold phenomenological investigation as practiced by Lanigan (1988), Langellier and Hall (1989), Nelson (1989), and Macke (1991). As described earlier, Hymes borrows a three-phase reflexive method from linguistics and adapts it to his ethnography of speaking. Carbaugh and Hastings develop a scheme for the ethnographic investigation of interpersonal communication that includes the reflexive use of four stages: Basic theoretical orientation, Activity theory or theory of a communicative phenomenon, Situated theory of a sociocultural case, and Evaluation theory (BASE) (1992, p. 160).[21] To the extent that natural sciences and mathematics progress by using contemporary findings to alter their presuppositions, they also engage in a version of the hermeneutic circle, thus linking both the natural and human sciences through a hermeneutic understanding of rational reflection.

Romantic hermeneutics limits reflexivity to the epistemological shifts engendered through rational reflection. Thus, the reflexivity of the hermeneutic circle is not distinctively postmodern. The reflection on method is, by itself, a modernist tendency. Postmodernists typically reject romantic hermeneutics as too nostalgic for origins, a telos, and goals that axiomatically ground inquiry. Postmodernists take reasoned reflection to be one aspect of the general reflexivity of understanding that includes the reflexivity of action, image, and desire as well as reason.

Three features of the hermeneutic circle bring it in closer proximity to postmodern thought. First, the hermeneutic circle results in the clarification of the research problematic, not in a move to a more perfect or valid knowledge of a given reality. Postmodernism rejects the need to adopt a single metaphysical or ontological position. Pragmatically oriented postmodernists understand that the assumptions of a discoverable stable reality, the ability of the knower to construct theories based on nonambiguous statements, and the progressive accumulation of knowledge are heuristic strategies that can be evaluated relative to the concerns of a specific research context. Ontological assumptions about the nature of knowledge are not understood as axiomatically guiding metatheoretical criteria. They are merely handy conceptual tools that may be abandoned if they are not concordant with local circumstances of inquiry. Postmodern social science is a collection of strategies rather than a unified philosophy, set of goals, or theoretical assumptions.

Second, the reflexivity of the hermeneutic circle is understood as a fundamental property of language and consequently of all inquiry. The language we use to understand ourselves and the world is conceived as a network of terms that define each other through a complex web of semantic and syntactic relationships. Changing part of the system of terms shifts the relationships among the other terms, resulting in shifts in their definitions. The modernist version of this web of meaning supposes that the system as a whole is rationally understandable through descriptions of its systemic characteristics, as in structuralism and General Systems Theory. For postmodernists, the result of the interrelatedness of signification is that meaning is inherently unstable, determined by a vast array of influences that could never be completely articulated because the very effort would shift the web of relationships. Understanding of this web of significance is progressive in the sense of enriching experience rather than accumulating bits of knowledge. Consequently, only local subsystems of the whole can be understood as coherent, and even these systems of meaning carry within them the contradictions and tensions entailed by their embeddedness in the larger, noncoherent context.

These two ways of understanding the hermeneutic circle have the respective advantages of opening inquiry to a wide range of methods and theoretical assumptions and drawing our attention to the role that language plays in the construction of what we count as knowledge. A third version of reflexivity includes the reflexivity of action and image as well as language. For instance, Conquergood emphasizes the rhetorical function of the hermeneutic circle and is thereby prompted to explore its language dimensions. In addition, his concern for developing a critical ethnography leads him to a more broadly conceived performative reflexivity. Conquergood rejects the view that only a reflexivity of language is involved in a critical understanding.

> To be sure, ethnography on the page constrains and shapes performance in the field. But it is also true, I believe, that experiential performance sometimes resists, exceeds, and overwhelms the constraints and strictures of writing. It is the task of rhetorical critics to seek out these sites of tension, displacement, and contradiction between the Being There of performed experience and the Being Here of written texts. (p. 193)

Conquergood's call for investigating the tension between field experience and the ethnographic text gets more to the point of postmodern ethnography, it seems to me, that Turner's and Tyler's call for presentational rather than representational ethnography. The issue is not which mode of inquiry or expression is inherently more liberating or oppressive, but rather what power relations emerge and are maintained through ethnography as a practice. The practice of ethnography includes the encounter between researcher and researched, their co-production of a text, and its presentation to both of their communities. Postmodern reflexivity is a hermeneutic circle of pragmatically situated action and image as well as language.

Conclusion

Realist, romantic hermeneutic, and postmodern ethnography all offer alternatives to experimental approaches to interpersonal communication. I have argued that realist ethnography offers alternative methods but does not differ from more traditional positivist research in its fundamental assumptions about the nature of communication or the relationship between researcher and researched. Romantic hermeneutics does accomplish a partial shift from a positivist paradigm, but leaves in place the assumption of subject-object dualism, favoring the investigation of subjective experience over objective fact. Retaining these assumptions results in approaches that fail to account for communication as accomplished by embodied subjectivities. Postmodern subjectivities collaboratively establish and interpret boundaries and borderlands through inventive performance and reflexively alter both their rational understanding of their relationships and their understanding as expressed in action and images.

The postmodern turn in ethnography opens a number of possibilities for the study of interpersonal communication. First, postmodern ethnography focuses on the density of everyday life, not just as an exemplar of general cultural norms but as an expression of how persons within a localized context negotiate and invent responses to particular situations. Second, postmodernism rejects the positivist-humanist dualism as dictating methods of research. Both qualitative and quantitative methods may be employed within the methodological pluralism that postmodernism encourages. Axiomatic assumptions of positivism and humanism are rejected in favor of a hermeneutically reflexive pragmatism. Third, postmodernism's emphasis on collaboration of researcher and researched opens a wide range of ethical and political questions about the nature and function of inquiry as an interpersonal (face-to-face encounter). Considering the ethics of collaborative research not only raises ethical questions about the politics of research, but also can be one avenue for exploring interpersonal ethics in our age of cultural diversity. Collaboratively produced texts function as the boundaries and borderlands of a common understanding between members of different communities. Forth, postmodern ethnography encourages broadening the range of expressions that might emerge from research efforts. The emphasis on communication as collaborative performance, and the sensitivity to the varieties of communicational reflexivity, invites the development of nonprint and multimedia projects. The very process of cooperatively engaging in performative efforts with others can deepen our understanding about how communication can be accomplished. These co-productions of researcher and researched have the potential to break the usual academic assumptions about what modes of communication are acceptable for demonstrating knowledge and understanding. Fifth, postmodern ethnography can help avoid some of the colonialist impact of the distanced observer who either partially or completely hides his or her research agenda.[22]

A postmodern ethnography of interpersonal communication challenges researchers to conceive of different avenues of expression and different ways of evaluating those expressions. It invites greater participation as researchers in the everyday concerns of communicators. Postmodern ethnography also offers a means by which the sense of self of both researcher and researched can be explored, thematized, and articulated in cooperative attempts to build and maintain communities.

NOTES

1. I will place quote marks around "native" to emphasize that contemporary ethnographies are often written about members of one's own culture. In this case, the self-other *opposition* often implied by

"ethnographer" and "native" clearly does not hold. The researched subject and the researcher share a general cultural context, even if the subjects of research are members of a "deviant subculture." The significance of the self-other dialogue is a problematic of postmodern ethnography that informs later themes of this chapter.

2. Malinowski's (1967) posthumously published *A Diary in the Strict Sense of the Term* stirred controversy over the ethnographic method as he had inspired it. This work has been the occasion for the critical reflection on ethnography and the elaboration of some interpretive approaches (see, for instance, Clifford Geertz, 1983, pp. 55–70).

3. The distinction between cultural and social anthropology has a long and complex history. In one version, social anthropology is simply one branch of cultural anthropology, archeology being the other major branch. In another version, the distinction harkens back to debates between Malinowski's reductive functionalism and perspectives that emphasize primarily the symbolic levels of culture. I will refer to that branch of anthropology that investigates the communicative processes and events of culture as social anthropology.

4. According to Rose (1990), "Ethnographers' lives, like the works they have written, have been standardized carefully at least since Malinowski: a summer in the field, two years in the field, subsequent summers in the field, and an occasional semester" (p. 17).

5. I appreciate the frustration of some "traditional" researchers that resist the designation "positivist." Certainly few if any contemporary scholars hold all of the views promoted by positivist philosophers such as Comte, Russell, and the early Wittgenstein. As I use the term, *positivism* is shorthand for any view that espouses accomplishing the following goals: (1) the one-to-one correspondence between observational terms and data, (2) discovery of logically coherent evidence sufficient for warranting claims about observations and causal relations as valid according to a correspondence theory of truth, (3) the use of a value-neutral language for observation and theory building, (4) the treatment of observational and theoretical language as, a priori, different logical type levels, and (5) an additive conception of the accumulation and progress of knowledge. I take these *goals* to define research inspired by the philosophies of positivism, including inductive probability and hypothetico-deductive research, and potentially qualitative as well as quantitative methods, whether or not investigators claim that the goals are completely attainable.

6. The authors are somewhat equivocal about what they mean by "interpretive" research. Sometimes they treat it as synonymous with qualitative methodology and sometimes they treat the two as different levels of research design that might be mixed and matched with others.

7. I do not mean to imply that Philipsen is entirely hostile toward perspectives that I would call interpretive. In another section of the review, Philipsen does call a chapter on phenomenological research "excellent" and "interesting." My point is simply that the evaluation of research often arbitrarily shifts from the level of method to the level of paradigmatic assumptions.

8. Although Kuhn's work is often cited in support of interpretive approaches to the history of science, it is worth remembering that Kuhn's *The Structure of Scientific Revolutions* was published as a monograph in a series entitled Foundations of the Unity of Science: Toward an International Encyclopedia of Unified Science. Otto Neurath was the founding editor, and Rudolf Carnap and Charles Morris were the associate editors. Kuhn's work does raise important implications that lend themselves to an interpretive perspective. However, his project also has some strong positivist leanings. Perhaps this just indicates, in Kuhn's terms, that a paradigm shift in the history of science is in progress. It may also suggest that paradigms do not necessarily tend to become closed systems of thought.

9. See the Chapter by Kelly Coyle for a postmodern interpretation of the project of ethnomethodology.

10. Legge and Rawlins (1992) partially rely on Bochner's chapter as defining in what sense they are employing an interpretive analysis. I would refer to Legge and Rawlins's article as employing a qualitative method but not within an interpretive paradigm. I am not sure that the Legge and Rawlins method could be considered interpretive in any of the senses that Bochner had in mind. As in the Legge and Rawlins article, the designation "interpretive" is frequently used by researchers when they rely on qualitative methods of collecting data such as self-reports or when they extend analysis beyond inductively or deductively arrived-at conclusions. The everyday sense of interpretation is conflated with the use of the term as designating a theoretical paradigm. Although there are certainly important relationships between everyday processes of interpretation and interpretation as practiced within phenomenological or hermeneutic research, collapsing the two without discussion obscures important issues.

11. The interpretive reliance on multiple perspectives to enrich understanding and establish saliency should not be confused with the qualitative method of triangulation to determine the objective validity of truth claims within a positivist paradigm. The two approaches belong to different paradigms and have different research objectives.

12. Lasch believes that humanist psychology and the human potential movement in general are entrenchment strategies that we have adopted in the face of a hostile, fragmented, and frustrating social

environment. In this sense, Lasch interprets the concerns with the self, typical of humanist psychology, as a desperate but understandable coping mechanism rather than as an expression of a pathology. Lasch remarks that "to avoid confusion, what I have called the culture of narcissism might better be characterized, at least for the moment, as a culture of survivalism" (1984, p. 57). The problem for Lasch is that the location of the struggle for meaning in the individual as an isolated psychological personality not only misconstrues effect for cause, but also exacerbates the problem by conceiving of selfhood independent of relational, social, and historical context.

13. Because we try to symbolize our desires for ourselves in the attempt to construct a sense of self, our self also remains an enigmatic Other with evocative powers of our-its "own." The elaboration of a postmodern theory of self is a theme that I am developing in a work in progress.

14. Frank J. Macke (1991) comments on the history of the speech discipline from the perspective of speech as embodied subjectivity. He contends that the role of the sensuous body as part of the communication process has been subdued and that the field of study could benefit from a postmodern revitalization of teaching speech performance.

15. My spatial metaphor might imply a model of communication based on overlapping Venn diagrams, indicating that communication takes place when two or more people share a common set of experiences. However, borderlands do not "belong" to anyone (they are not simply an area of overlap of my experiences and the other's). Nor do boundaries mark sets of unambiguously identifiable experiences. The objectification of experience retains an enigmatic dimension of meaning partly because of its understanding through embodied subjectivity and partly because of the constitutive role of communication. The spatial metaphor is meant to draw attention to aspects of the lived experience of geographic space that are particularly relevant to communication. It is not meant to model logical relationships (as do Venn diagrams).

16. Here, "should" is an ethical imperative, not a theoretical one. I believe that such ethical imperatives emerge from encounters with others, not as a priori transcendental implications of communication taken as a telos, as Habermas argues, but from the work of text co-production, the evocative character of texts, and the life-world of the interlocutors taken together.

17. The partial exceptions to this tendency are studies in the ethnography of communication and discourse analysis. These exceptions have some implications for the postmodern study of interpersonal communication, but as already mentioned, they are usually conducted as

either traditional social science research or as qualitative research informed by the positivist paradigm.

18. Schrag (1989) also attempts to articulate a general concept of the text while accounting for its dynamic and semantically rich character. He chooses the term *texture* to express the weaving of meaning that objectifying consciousness accomplishes.

19. Wilden (1972, 1987) has done the most to articulate a postmodern version of systems theory. Lanigan (1988) provides an integration of postmodern systems theory, Frankfurt School critical theory, semiotics, and phenomenology in an approach that he variously calls *semiotic phenomenology* and *communicology*.

20. In fairness to systems theorists, General Systems Theory does include a term for systems that undergo internal structural change. Such systems are called *morphogenic*. I would suggest that the ramifications of this concept are epistemologically and ontologically profound in a way that systems theorists rarely discuss. The notions of morphogenisis and open systems, when taken together, problematize the ability to locate a system identity that is coherent over time and has clear boundaries. In short, these concepts throw into doubt the validity of the concept of identity in general, when applied to the "system" called *human being*.

21. Carbaugh and Hastings's approach relies on a mix of qualitative and interpretive assumptions. For instance, the authors describe the Basic theoretical orientation and Activity theory phases as "acontextual and acultural," even though they include these phases within a reflexive methodology that closely resembles the hermeneutic circle.

22. Rose (1990), someone who otherwise fits my characterization of a postmodern ethnographer, suggests that letting go of the dualism between researcher and researched means the researcher can let himself or herself "go native" without informing researched persons of the researcher's role and then write a research report about the role ambiguities thus experienced. This version of postmodern ethnography treats the notion of collaboration at a theoretical level without incorporating it into research methodology. Consequently, it is a version that I would reject. Not only is it not fully collaborative, but it seems to aim at reporting about an empathetic but monological understanding more consistent with romantic hermeneutics than the explorations of self-other boundaries and borderlands.

REFERENCES

Arac, J. (Ed.). (1986) *Postmodernism and politics*. Minneapolis: University of Minnesota Press.

Atkinson, P. (1990). *The ethnographic imagination: Textual constructions of reality.* London and New York: Routledge.

Barthes, R. (1975). *The pleasure of the text.* New York: Hill and Wang.

Baudrillard, J. (1983). *Simulations.* New York: Semiotext(e).

Berger, P., & Luckmann, T. (1966). *The social construction of reality.* Garden City, NY: Doubleday Books.

Bochner, A. (1985). Perspectives on inquiry: Representation, conversation, and reflection. In M. L. Knapp & G. R. Miller, (Eds.), *Handbook of interpersonal communication* (pp. 27–58). Beverly Hills, CA: Sage Publications.

Bormann, E. G. (1989). *Communication theory.* Salem, WI: Sheffield Publishing Co.

Bostrom, R., & Donohew, L. (1992). The case for empiricism: Clarifying fundamental issues in communication theory. *Communication Monographs, 59*(2), 109–129.

Bruner, E. M. (1986). Experience and its expressions. In V. W. Turner & E. M. Bruner (Eds.), *The anthropology of experience* (pp. 3–30). Urbana and Chicago: University of Illinois Press.

Carbaugh, D., & Hastings, S. O. (1992). A role for communication theory in ethnography and cultural analysis. *Communication Theory, 2*(2), 156–165.

Collins, R. (1986). *Media, culture, and society: A critical reader.* London: Sage Publications.

Conquergood, D. (1991). Rethinking ethnography: Towards a critical cultural politics. *Communication Monographs, 58*(3), 179–194.

Deleuze, G., & Guattari, F. (1977). *Anti-Oedipus, capitalism and schizophrenia.* New York: Viking Press.

Derrida, J. (1974). *Of grammatology.* Baltimore: Johns Hopkins University Press.

Featherstone, M. (1991). *Consumer culture and postmodernism.* Newbury Park, CA: Sage Publications.

Fisher, W. R. (1987). *Human communication as narration: Toward a philosophy of reason, value, and action.* Columbia: University of South Carolina Press.

Foster, H. (Ed.). (1983). *The anti-aesthetic: Essays on postmodern culture.* Port Townsend, WA: Bay Press.

Geertz, C. (1983). *Local knowledge: Further essays in interpretive anthropology.* New York: Basic Books.

Goodall, L. (1990). A cultural inquiry concerning the ontological and epistemic dimensions of self, other and context in communication scholarship. In G. M. Phillips & J. T. Wood (Eds.), *Speech communication: Essays to commemorate the 75th anniversary of the speech communication association* (pp. 264–292). Carbondale: Southern Illinois University Press.

Hall, S. (1985). Signification, representation, ideology: Althusser and the post-structuralist debates. *Critical Studies in Mass Communication, 2,* 91–114.

Hall, S., Hobson, D., Lowe, A., & Willis, P. (1981). *Culture, media, language.* London: Hutchinson.

Hymes, D. (1962). The ethnography of speaking. In T. Gladwin & W. Sturtevant (Eds.), *Anthropology and human behavior* (pp. 15–53). Washington DC: Anthropological Society of Washington.

Hymes, D. H. (1978). *What is ethnography?* Sociolinguistic Working Paper 45. Austin: Southwest Educational Development Laboratory.

Knapp, M. L., & Miller, G. R. (1985). Introduction: Background and current trends in the study of interpersonal communication. In M. L. Knapp & G. R. Miller (Ed.), *Handbook of interpersonal communication* (pp. 7–26). Beverly Hills: Sage Publications.

Lacan, J. (1977). *Écrits: A selection.* New York: W. W. Norton and Company.

Langellier, K., & Hall, D. L. (1989). Interviewing women: A phenomenological approach to feminist communication research. In K. Carter & C. Spitzack (Eds.), *Doing research on women's communication: Perspectives on theory and method* (pp. 193–220). Norwood, NJ: Ablex.

Lanigan, R. L. (1988). *Phenomenology of communication.* Pittsburgh: Duquesne University Press.

Lannamann, J. W. (1991). Interpersonal communication research as ideological practice. *Communication Theory, 1*(3), 179–203.

Lasch, C. (1979). *The culture of narcissism: American life in an age of diminishing expectations.* New York: Warner Books.

Lasch, C. (1984). *The minimal self: Psychic survival in troubled times.* New York: W. W. Norton & Company.

Lash, S. (1990). *Sociology of postmodernism.* New York: Routledge.

Legge, N. J., & Rawlins, W. K. (1992). Managing disputes in young adult friendships: Modes of convenience, cooperation, and commitment. *Western Journal of Communication, 56*(3), 226–247.

Littlejohn, S. W. (1992). *Theories of human communication* (4th ed.). Belmont, CA: Wadsworth Publishing Co.

Lyotard, J. (1984). *The postmodern condition: A report on knowledge.* Minneapolis: University of Minnesota Press.

Macke, F. J. (1991). Communication left speechless: A critical examination of speech communication as an academic discipline. *Communication Education, 40*(2), 125–143.

Malinowski, B. (1967). *A diary in the strict sense of the term.* London: Routledge and Kegan Paul.

Marcus, G. E., & Fischer, M. M. J. (1986). *Anthropology as cultural critique: An experimental moment in the human sciences.* Chicago: University of Chicago Press.

McLuhan, M. (1964). *Understanding media: The extensions of man.* New York: McGraw-Hill.

Nelson, J. (1989). Phenomenology as feminist methodology: Explicating interviews. In K. Carter & C. Spitzack (Eds.), *Doing research on women's communication: Perspectives on theory and method* (pp. 221–241). Norwood, NJ: Ablex.

Ong, W. J. (1982). *Orality and literacy: The technologizing of the word.* New York: Methuen Books.

Penniman, T. K. (1974). *A hundred years of anthropology.* New York: William Morrow & Company.

Philipsen, G. (1992). Recent books in qualitative research. *Communication Education 41*(2) 240–245.

Philipsen, G., & Carbaugh, D. (1986). A bibliography of fieldwork in the ethnography of communication. *Language and Society, 15,* 387–398.

Poole, M. S., & McPhee, R. D. (1985). Methodology in interpersonal communication. In M. L. Knapp & G. R. Miller (Eds.), *Handbook of interpersonal communication* (pp. 100–170). Beverly Hills, CA: Sage Publications.

Presnell, M. (1989, November). *Postmodernism and the discontinuity of rhetoric and philosophy.* Paper presented at the Speech Communication Association Convention. San Francisco.

Putnam, L., & Pacanowsky, M. E. (1983). *Communication and organization: An interpretive approach.* Beverly Hills, CA: Sage Publications.

Rose, D. (1990). *Living the ethnographic life.* Newbury Park, CA: Sage Publications.

Schrag, C. (1989). *Communicative praxis and the space of subjectivity.* Bloomington: Indiana University Press.

Stewart, J. R. (1986). Speech and human being: A complement to semiotics. *Quarterly Journal of Speech, 72*(1), 55–73.

Stewart, J., & Philipsen, G. (1984). Communication as situated accomplishment: The case of hermeneutics and ethnography. In B. Dervin & M. J. Voigt (Eds.), *Progress in communication sciences* (pp. 177–217). Norwood, NJ: Ablex.

Stocking, G. W., Jr. (Ed.). (1991). *Colonial situations: Essays on the contextualization of ethnographic knowledge.* Madison: University of Wisconsin Press.

Turner, V. W. (1986). Dewey, Dilthey, and drama: An essay in the anthropology of experience. In V. W. Turner & E. M. Bruner (Eds.), *The anthropology of experience* (pp. 33–44). Urbana and Chicago: University of Illinois Press.

Tyler, S. (1986). Post-modern ethnography: From document of the occult to occult document. In J. Clifford & G. Marcus (Eds.), *Writing culture: The poetics and politics of ethnography* (pp. 122–140). Berkeley: University of California Press.

Van Maanen, J. (1988). *Tales of the field: On writing ethnography.* Chicago: University of Chicago Press.

Wilden, A. (1972). *System and structure: Essays in communication and exchange.* London: Travistock Publications.

Wilden, A. (1987). *The rules are no game: The strategy of communication.* New York: Routledge & Kegan Paul.

2

An Interpretive Approach to Validity in Interpersonal Communication Research

JOHN STEWART

VALIDITY IS A PRIMARY CRITERION used to evaluate the results of research both by those who believe that "experimentation . . . [is] the only available route to cumulative progress" (Campbell & Stanley, 1966, p. 3) and those committed to the "many variants of 'qualitative' and interpretive research—ethnographies, case studies, ethnomethodological and grounded-theory inquiries, and analyses of texts and discourses" (Mishler, 1990, p. 416). Scholars and laypeople agree that validity is something good advice, sound organizational policies, and worthwhile research findings should have, but there is no universal agreement about what it "is" or how one "gets it." Not only does the research literature include dozens of direct discussions of validity as a construct (e.g., Blalock, 1982; Campbell & Stanley, 1966; Cook & Campbell, 1979; Cronbach, 1972; LeCompte & Goetz, 1982; Lincoln & Guba, 1985; Mishler, 1990), but other disputes, such as the debate over the use of examples to establish claims from conversation analytic research, are also centrally about the validity of methods and findings (Pomerantz, 1990; Cappella, 1990; Jacobs, 1990).

One reason for the lack of consensus is conceptual slippage; there are at least three general accounts of validity in the research literature: the classical, pluralist, and interpretive perspectives. None of these perspectives includes a thorough explication of the ontological and epistemological assumptions underlying it. But all validity claims involve explicit or implicit arguments about how confidently one can accept a knowledge claim (epistemology) or what "actual world" the claim is

45

about (ontology). Therefore a discussion of validity that does not address these issues is inherently incomplete. Fortunately, thorough discussions of these assumptions can be found in some recent philosophical works, and these discussions can usefully inform the approaches to validity taken by some interpersonal communication scholars. After sketching the three accounts and characterizing what is at stake philosophically, this chapter reviews two interpretive approaches to validity taken by the prominent philosophers, Charles Taylor (1985a, 1985b, 1988) and Hans-Georg Gadamer (1976, 1989a, 1989b). The primary goal of this review is to illustrate how philosophical analyses can aid in clarifying theoretical and methodological issues in interpersonal communication research. The final section of the chapter employs the philosophies of Taylor and Gadamer to elucidate two recent discussions of validity in the interpersonal literature, the argument for "representational" validity in interpretive content analysis (Baxter, 1991; Folger, Hewes, & Poole, 1984; Folger & Poole, 1982; Rogers & Millar, 1982) and the debate over the use of examples in conversation analysis (Jackson, 1986; Jacobs, 1986, 1990; Pomerantz, 1990; Cappella, 1990).

THREE VERSIONS OF VALIDITY

The classical definition of validity captures what for many social scientists are the central features of the construct:

> validity is concerned with the accuracy of scientific findings. Establishing validity requires determining the extent to which conclusions effectively represent empirical reality and assessing whether constructs devised by researchers represent or measure the categories of human experience that occur. Internal validity refers to the extent to which scientific observations and measurements are authentic representations of some reality. External validity addresses the degree to which such representations may be compared legitimately across groups. (LeCompte & Goetz, 1982, p. 32)[1]

In the classical view, validity claims are about the *correspondence* between conclusions and constructs, on the one hand, and "empirical reality" or "the categories of human experience," on the other. Here validity is a measurement of the accuracy of certain *representations*.

In their book-length treatment of validity, Brinberg and McGrath (1985) resist the classical perspective, because they believe it is oversimplified. They propose instead a pluralistic approach. Their review of social scientific literature identifies over a dozen kinds of validity including construct, content, convergent, criterion-related, discriminant, ecological, explanatory, external, face, internal, methodological, predictive, and statistical conclusion validity. They attempt to cope with this terminological hodgepodge, first by arguing that validity should not be treated as a clearly definable, quantifiable feature that can be determined to be either present or absent in a given study and then by proposing a pluralist version of the construct. They distinguish among three research "domains" (conceptual, methodological, and substantive), three "levels" (elements, relations, and an embedding system), three "stages" (generative, central, and follow-up), three "paths or styles for conducting the central stage" (experimental, theoretical, and empirical), and three research "orientations" (basic, applied, and technological) (Brinberg & McGrath, pp. 15–21). Brinberg and McGrath argue that "the concept of validity takes on fundamentally different meanings in each of the three stages" of research (p. 16). In the preparatory stage, "validity means *value* or worth"—how important, significant, useful, or desirable the research is. In the central stage—data gathering, analysis, and interpretation—"validity means *correspondence* or fit" between elements of the substantive, conceptual, and methodological domains. In the third, follow-up or replication stage, "validity means *robustness* [or] *generalizability* (pp. 19–20).

A third influential contemporary approach to validity begins by distinguishing between two research paradigms—"positivist," "experimental," or "hypothesis testing," on the one hand, and "naturalistic" or "inquiry guided," on the other. From this perspective, validity for the latter paradigm is synonymous with "trustworthiness" (Mishler, 1990, Lincoln & Guba, 1985). Mishler (1990) observes that "Those . . . in the social sciences who do inquiry-guided research have long been aware that the standard approach to validity assessment is largely irrelevant to our concerns and problems" (p. 416). He acknowledges that, "[l]ike the fabled Gordian Knot, validation is a mess of entangled concepts and methods," and in what may be a reference to Brinberg and McGrath (1985), Mishler contends that "[s]ophisticated, technical procedures pulling out and straightening each thread, one at a time, seem to leave the knot very much as it was" (p. 416). His alternative is to adopt "trustworthiness" as a way of "reformulating validation as the social construction of knowledge." He anchors this reformulation primarily in recent studies of "actual practices of scientists rather than on textbook idealizations" (p. 417). These studies, he argues, reveal that

> First, no general, abstract rules can be provided for assessing overall levels of validity in particular studies or domains of inquiry. Second, no formal or standard procedure can be

determined either for assigning weights to different threats to any one type of validity, or for comparing different types of validity. These assessments are matters of judgment and interpretation. And these evaluations depend, irremediably, on the whole range of linguistic practices, social norms and contexts, assumptions and traditions that the rules had been designed to eliminate. (p. 418)

Thus the interpretive approach holds that validity assessments are situationally and communicatively accomplished. As Mishler (1990) puts it, "reformulating validation as the social discourse through which trustworthiness is established elides such familiar shibboleths as reliability, falsifiability, and objectivity" by clarifying that they are outcomes of rhetorical and interpretive strategies (p. 420). Lincoln and Guba's (1985) account of validity as trustworthiness also highlights the interpretive, situationally accomplished, and persuasive dimensions of the construct, and in the interpersonal communication literature, Jackson's (1986) and Jacobs's (1986, 1990) discussions similarly emphasize the rhetorical nature of validity claims.

A PHILOSOPHICAL CHOICE WITH LITTLE PHILOSOPHICAL GUIDANCE

So how does one select from among classical, pluralist, and interpretive approaches to validity? Typically the experienced researcher adopts the approach and conventions that, over time, have become most accepted by those in his or her primary professional network—others doing similar work, editorial boards of salient journals, and often-cited authorities. The beginning scholar tends to follow the lead of his or her research methods professor or mentor. But seldom does one find an argument for an approach to validity that clearly explicates its philosophical grounds. In fact, the opposite is more common. For example, Lincoln and Guba (1985) explicitly claim to "make no real effort to ground the writing in the philosophical and epistemological literature that is so relevant" (p. 9). Similarly, Brinberg and McGrath (1985) explain that they "will not examine epistemological issues in depth, but only discuss those issues briefly, insofar as needed to describe our schema" (pp. 9–10). They then offer a 14-line sketch of their tendency to "lean heavily toward a philosophy of 'hypothetical realism,'" which they attribute to Donald T. Campbell (Campbell, 1981). In their words, this position in essence says that we do not know whether there is really a "real world." We are confident that, if there is a "real world" we can know it only "through a glass darkly." But at the same time, we believe that the underjustified presumption of the existence of a real world makes sense to use for those intellectual endeavors we call science, just as it does for our everyday experience. (Brinberg & McGrath, 1985, p. 10)

Virtually the only other epistemological comment these authors make occurs in their discussion of the "substantive domain" of research, where they identify "the basic unit of study for the social and behavioral sciences as 'actors behaving toward objects in context' " (Brinberg & McGrath, 1985, p. 33).[2]

Their avoidance of philosophical issues helps prevent Brinberg and McGrath from recognizing that their three senses of validity reflect two incommensurable epistemologies. When validity is treated as "correspondence" or "generalizability-robustness," the implicit epistemological assumption is that theoretical propositions and research findings are fundamentally different from the objective realities they are "about." Thus the correspondence view assumes that research findings can be tested by assessing how well they correspond with, represent, reflect, or are applicable to an objective reality. This analysis is consistent with hypothetical realism and similarly naturalistic ontologies. When validity is treated as "value or worth," on the other hand, there is no such assumption about the distinction between a claim and what it is about. In this case, validity assessments *embody* cultural and social preferences rather than *representing* a "hypothetical reality." Moreover, these preferences are communicatively accomplished, so the epistemological ground in this case is interpretive rather than realistic or naturalistic. Given their pluralism, Brinberg and McGrath (1985) may actually want to embrace two fundamentally different epistemologies. But their comments about hypothetical realism and about "actors behaving toward objects in context" suggest otherwise.

The tendency to gloss over epistemological issues is also evident in the work of LeCompte and Goetz (1982). They do not explicitly express disinterest in philosophical topics, but their discussion of reliability and validity also illustrates how confusion can arise when such issues are ignored. For example, they purport to *contrast* "the tenets of external and internal validity and reliability as they are used in positivistic research traditions" with those applied "by ethnographers and other researchers using qualitative methods" (p. 31). They highlight how "ethnographic research differs from positivistic research" (p. 32) and attempt to "translate" reliability and validity concerns from the positivistic to the ethnographic paradigm in ways that affirm these differences.

The problem with their account is that they present what they refer to as distinct approaches to validity as if they are both grounded in the same epistemology. As the "classical" definition cited earlier indicates, LeCompte and Goetz (1982) treat validity in both experimental and ethnographic research as a matter of determining the correspondence, match, or degree of representativeness between research constructs or findings and "empirical reality" (p. 32). "Validity," they claim, "necessitates demonstration that the propositions generated, refined, or tested match the causal conditions which obtain in human life" (p. 43); and again, "researcher designated constructs . . . should be grounded in and congruent with actual data" (p. 47).

Like hypothetical realism, this analysis assumes that human subjects can be accurately understood as existing over against an independent world of objects that they can more or less accurately represent in their language or cognitions. This epistemology clearly embodies the so-called Cartesian-Kantian, subject-object distinction that first became prominent in the 17th century. A great deal of philosophical analysis over the past 60 years has questioned this subject-object distinction and the view of knowledge as representation based on it. But LeCompte and Goetz (1982) do not appear to be aware of this literature. Much of this philosophical work has clarified the radical differences between the Cartesian assumptions that ground representational epistemologies and post-Cartesian assumptions that ground interpretive accounts of validity. For example, in their analyses post-Cartesian philosophers have seriously questioned both the notion of "the sovereign, rational subject" and claims about the existence of objective "brute data." Their consensus, as one philosopher (McCarthy, 1987) summarizes it, is now that (1) because it is no longer possible to deny the influence of the unconscious on the conscious or the intrinsically social character of consciousness,

> the epistemological and moral subject has been definitively decentered. . . . Subjectivity and intentionality are not prior to but a function of forms of life and systems of language; they do not "constitute" the world but are themselves elements of linguistically disclosed world. (p. 5)

Moreover, (2) subject and object cannot be set off from one another as Descartes and Kant attempted to do. It is impossible to make sense of the idea of a linguistically naked "given" that is interpreted in various more or less adequate ways, or of "an invariant 'content' that is incorporated into different 'schemes'—the final dogma of empiricism" (p. 5). As a result, it is now acknowledged (3) that objects of knowledge are always already preinterpreted, "situated in a scheme, part of a text, outside which there are only other texts. [And] . . . the subject of knowledge belongs to the very world it wishes to interpret" (p. 5).

In other words, the philosophers whom McCarthy (1987) summarizes argue that there are problems with both the "subject" and the "object" poles of the Cartesian-Kantian picture of the world and thus with the representational accounts of validity based on it. On the one hand, they contend, there is literally no such thing as the autonomous "subject," "self," or "individual." These constructs obscure both the unconscious and the inherently social features of humans. For one thing, humans are beings in relation, physiologically, psychologically, socially, and culturally. Though humans are obviously individually embodied, the boundaries of our skin are not the boundaries of our "selves." Our identities are relational, social, historical, cultural, and interpersonal; we are not simply "subjects" but "intersubjective" (Mead, 1934; Sullivan, 1953; Buber, 1965; Shotter, 1984). Moreover, what we call "objects" are not, in McCarthy's words, "linguistically naked 'givens.' " A great deal of perception and cross-cultural research—to say nothing of the testimony of countless eyewitnesses to crimes and accidents—has verified that "what" one senses depends in part on his or her agendas. Physiological constraints, cultural values, expectations, linguistic competencies, conformity pressures, and other factors affect the identification and definition of "what's out there" or "the objective world."

If reminded of these arguments and conclusions, LeCompte and Goetz (1982) would probably acknowledge and even agree with them. But, at least partly because they do not address central philosophical concerns, these authors do not appear to recognize either how thoroughly these critiques of the subject-object distinction challenge their view of validity or how difficult it would be to integrate this analysis into their approach. The central problem is this: given these difficulties with the constructs "subject" and "object," what can it now mean to say that validity means "correspondence or fit" between elements of the conceptual (subjective) and the substantive (objective) domains (Brinberg & McGrath, 1985, p. 20), or that a construct or finding "accurately represents reality" or "corresponds with the causal conditions which obtain in human life" (LeCompte & Goetz, 1982, p. 32)?

This question is also not answered by those who, following Campbell (1981), adopt tentative versions of the Cartesian-Kantian view. Their "hypothetical realism" is based on the same dichotomy between subjects and objects that many post-Cartesian philosophers critique. Although hypothetical realists appear to escape the representational problem by expressing uncertainty about whether there is actually something that "gets represented," in fact they only avoid it by presuming that data are out there even though one cannot know for sure. Having begun with this assumption, they then develop an approach to validity that is subject to the same challenges as those sketched previously. But, primarily because they have chosen not to "examine epistemological issues in depth" (Brinberg & McGrath, 1985, p. 9), these scholars appear to be unaware of the extent to which either the critiques of the subject-object split or the classical and pluralistic accounts of validity are incoherent.[3]

Interpersonal scholars' understanding of validity may therefore be enhanced by a discussion of some philosophical issues central to this construct. Such a discussion is relevant to researchers in all the human studies, but it is particularly so for communication scholars. First, because of the inherently interdisciplinary nature of communication research, it is especially important for these scholars to be able to identify the most appropriate and productive approaches to their research questions and to evaluate competing claims grounded in different methodologies. This is exactly the enterprise that engages Pomerantz (1990), Cappella (1990), and Jacobs (1990). In addition, because of the complex, situated, and relational nature of their subject matter, communication researchers are especially vulnerable to claims that only research approaches grounded in *post*-Cartesian philosophy can do justice to their research questions. Leeds-Hurwitz (1989) and I (Stewart, 1991) have argued for this approach, and Baxter (1991) grapples with this issue as she explores interpretive or qualitative enhancements of classical content analysis research methods.

I offer a discussion of some of these philosophical issues here in the form of a review of two approaches to validity taken by the post-Cartesian interpretive philosophers: Charles Taylor (1985a, 1985b, 1988) and Hans-Georg Gadamer (1976, 1989a, 1989b). Both are students of Heidegger, and both argue against what Taylor (1985b) calls "the ambition to model the study of [the hu]man on the natural sciences" (p. 1). But each develops a distinct program. Taylor writes in the tradition of British philosophers of language and focuses explicitly on philosophy of the human sciences, whereas Gadamer works out of the German tradition of Hegel and Humboldt as he develops his version of an ontologically–focused philosophical hermeneutics. My goal in reviewing selected works by these philosophers is first to demystify their discussions of validity in an effort to encourage more interpersonal scholars to address these issues. In addition, I hope to demonstrate the usefulness of these philosophical analyses by applying Taylor's and Gadamer's approaches to the two already-mentioned discussions of validity in the communication literature. I hope that this application will illustrate how interpersonal scholars' discussions of validity issues can be fruitfully informed by post-Cartesian, interpretive works.

CHARLES TAYLOR'S APPROACH TO VALIDITY

To summarize Charles Taylor's perspective on validity I review his central ideas about the "subject" and the "object" in the Cartesian model, and then sketch the approach to validation that he develops from these ideas. Taylor's post-Cartesian orientation is evident when he argues that the central issues confronting the human sciences are not epistemological, as Descartes maintained. They are ontological, he contends, because they embody an "understanding of human agency, of a person or self" (Taylor, 1985b, p. 3). "We might say," he also writes, that what is at stake "is an ontological issue which has been argued ever since the seventeenth century in terms of epistemological considerations which have appeared to some to be unanswerable" (1985b, p. 17).

The Subject

Taylor's central ontological claims about the "subject" are that persons are "self-interpreting animals," which is to say that "our self-interpretations are partly constitutive of our experience" (Taylor, 1985a, p. 37), and that human agents are characterized by "the significance feature," which is to say that "things *matter* for them" in a unique, nonderivative way (Taylor, 1985a, pp. 98, 197). To say that persons are "self-interpreting" is in part to acknowledge that human identity is situation-specific—that is, continually changing—and that it is culturally and socially negotiated. Hence subjectivity cannot simply be construed as a Cartesian "consciousness" or "cogito." That persons are self-defining also affects the understanding of language. As Taylor (1985b) explains,

> If we are partly constituted by our self-understanding, and this in turn can be very different according to the various languages which articulate for us a background of distinctions of worth, then language does not only serve to *depict* ourselves and the world, it also helps *constitute* our lives. (p. 9)

For instance, a certain linguistically negotiated self-understanding, undergirds the subjectivity of a Christian ascetic; another self-understanding is required to be a university president. Successful "being" either requires working out a particular discursive self-understanding.

Taylor (1988) highlights the second distinctive feature of humans in his arguments against the basic project of artificial intelligence (AI) researchers. Unlike computers, he writes, "things matter" to humans. "Things can go well or ill for them; they have purposes, ends they strive for, which are being fulfilled or frustrated. They also, above some phylogenetic level, feel. None of this is true of my desk calculator" (p. 450). Although this difference between humans and machines cannot be understood in terms of "consciousness," which Descartes treated as a power to frame representations, AI researchers, Taylor argues, maintain a version of this representational perspective. Taylor's alternative is to argue that the inherently self-defining and valuing features of human beings make it impossible to reduce *thinking* or *intelligence* to *calculating*. There is a fundamental difference, he argues, and "believing that computers think is ignoring the difference." How does this ignoring happen? "The reasons lie deep in the hold of us of rationalist-empiricist epistemology, according to which knowing the world is having a correct inner representation of outer reality" (Taylor, 1988, p. 451). In several of his essays Taylor claims that self-defining and valuing are not just contingent facts about human agents but are "essential to what we would understand and recognize as full, normal human agency" (1985b, p. 3).

Objects

Taylor develops his view of the Cartesian "object" and introduces his direct account of validity in his discussion of the senses in which the human sciences are "hermeneutical." Because "hermeneutical" has traditionally meant "based on interpretation," he raises the central question, "what are the criteria of judgment in a hermeneutical science? A successful interpretation is one which makes clear the meaning originally present in a confused, fragmentary, cloudy form. But how does one know that this interpretation is correct" (Taylor, 1985b, p. 17)? Traditionally, he notes, one responded to this question—and thus established the validity of an interpretation—by appealing to the "brute data" that the interpretation purports to render understandable. "By 'brute data,'" he writes, "I mean here and throughout data whose validity cannot be questioned by offering another interpretation or reading, data whose credibility cannot be confounded or undermined by further reasoning" (1985b, p. 19). But, Taylor points out, an interpretation can make sense of the original text only by appealing to our understanding of the language of expression of both the text and the interpretation.

> Our conviction that the account makes sense is contingent on our reading of action and situation. But these readings

cannot be explained or justified except by reference to other such readings, and their relation to the whole. If an inter-locutor does not understand this kind of reading, or will not accept it as valid, there is nowhere else the argument can go. Ultimately, a good explanation is one which makes sense of the behavior; but then to appreciate a good explanation, one has to agree on what makes good sense; what makes good sense is a function of one's readings; and these in turn are based on the kind of sense one understands. (Taylor, 1985a, p. 24)

In short, we can convince an interlocutor of the validity of a reading only by further reading. If he or she does not share our understanding of the language concerned, "there is no further step to take in rational argument; we can try to awaken these intuitions in [the person] or we can simply give up; argument will advance us no further" (Taylor, 1985b, p. 18). Taylor's point is that there is no way to "break out" of this interpretive circle to connect with "brute data." In the human sciences there is no Archimedean point from which a researcher can directly contact such data. Or to hypostasize the construct, there *are* no "brute data."

Validity

These views of "subjects" and "objects" coalesce in Taylor's account of "how we validate social theories" (Taylor, 1985a, p. 91). He develops three major claims about validation. First, natural science theory should not be taken as a model for social theory because of

the nature of the common-sense understanding that [social] theory challenges, replaces, or extends. There is always a pre-theoretical understanding of what is going on among the members of a society, which is formulated in the descriptions of self and other which are involved in the institutions and practices of that society. (Taylor, 1985b, pp. 92–93)

In other words, the self-descriptions that are an inherent feature of persons constitute an important part of the frame or context of any particular social theory. *Like* natural science theories, social theories claim to tell us what is really going on. But *unlike* those theories, the commonsense view that a social theory upsets or extends "plays a cru-cial, constitutive role in our practices." As a result, "the alteration in our understanding which theory brings about can alter these practices; so that, unlike with natural science, the theory is not about an indepen-dent object, but one that is partly constituted by self-understanding"

(Taylor, 1985b, p. 98). This is one vitally important implication of his claim that there are no such things as "brute data."

Taylor's second point is that, because the practices that social theories are about are partly constituted by self-understandings, "to the extent that theories transform this self-understanding, they undercut, bolster or transform the constitutive features of practices" (Taylor, 1985b, p. 101). This is the sense in which social theories are not about "independent objects" in the way natural science theories are. As a result, the validation of social theory cannot employ a correspondence model, "where the theory is true to the extent that it correctly characterizes an independent object" (1985b, p. 101). Certainly some simple social actions are regular enough to be accounted for with theories that follow a natural science model. "But this could never be the general model for social science" (1985b, p. 104). So how can social theories be validated?

Taylor's third point is that social theories are validated by being tested in practice. That is, "because theories which are about practices are self-definitions, and hence alter the practices, the proof of the validity of a theory can come in the changed quality of the practice it enables. Let me introduce terms of art for this shift of quality, and say that good theory enables practice to become less stumbling and more clairvoyant" (Taylor, 1985a, p. 111). *More clairvoyant* does not necessarily mean more successful; a social theory may reveal why and how a practical enterprise is not worth continuing. But the central point is that, because of the self-defining nature and praxical orientation of the beings whose behavior social theories attempt to explain, these theories can be validated only by assessing their impact on the practices of the persons to whom they are applied. But importantly, "to test the theory in practice means . . . not to see how well the theory describes the practices as a range of independent entities; but rather to judge how practices fare when informed by the theory" (1985b, p. 113). So Taylor's practical test consists mainly of (1) applying the theory to the practices it purports to explain and (2) determining how, if at all, the practices change when informed by the theory.

Taylor (1985b) concludes his account of validation by citing the example of the 1970–1980 debate about economic theories of inflation. Early in this period, he notes, economists argued that inflation could be explained by factors that could be manipulated, "that is, by factors which could be adjusted without any change in people's self-definitions: the level of demand, levels of taxation, size of government deficit, growth of money supply." But by the early 1980s they were arguing that inflation is "largely fuelled by our political relations, in other words, in part by the self-definitions implicit in our dominant practices" (p. 115). In this case, he argues, economic theory began to be validated only when it acknowledged the centrality of self-definitions on the economic practices it purported to explain.

In sum, Charles Taylor offers an approach to validity that begins by radically reformulating the Cartesian categories that ground the traditional accounts I reviewed. The "subject" is no longer a "conscious pole" existing over against a world of objects, because he or she is continually self-defining and these definitions help constitute the world he or she inhabits. Correlatively, there is no world of "objects"—brute data—because "what is" is *for* a self-defining subject. Because there is no Archimedean point, in practice there are no brute data. As a result, correspondence approaches are obviated and validity becomes a criterion used to assess how well a theory informs the practices it is designed to explain. Validity is thus not established by determining how well a finding "fits objective reality" but by employing the finding and assessing how effectively it "enables practice to become less stumbling and more clairvoyant."

One need not accept all of Taylor's arguments to exploit his insights about validity in the human sciences. But his work is one example of how a philosopher approaches validity by directly addressing relevant epistemological and ontological considerations. In the final section of this chapter, I illustrate some ways Taylor's approach can be used by interpersonal communication researchers.

HANS-GEORG GADAMER'S APPROACH TO VALIDITY

Validity issues figured prominently in the book that first introduced Gadamer's hermeneutics to English-speaking readers. Palmer (1969) demonstrated that the then-prominent versions of hermeneutics developed by Emilio Betti and E. D. Hirsch were grounded in the conviction that one could trust the validity of an interpretation only to the degree that it faithfully recaptured its author's original intent. These writers maintained that the central question of hermeneutics is, "How can one obtain a valid interpretation?" and the answer is that one assesses the correspondence between it and the determinate, changeless, reproducible author's meaning (Hirsch, 1967, p. 46). But as Palmer (1969) explained, Heideggerian-Gadamerian hermeneutics began from a fundamentally different question: "What is the nature of understanding itself?" (Palmer, 1969, p. 66). Thus, like Taylor's program, Gadamer's is more ontological than epistemological, although, partly because he rejects the Cartesian foundations of many of his predecessors (Gadamer, 1984, pp. 57–58), Gadamer does deal directly with validity issues.

Like Taylor, Gadamer critiques traditional accounts of the subject, objects, and knowledge as representation. But there are several distinctive aspects of Gadamer's approach to validity that can best be displayed by reviewing three general characteristics of his program, which are embedded in the title of his major work, *Truth and Method:* (1) its universal scope, (2) his disconnection of validity from methodology, and (3) his insistence on anchoring validity tests in communication rather than consciousness. Gadamer also develops three specific arguments that follow from his general perspective.

Truth, Method, and Validity

As the first word in the book's title suggests, Gadamer's concerns are universal in scope. "Understanding and interpretation," he writes

> have to do with the general relationship of human beings to each other and to the world. . . . The ability to understand is a fundamental endowment of [the hu]man, one that sustains his [or her] communal life with others and, above all, one that takes place by way of language and the partnership of conversation. In this respect, the universal claim of hermeneutics is beyond all doubt. (1989b, p. 21)

So when Gadamer writes about how one pursues truth or develops confidence in research findings, he is addressing not only qualitative researchers or those in the human sciences; his claims are about human understanding generally—across disciplines and ways of knowing.

The title of Gadamer's (1989a) work also emphasizes that no method, scientific or otherwise, can guarantee certainty, validity, or truth. In the final paragraph of this work he summarizes.

> Throughout our investigation it has emerged that the certainty achieved by using scientific methods does not suffice to guarantee truth. This especially applies to the human sciences, but it does not mean they are less scientific, on the contrary, it justifies the claim to special humane significance that they have always made. The fact that in such knowledge the knower's own being comes into play certainly shows the limits of method, but not of science. Rather, what the tool of method does not achieve must—and really can—be achieved by a discipline of questioning and inquiry, a discipline that guarantees truth. (pp. 490–491)

This "discipline of questioning and inquiry" is Gadamer's philosophical hermeneutics. He maintains that it is "a discipline that guarantees truth," but not by prescribing a methodology or series of steps to be followed.

A third general feature of Gadamer's approach to validity is that it begins from the originary event of language rather than from the indubitability of the cogito. In a major essay Gadamer (1989b) echoes some of Taylor's central concerns as he contrasts his program with Cartesian ones that begin with the assumption

> that the subject takes hold of empirical reality with method-ological self-certainty by means of its rational mathematical construction and . . . then expresses this reality in propositional statements. In this way the subject fulfills its true epistemological task, and fulfillment climaxes in the mathematical language with which natural science defines itself as universally valid. (p. 29)

The central problem with this approach, Gadamer argues, is that "the midworld [Zwischenwelt] of language is left out of consideration here in principle" (1989b, p. 29). The Cartesian program elevates self-consciousness to an "almost mythical status," of "apodictic self-certainty and [of] the status of origin and justification of all validity." Gadamer's alternative emphasizes "the priority of the domain of language, a domain that we cannot undermine and in which all consciousness and all knowledge articulates itself." The irreducible reality from which inquiry begins, in other words, is not the "conscious subject" but "language" construed as the *event of conversing.*

So, according to Gadamer, one does not establish valid interpretations or findings by being a technical virtuoso of method. Instead, if one observes how validating actually occurs, one can recognize that it emerges when thinkers (1) encounter "something that asserts itself as truth" (1989a, p. 489), (2) apply it to its relevant practices (pp. 332–334, 339–341), and (3) assess what it "comes to in being worked out" (p. 267). Gadamer clarifies how these three validity moves work as he discusses the roles of closure and certainty, the nature of validating experience, and the qualitative features of validating conversation.

Closure and Certainty

First, he argues that an "encounter with something that presents itself as truth" does not typically lead the inquirer to closure or to what is normally thought of in this context as certainty. Throughout his work Gadamer emphasizes the finite quality and incomplete nature of human understanding. When he argues (1989a) that play is a "clue to ontological explanation," for example, he notes in part that "the movement of playing has no goal that brings it to an end; rather it renews itself in constant repetition" (p. 103). Just as on game of football, chess, or poker is the "final" or "definitive" one, so understanding can be only complete–given–the–circumstances or adequate–for–present–purposes. The U. S. Bill of Rights was certainly "understood" when it was drafted in 1791, but we understand it differently today, after 200 years of application and court interpretation, and it will be understood still differently on its tri- and quadricentennials.

As I noted earlier, the final four words of *Truth and Method* (Gadamer, 1989a) characterize philosophical hermeneutics as "a discipline that guarantees truth" (p. 491). Clearly Gadamer believes in a kind of certainty. But he contrasts the "certainty acquired in life," the "immediate and living certainty that all ends and values have when they appear in human consciousness with an absolute claim" with "the kind of certainty afforded by a verification that has passed through doubt." One difference is that "scientific certainty always has something Cartesian about it. It is the result of a critical method that admits only the validity of what cannot be doubted" (p. 238). So he does not promise—and in fact does not even encourage the pursuit of—any certainty guaranteed by a methodology. But he does argue that a high degree of confidence can be attained by the person who pursues understanding via encounter, application, and assessment.

Erlebnis and Erfahrung

A second specific feature of Gadamer's approach to gaining confidence in an understanding is embedded in the distinctions between the German terms *Erlebnis* and *Erfahrung*. Both translate into English as "experience," but they differ significantly. *Erlebnis* labels an experience one "has" of something. The use of *Erlebnis*, says Gadamer, was especially developed by Wilhelm Dilthey as part of his effort to establish an epistemological foundation for the human sciences that contrasted with the natural sciences. Dilthey's account of Erlebnis assumed the validity of Descartes's distinction between *res cogitans* (the subjective) and *res extensa* (the objective), and thus this "concept of experience is the epistemological basis for all knowledge of the objective" (Gadamer, 1989a, pp. 65–66). Gadamer also describes how this account of experience as Erlebnis dominated classical and romantic aesthetic theory and led to the treatment of aesthetic experience as a grasping of "the infinite whole" (p. 70).

Whereas *Erlebnis* designates experience as something a subject "has" of an object, *Erfahrung* is the term for experience as something one *undergoes* or is *subject to*. Gadamer highlights this distinction and suggests some of its implications:

> Dilthey . . . was not able to escape his entanglement in traditional epistemology. Since he started from the awareness of "experiences" (Erlebnisse), he was unable to build a bridge

to the historical realities, because the great historical realitities of society and state always have a predeterminate influence on any "experience." Self-reflection and autobiography—Dilthey's starting points—are not primarily and therefore not an adequate basis for the hermeneutical problem, because through them history is made private once more. In fact history does not belong to us; we belong to it. Long before we understand ourselves through the process of self-examination, we understand ourselves in a self-evident way in the family, society, and state in which we live. The focus of subjectivity is a distorting mirror. The self-awareness of the individual is only a flickering in the closed circuits of historical life. (p. 276)

So experience as Erfahrung happens *to* us; the individual does not wholly control it or engage in it as a subject grasping an object. Because it happens to us, this kind of experience cannot be confirmed by being repeated or replicated. For one thing, we cannot determine all the conditions that create experience and to repeat it would, as Gadamer (1989a) notes, "abolish history and thus itself" (p. 347). It follows that this kind of experience

is experience of human finitude. The truly experienced person is one who takes this to heart, who knows that he [or she] is master neither of time nor the future. The experienced [hu]man knows that all foresight is limited and all plans uncertain. . . . Real experiences is that whereby [the hu]man becomes aware of his [or her] finiteness. (p. 357)

In sum, Gadamer's detailed history of how humans come to understand human artifacts and actions and how we validate our understanding shows that correspondence methods of developing confidence in knowledge claims constitute only a very narrow route to validity. Two features of the broader route he proposes are (1) that it substitutes tentative, context dependent, and experientially based confidence for methodologically guaranteed certainty and (2) that it privileges receptivity and responsiveness over instrumental domination. Undergoing the experience of a finding, letting a finding happen to us, and then following it through in application is a legitimate—and in fact predominant—way to validate it.

Conversation

Ultimately Gadamer argues that truth emerges in finite, situated, thoughtful conversation. Just as no clearly delineated method guarantees that a conversation will produce agreement, satisfaction, conflict resolution, or closure, no method guarantees truth, validity, or absolute confidence in an interpretation or finding. But just as thoughtful conversation commonly produces insights, problem definitions, and solutions which are entirely adequate for the interlocutors' purposes, so it can produce similarly adequate validity assessments.

Because for Gadamer validity ultimately emerges in and from conversation, it is important to understand what he means by this term. Six properties are crucial: Gadamerian conversation (1) is somewhat uncommon, though not rare; (2) includes critique; (3) focuses on subject matter not on those conversing; (4) pursues increased insight over self-defense; (5) develops each interlocutor's strongest case; and (6) acknowledges incompleteness.

VALIDATING CONVERSATION IS UNCOMMON THOUGH NOT RARE Like most philosophers, Gadamer purports to be reflectively reporting his experience. He does not mean to prescribe a form of conversation in which scholars "should" engage, but to summarize the qualities or features of thoughtful conversations he has lived—participated in and observed between others in face-to-face and written exchanges. He admits, though, that this quality of contact is often experienced as wheat surrounded by considerable chaff. As he writes,

> To be sure the "binding element" in conversation, in the sense of that which produces itself in the form of the self-generating language of mutual comprehension, is by its very nature necessarily surrounded by *Gerede*, or idle chatter, and thus by the mere appearance of speaking. . . . Just this suggests the primacy that must be accorded to the kind of conversation that evolves as question and answer and builds up a common language. (1989b, p. 106)

VALIDATING CONVERSATION INCLUDES CRITIQUE Habermas (1970) claims that Gadamer has a naive, idealistic view of conversation that ignores the uncooperative, critical, manipulative, "antidialogic" or "anticonversational" realities of many exchanges. This issue has also been raised to explain the alleged failure of the planned "encounter" between Gadamer and Derrida in 1981. In response to his critics, Gadamer has maintained that his view of conversation definitely includes challenge and critique. For example, in response to Derrida's claim that his approach unrealistically assumes a dissolving of differences or a "covering-up of otherness," Gadamer (1989b) clarifies that, when he writes that understanding basically involves agreement, he does not mean by *agreement* the creation of an "abiding and identifiable 'one' (*Eines*], but just to what takes place in conversation as it goes along" (p. 119). Neither groupthink nor self-justification is the outcome of conversation as Gadamer conceives of it. "To be in a conversation," he writes, "means to be beyond oneself, to think with the other and to come back to oneself as if to another" (p. 110), thereby integrating critique.

VALIDATING CONVERSATION FOCUSES ON *DIE SACHE* NOT SUBJECTIVITIES   Gadamer distinguishes his view of conversation from the person-centered, therapeutically oriented conceptions elaborated by such writers as Karl Japsers (1955), Martin Buber (1965), Emannuel Levinas (1969), Gabriel Marcel (1949), Carl Rogers (1980), and Abraham Maslow (1970). At several points in *Truth and Method*, he underscores his interest, not in the subjectivities or personal growth of the dialogue partners but in *die Sache*, the issue or subject matter at the heart of the exchange. The "truth" of the words spoken in genuine conversation, he writes,

> lies in what is said in them, and not in an intention locked in the impotence of subjective particularity. Let us remember that understanding what someone says is not an achievement of empathy in which one divines the inner life of the speaker. Certainly it is true of all understanding that what is said acquires its determinacy in part through a supplementing of meaning from occasional sources. But this determination by situation and context, which fills out what is said to a total-ity of meaning and makes what is said really said, pertains *not to the speaker but to what is spoken* [italics added]. (1989a, p. 489)

So the conversation that Gadamer views as paradigmatic of human understanding is not about individual feeling states but matters beyond the subjectivities of the interlocutors. "The dialogical character of lan-guage, which I tried to work out, leaves behind it any starting point in the subjectivity of the subject, and especially in meaning-directed inten-tions of the speaker" (Gadamer, 1989b, p. 26). "In a conversation, it is *something* that comes to language, not one or the other speaker" (1989b, p. 122).

VALIDATING CONVERSATION PURSUES INCREASED INSIGHT Not only is the topic larger than or separate from the individuals, but the goal of the interchange is also. The point is not to "win," "excel," or defend one's position, but to further the articulation of a problematic and to test findings and insights. "To conduct a conversation . . . requires that ones does not try to argue the other person down but that one really considers the weight of the other's opinion. Hence it is an art of testing. But the art of testing is the art of questioning" (Gadamer, 1989a, p. 367). "The speaker is put to the question until the truth of what is under discussion finally emerges. . . . What emerges in its truth is the logos, which is neither mine nor yours" (p. 368). "One must seek to understand the other, and that means that one has to believe that one could be in the wrong" (1989b, p. 119).

VALIDATING CONVERSATION DEVELOPS EACH STRONGEST CASE   Philosophical hermeneutics, Gadamer (1985) summarizes, "insists that there is no higher principle than holding oneself open in a conversation. But this means: Always recognize in advance the possible correctness, even the superiority of the conversation partner's position" (p. 189). In his reply to Derrida's criticism of his discussion of "good will," Gadamer (1989b) notes that he is not relying on the Kantian formula but rather on what Plato called *eumeneis elenchoi,*

> that is to say, one does not go about identifying the weaknesses of what another person says in order to prove that one is always right, but one seeks instead as far as possible to strengthen the other's viewpoint so that what the other person has to say becomes illuminating. (p. 55)

This kind of conversation "is not the art of arguing (which can make a strong case out of a weak one) but the art of thinking (which can strengthen objections by referring to the subject matter)" (1989a, p. 367).

VALIDATING CONVERSATION ACKNOWLEDGES INCOMPLETENESS When one affirms the finitude of all human understanding, one recognizes that the pursuit of any genuinely substantive problematic will necessarily be incremental and therefore that one needs to remain committed to the conversation. Importantly, the point is not that one is willing to persevere because of the naive belief that all differences will be overcome. Instead, one perseveres because one recognizes that incompleteness and imperfection are the nature of the human condition. One accepts—and even gratefully lives in—the tension created between a recognition of the importance of *die Sache* and the realization that one will never attain the certainty that would completely "answer" the question. In short, the researcher substitutes for the pursuit of closure, certainty, and control a recognition of the incompleteness of human knowledge and a concomitant commitment to the ongoing scholarly conversation.

Gadamer's account of validity is supported by a recent description of the research activities of a group of geneticists at the Center for Molecular Genetics in Heidelberg. As part of a forum on Representation in Scientific Practice, Amann and Knorr Cetina (1988a) describe how "data" and "evidence" are coconstituted in talk between and among researcher-interlocutors. In their description of how the scientists "see" or "read" the autoradiograph film they work with, the authors explain that "The resulting perceptual identification is . . . the product of conversational talk. What difference does this make? When embedded in talk, 'seeing' is interactively accomplished" (p. 138). In other words, these scientists confirm Gadamer's account as they negotiate valid understandings and interpretations in talk; the "interactional organization" and "conversational devices" they employ mirror the qualities of conversation Gadamer highlights. For example, there is no one prescribed method for achieving valid understanding (Amann & Knorr Cetina, 1988a, p. 144), and interlocutors "use their disagreement to produce novel (not previously obvious) features of the phenomenon discussed" (p. 152). Other ethnographies of scientific work are similarly congruent with Gadamer's account (Amann & Knorr Cetina, 1988b; Lynch, 1988; Woolgar, 1988).

AN INTERPRETIVE APPROACH TO VALIDITY

As I noted, it is not necessary to accept all of Taylor's or Gadamer's arguments to profit from their analyses of validity. But it is instructive to compare the approaches by LeCompte and Goetz (1982), Brinberg and McGrath (1985), and Mishler (1990) which I summarized earlier with Taylor's and Gadamer's approaches (see Table 2.1).

Like classical approaches to validity, these interpretive ones respond to the central question, "How do we know that the researcher has gotten it right?" or "How can we develop confidence in research designs and findings?" Unlike earlier approaches, however, these argue that validity is not determined by assessing the *correspondence* or degree of *representativeness* between some more-or-less "subjective" proposition or finding and an aspect of the "real" or "objective" world, but is accomplished in interpretive praxis and ongoing shoptalk. Approaches that construe validity as "trustworthiness" and emphasize the rhetorical dimensions of the validity-assessment process (Lincoln & Guba, 1985; Jackson, 1986; Jacobs, 1986; Mishler, 1990) obviously parallel these interpretive perspectives. But Taylor and Gadamer provide a much more fully worked-out rationale for this approach and thus can enable com-

Table 2.1.   Two Interpretive Approaches to Validity

Charles Taylor	Hans-Georg Gadamer
Rejects Cartesian subject-object analysis; central issues are ontological not epistemological.	Develops a post-Cartesian hermeneutics interrogating "understanding" ontologically rather than treating it as an epistemological achievement.
Treats "subjects" as self-interpreting hence self-constituting.	Treats understanding as a universally distinctive feature of the person.
"Objects" qua "brute data" do not exist, because humans cannot get "behind" or "beyond" interpretations.	Disconnects validity or "truth" from method, because no method guarantees truth.
Rejects a Cartesian analysis of validity as correspondence between cognition or proposition and "brute data."	Develops a conversational model of validity assessment.
Natural science versions of validity cannot be the model for social theory.	The event of conversation, not consciousness, is the primary human reality: Validating conversation does not produce closure or certainty.
Social theories are about practices constituted in part by self-understandings.	This conversation happens to one—it is experience as *Erfahrung.*
Social theories can be validated only in practice. The test: "A good theory enables practice to become less stumbling and more clairvoyant."	Validating conversation is not idle chatter, naive consensus, or person-centered therapy.
	This conversation involves the thoughtful pursuit of substantive questions, commitment to insight not self-aggrandizement, interest in the other's strongest case, tentativeness, and the willingness to persevere.
Informed and thorough validity assessments emerge from this kind of test–in–practice.	Informed and thorough validity assessments emerge from this kind of conversation.

munication scholars to reflect much more cogently and thoroughly on validity issues. To illustrate these practical benefits of their interpretive perspectives, I conclude with a reading of two recent discussions of this problematic. The first calls attention to a single issue raised by Taylor and Gadamer, and the second thematizes several interrelated issues.

INTERPRETIVE VALIDITY AND INTERPERSONAL COMMUNICATION RESEARCH

Representational Validity of Content Analysis

Baxter (1991) argues that traditional "manifest content analysis" could usefully be developed into "interpretive content analysis" by broadening the analyst's interest in *meaning*. Such a move would require that the researcher give attention to the reliability and validity of coding categories. "The criterion by which to determine the validity of the categorizations in an interpretive content analysis," Baxter argues, is that the categories should "capture 'the native's point of view' " (p. 243, citing Geertz, 1973). This interest in the "native's point of view," she notes, "shows remarkable conceptual similarity to *representational validity*. This form of validation refers to whether one's categorizations capture the conventional meanings that would be ascribed to the content by members of the speech community" (p. 243).

Baxter (1991) comments that this kind of representational validity has been discussed by Folger, Hewes, and Poole (1984) as an important means of validation of coding in what they call the "experiencing" (as contrasted with the "experienced" and the "experiencer") mode of research observation (pp. 141–153). She also briefly reviews the dispute over the appropriateness of representational validity as a criterion for assessing relational coding schemes (Folger & Poole, 1982; Rogers & Millar, 1982). Baxter mentions Rogers and Millar's (1982) argument that representational validity is not appropriate for their research enterprise, and she concludes, "without taking a position one way or the other on this particular debate, it is simply worth noting that neither side to the debate challenged . . . the value of representational validity when the content analyst claimed to interpret meanings . . . " (p. 244).

Taylor's and Gadamer's discussions of validity can help clarify one way in which Baxter's analysis is incomplete by highlighting an issue that is central to the applications being made by all these scholars but almost completely overlooked in their discussions. The issue is this: *When assessing representational validity, exactly what is to be "represented"? And if it is impossible to specify what is represented, can the construct of representational validity itself be coherent?* As I have already noted, this issue is raised by the Cartesian bias of an epistemology, which treats knowledge as a matter of the subject more or less accurately "representing" aspects of "objective reality" and validity as correspondence between such "representations" and some "represented."

Folger and Poole (1982) claim that the validity of relational coding schemes is weak because researchers work from observer-defined constructs that are not checked against subjects' understandings. So in their view, that which is "represented" is something like "the shared, relational functions of messages" (p. 238), or "subjects' shared interpretations" (p. 243). They claim that to establish representational validity the researcher must simply "(a) determine what representation of interaction subjects' shared interpretations yield, (b) determine what representation of interaction a coding scheme yields, and (c) draw an empirical comparison between the two representations" (p. 243). Rogers and Millar (1982) reject Folger and Poole's (1982) criticism of the validity of their coding scheme primarily by distinguishing between others' studies of *meaning* and their studies of behavioral *patterns*. They ague that validating coding against subject interpretations is unnecessary when one is studying behavior patterns, primarily because "relationships are immanent in messages, rather than expressed by messages" (pp. 250–251, citing Bateson, 1972, p. 245). In other words, when the focus of the researcher's inquiry is *present in* the phenomenon being studied, rather than cognitively "behind" it, it is neither necessary nor appropriate to validate research findings by assessing the degree to which they correspond with or represent some other psychological phenomenon. Then Rogers and Millar argue that the best way to test their findings is to assess "which types of data . . . account for the most variance (a) in which relational contexts, (b) with what types of people, (c) on what content areas, and (d) when in the development, maintenance and change of interpersonal relationships" (p. 251). This appears to be an approach to validation which tests findings by determining what they come to in being worked out. But this suggestion is left undeveloped.

In short, Rogers and Millar claim that the interpretive meaning against which Folger and Poole want them to validate their coding cannot be decided upon, which is to say that for all practical purposes the "represented" of "representational validity" does not exist—or at least it is inaccessible. In addition, they propose an approach to testing findings that appears to rest on ontological assumptions consistent with those explicated by Taylor and Gadamer. But the issues are not explicitly worked through, despite the fact that they are absolutely central to the point at issue. The reader is left wondering whether or not there is something for representational validity to represent.

In a subsequent contribution to this debate, Folger et al. (1984) provide a much more extensive discussion of coding, but their account of representational validity is similarly problematic with respect to this central issue. Like Folger and Poole (1982) they characterize what is represented as "shared interpretations of interactors" (p. 144). But importantly, Folger et al. (1984) acknowledge the problematic nature of the construct, "shared interpretations of interactors," and they cite Charles Taylor's work as support. They note Taylor's (1971) claim that researchers often force subjects to make "unnatural" responses along dimensions of their own creation (p. 249). And they asset that it is

> imperative that we evaluate the degree to which the subject representation is held in common by subjects. There is simply no way of knowing whether any method—no matter how rigorous or conceptually strong it might be—will generate a subject representation that indexes shared interpretive schemes. We can only make such a determination a posteriori, for specific shared constructs and specific cultures, and we must collect and analyze our data in such a way that determination of commonality is possible. (pp. 149–150)

Later they spell out, again with Taylor's help, why it is so difficult to generate an accurate "representation" of "shared interpretive schemes."

> To code language in its social context is to code within the context of commonly held interpretive schemes; it is to interpret (either explicitly or implicitly) the intersubjective meanings that are "constitutive of the social matrix in which the individuals find themselves and act" and that "are not the property of a single person because they are rooted in social practice." (pp. 151–152, citing Taylor, 1971, p. 48)

Here Folger et al. clearly sense the difficulty of identifying what is to be "represented" when assessing "representational validity," but they appear to have grasped only part of Taylor's point. As noted earlier, Taylor's central claim is that humans are uniquely self-interpreting, self-defining animals, Hence, the "social practices" that constitute their meaning making are praxical and in flux. A researcher may be able to reify some aspects of these practices into a phenomenon labeled *subjects' meanings*, but there is no one-to-one relationship between that artifact of research methodology and the experiences and outcomes of the practices themselves. This is why Folger et al. (1984) are correct when they note that "there is no way of knowing" whether a method will generate "a subject representation that indexes shared interpretive schemes" (p. 149). But they are incorrect about the possibility of generating such a representation "a posteriori." The same basic problems that undercut any attempts to establish representational validity during the study also undercut later efforts to do the same thing.

This problem also threatens Baxter's (1991) appropriation of representational validity for interpretive content analysis. Although she acknowledges both Rogers and Millar's (1982) rejoinder to Folger and Poole (1982) and Folger et al.'s (1984) analysis, she does not work out the problems with representational validity that Taylor's work raises. She mentions, for example, the need for the researcher "to seek understanding from the informant perspective, not the researcher perspective" (p. 246), and she cites with approval a study by Douglas (1987) that, she argues, achieved representational validity by presenting to informants "three examples from the initial pool of 101 strategies that represented each category type" (Baxter, 1991, p. 247) so they could sort them into like-kind clusters. Her claim is that, because the informants' clusters corresponded statistically with the researcher's clusters, it is safe to conclude that the researcher's interpretations accurately *represented* the informants'. But Taylor's analysis suggests that some important elements are omitted in this account, namely the self-defining, self-interpreting nature of the informants. Like Folger et al. (1984), Baxter appears to be overlooking the degree to which self-interpreting keeps both "the representation" and "the represented" indeterminate or in a state of flux. One could also construct a parallel rebuttal of Baxter's conclusion based on Gadamer's claim that, when reconstructions are assumed to match the original constructions, one is, in effect, "abolishing history" and thus distorting the character of human—and hence inherently historical—phenomena being studied.

In sum, had these writers been informed by Taylor's and Gadamer's discussions of validity, they might have been able, first, to recognize the central ontological issue that their analyses raised and, second, to discuss it in a way that is conceptually more coherent and complete. The result would have been a significantly different discussion of representational validity.

Interaction-Discourse-Conversation Analytic Claims

In a forum published in *Communication Monographs,* Pomerantz (1990), Cappella (1990), and Jacobs (1990) exchange views of "the validity and generalizability of conversational analysis methods." This discussion extends earlier analyses by Jackson (1986) and Jacobs (1986, 1988). The treatments of validity provided by Taylor and Gadamer can contribute to this discussion by sharpening the issues among these scholars and by clarifying some ambiguities in their positions.

Jacobs and Jackson explicitly begin from the conviction that, as Jackson (1986) puts it, "No set of mere rules will prove to be sufficient guarantors of truth. Methodology is better seen as a way of reasoning about the phenomena, a way of generating arguments for what we believe to be true" (p. 145). This, of course, is exactly Gadamer's point in *Truth and Method* (1989a); he emphasizes the first claim more than the second, but both are wholly consistent with his perspective. As the communication scholars' discussion illustrates, this is also a very important claim.

One way to illustrate its importance is to observe what happens to it in Pomerantz's argument. She begins by citing Jacobs's (1988) expression of it: "The rationality of any research enterprise is guaranteed not by some set of established procedures," but by argument (Pomerantz, 1990, p. 231). But then, as Pomerantz moves to the question-answer sections of her essay, which most directly address validity issues, she seems to treat validity much more as a function of following methodological rules or techniques than as a product of rhetorical argument. For example, in response to the question, "Why don't you validate your characterizations by surveying?" she responds that "characterizations" usually do not need to be validated because they are propadeutic, but that they "hopefully lead to analyses," (p. 232), which, she implies, may well employ standard social scientific methods of validation. To the question, "Why don't you validate by using the method of checking with the informant who provided the sample of talk?" she responds that this method of asking may not get at the unconscious reality *behind* the talk. To the question, "What warrant do you have for saying that [a feature] is used regularly?" she responds that she waits until she has come across "perhaps a half dozen of them," which indicates that she has "located a phenomenon" (p. 233). Despite this apparent interest in "*n*," she emphasizes, however, that claims about regularity are "not the news, or value, of the analysis" (p. 233). And to the final question, "How would you test your predictions?" she replies that if she wanted to "test" them in this sense, she would need different *methods*: "different collections of data . . . control environments and . . . adequate samples . . . " (p. 234). It is possible to interpret all of these responses as appeals to methodological choices. Moreover, a commitment to some kind of correspondence test appears to be implicit in Pomerantz's interest in "analyses" that follow up initial characterizations and unconscious realities "behind" the talk, and a related assumption about method appears to ground the fact that she trusts "half a dozen" cases more than she trusts a single one. In these ways, Pomerantz's responses do not appear to be wholly consistent with her original distinction between anchoring validity in method and anchoring it in argument.

One might expect Cappella (1990), given his defense of "older methodologies" (p. 241), to adopt the view of validation via method common to many of those approaches. But through most of his essay he works within Jackson's (1986) characterization. For example, he explains that one of his central points "is not to deny that arguments from example can be useful; it is to deny that argument from example is as strong an argumentative principle as argument from frequency (plus baseline expectation)" (p. 239). He also offers two specific criticisms of the argumentative force of examples in interaction analysis studies (pp. 239–241). There is some ambiguity on this point in Cappella's conclusion. "The claim that methods are arguments," he writes, "does not entail the claim that arguments are methods." He continues, "The conclusion that there exist arguments for claims other than those generated by scientific or quantitative methods does not entail the conclusion that these other argumentative strategies are preferable to or even equivalent to those generated by *standard scientific practice*" (p. 241, italics added). It appears here that he may be contrasting "standard scientific practice," that is, methods, with "argumentative strategies." But he maintains that the criterion for acceptance of one or the other set of methodologies ought to be plausibility, and he concludes that "there are good reasons to disprefer the methodology of proof by example" (p. 241) because of the weakness of its claims. So it appears that Cappella adopts the view that methods provide arguments for the validity of claims, not techniques that guarantee their truth.

Given Jacobs's and his coauthor's earlier work (Jacobs, 1986, 1988; Jackson, 1986; Jackson & Jacobs, 1980), it is not surprising that in this exchange Jacobs consistently maintains the position that methods provide arguments, not certain demonstrations. But Jacobs's discussion could also be sharpened by an awareness of the philosophical literature on this set of issues.

First, Jacobs's characterization of Capella's position could be clearer if he were to acknowledge that one central question is whether Capella's approach is fundamentally Cartesian or post-Cartesian. Jacobs (1990) argues that "Cappella and other quantitative interaction analysts' conceptualize structure and order "independently of any intrinsic meaningfulness to those events. Structure and order are equated with regularity of occurrence compared against a baseline of randomness" (p. 244). This claim could be understood as Jacobs accusing Cappella and others of treating structure and order as Cartesian "objects" that exist independent of any "subject's" interpretations of "*sense* and *meaningfulness*" (Jacobs, 1990, p. 244). Jacobs (1990) contrasts discourse analysts'

treatments with those of interaction analysts, because the former identify structures that are "observably present in discourse not because
they have a certain conditional probability of occurrence, but because
they are *interpretable* [italics added] forms made recognizable by the
communicative practices and commonsense reasoning principles of natural language users" (p. 245). In other words, for discourse analysts,
these structures are not (Cartesian) objects but (post-Cartesian) interpretations or construals. Jacobs seems to be arguing here that interaction analysts are committed to a Cartesian world of objects and discourse
analysts are not, because discourse analysts agree with Gadamer that
the irreducible human reality is not consciousness engaged with objects
but the paradigmatic event of conversation.

But it is not clear that Cappella takes the position Jacobs attributes to him. Cappella (1990) insists that interaction analysts must
study both "identifiable sequences" and "what events and sequences
'count as' . . . (to participants, to observers, to the cultures which sur-
round interactants)" (p. 238). Thus he clearly includes some version of
the "meaningfulness" Jacobs accuses him of ignoring, which means that
at least part of the time Cappella (1990) is not construing the focus of
his work as a kind of Cartesian object. On the other hand, when Cappella
argues that an example of talk chosen by a discourse analyst may be
nothing more than a "random event sequence" (pp. 240–241), he appears to be reinforcing Jacobs's view. Clearly this part of the disagreement between Jacobs and Cappella could be sharpened by both authors
clarifying their position on a central issue treated by Gadamer; namely,
whether discourse structure is something to be *discovered*—out there,
objectively in the discourse—or something to be *interpreted*—construed
from interlocutors' practical accomplishments. This difference is basic:
claims about discourse structure as an "objective" phenomenon will be
fundamentally different from claims that treat such structure as interpretively defined. Moreover, one's position on this issue will dramati-
cally affect the advice one offers about how to study, diagnose, and alter
this structure.

These authors' claims about the role of the public and of publication in validity assessments could also be clarified if these discussions
were anchored in the philosophical literature. As noted earlier, Gadamer
contends that findings need to be tested in application; those can be
discarded that "come to nothing in being worked out." He also contends that the mutually inquiring, topic-focused to and fro of serious,
public conversation is the model for validity assessment. Taylor concurs
when he emphasizes that the reason natural scientific validity tests are
inappropriate for social theories is that social theories are *practices*
constituted in part by the self-understandings of the persons involved.

He argues for validation via practice, which means that findings are applied to the public, community practices they attempt to explain in order to see if they help the practices become "less stumbling and more clairvoyant."

Many indirect references to this interpretive approach to validity are embedded in Jacobs's (1990) discussion. He claims that Cappella's doubts about "whether qualitative research can ever deliver secure claims about conversational structure" are groundless, because a large "community of researchers" has already subjected them "to public test" and they have turned out to be "manifest[ly] successful" (p. 243). "Readers can see" whether discourse analytic claims are reasonable, he argues (p. 245), and the "empirical corrective" for invalid claims is the "community of analysts who actively set out to falsify the analysis in any particular study" and the "tradition of studies" they develop (p. 247). Here Jacobs is describing exactly the kind of conversation that Gadamer contends is the primary site of validating events.

In his earlier work, Jacobs (1986) explicitly emphasizes the role of scholarly exchange by the informed public, and this discussion goes even further to highlight the legitimacy of *verisimilitude* as a validity criterion. Jacobs (1986) writes,

> Because examples are assumed to more or less publicly exhibit properties generated by the rules of language, any reader who has mastered those rules can evaluate the prima facie adequacy of any characterization of an example by inspecting that example and comparing the characterization to his [or her] own native intuitions. (p. 155)

He cites O'Keefe's (1982) account of the same criterion for ordinary language philosophy analyses: "The ground of my analysis... is my appeal to the reader's native sense of the concepts in question: if my intuitions... are idiosyncratic or skewed... [they] will not ring true to the reader's ear... " (see Jacobs, 1986, p. 155). Later in this essay Jacobs (1986) speaks of cases "that strongly resonate with the intuitions of any reader" (p. 156), and he concludes his response to Cappella with a reference to the test of "the extent that the cases fail to ring true with our own experiences... " (Jacobs, 1990, p. 248). Importantly, *intuition* can be a misleading term here. But, as was explained earlier, Gadamer and Taylor clarify how it is meant when they emphasize that one tests examples against lived experience, practical application, and the rigorous test of focused conversation, not simply against one's spontaneous hunches.

This distinction is clearer in Walter Fisher's (1987) discussion of verisimilitude as "narrative fidelity." Fisher's construct is a thoroughly post-Cartesian validity criterion. He offers no pretense that the validity of a construct or finding can be determined by assessing the extent to which it captures or measures what (i.e., the brute data) the researcher thought he or she was measuring. Instead narrative fidelity tests the fit between the researcher's arguments about his or her experiences and the reader's experience. But it is one's lived experience—situated, historical, concrete life learnings—not one's sixth sense or second sight against which one checks to see if the findings "ring true." Fisher's is one of the clearer accounts of how, in practice, validity is established interpretively, rhetorically, or narratively.

Unfortunately, the central roles of the public, of publication, of interpretation, and of rhetoric are more implicit than explicit in Jacobs's (1990) discussion, and partly as a result, it is difficult to discern how this centrally important idea affects Pomerantz's and Cappella's arguments. Partly because of her focus on techniques rather than arguments, Pomerantz (1990) misses the opportunity to highlight the roles that convention critics, editors, associate editors, referees, and ultimately readers of research reports play in validity assessment. She concentrates instead on attenuating the claims of conversation analysts and clarifying the applicability of various methods. Some of Cappella's (1990) arguments also seem to ignore this feature. He contends that the discourse analyst's example may not in fact be exemplary but a random occurrence, and he worries about trusting "the representativeness of an example chosen by the researcher . . . who is not blind to his or her own hypotheses" (p. 240). In each case he seems to overlook the effects of critical readers' evaluations. And if Cappella were to support his point by citing published research that was subsequently contradicted, that would be evidence for, not against, the role of criticism in validity assessment. After reading all three of these discussions, one is left with a less than complete understanding of the central role in validity assessment played by (1) informed conversation and (2) tests in practice or application. As a result, it is possible to think of validity as an assessment guaranteed by applying the right method rather than one worked out in discursive praxis. In this way the misleading picture painted by Descartes is once again allowed to influence researchers' and readers' understandings.

In sum, this exchange about validity among interaction, discourse, and conversation analysts could be more sharply delineated if it were informed by philosophical treatments of these issues. The participants could more readily recognize inconsistencies between a basic position and its development and could more effectively distinguish between central and ancillary claims. They could sharpen points of agreement and disagreement between their positions and those of their interlocutors. They could also more clearly and accurately situate their arguments in the ongoing conversation about these questions among philosophers interested in language, communication, and applied validity tests. In all these ways they would much better serve their readers' efforts to understand validity and to develop valid conversation analytic research.

CONCLUSION

Taylor and Gadamer are clearly not the only contemporary philosophers who can contribute to interpersonal communication scholars' discussions of validity. Works by, for example, Wittgenstein (1953), Habermas (1984, 1988), Rorty (1979, 1982), Ricoeur (1981, 1984), and Donald Davidson (1980, 1983) also deserve attention. In addition, as I noted earlier, one does not have to concur with all of Taylor's or Gadamer's arguments about validity to profit from their analyses. But one element they add to the validity debate is thoroughness; their works demonstrate that a careful treatment of validity issues includes a reconsideration of central ontological and epistemological issues, including the traditional Cartesian subject-object distinction and the traditional account of knowledge as representation based on it. Moreover, as carried out by these two writers, this reconsideration is not just grist for some philosopher's mill; it is directly applicable to interpersonal communication theorizing and research. Gadamer argues that the ontologically irreducible human event is conversation rather than consciousness and works out a conversational model of validity assessment. Taylor emphasizes the self-interpreting, and therefore communicatively accomplished nature of human beings and the subsequent centrality of communicative practice to validity assessment. It is a very short intellectual distance from these arguments to, for example, interpersonal communication scholars' concerns over the role of "representational" validity in interpretive content analysis and strategies for validating interaction- and conversation-analytic claims. Perhaps unfortunately, Taylor, Gadamer, and those who translate accounts like theirs into treatments of validity as "trustworthiness" do not provide a validity receipe—a comprehensive list of research strategies and tactics for guaranteeing the strongest possible argument. But each points clearly toward ways of thinking, research designs, and ways of arguing that can enable the interpersonal communication researcher to treat validity issues credibly and persuasively.

NOTES

1. LeCompte and Goetz cite J. F. Hansen (1979), *Sociocultural Perspectives on Human Learning An Introduction to Educational An-*

thropology (Englewood Cliffs, NJ: Prentice-Hall); and P. J. Pelto and G. H. Pelto (1978) *Anthropological Research: The Structure of Inquiry,* 2nd ed. (Cambridge: Cambridge University Press).

2. As I clarify later in this chapter, this statement by Brinberg and McGrath reflects a Cartesian-Kantian view of the subject-object split and implies a concomitant representational view of validity.

3. Though as I noted, Brinberg and McGrath's (1985) approach is avowedly pluralist, it often appears that they privilege "stage two" research, where validity means "correspondence" or "fit." Ultimately the other kinds of validity they mention, especially "robustness or generalizability," depend on relationships among the findings of a series of controlled "stage two" studies. See Brinberg and McGrath (1985), pp. 128–129 and 159–160.

REFERENCES

Amann, K., & Knorr Cetina, K. (1988a). The fixation of (visual) evidence. *Human Studies, 11,* 133–170.

Amann, K., & Knorr Cetina, K. (1988b). Thinking through talk: An ethnographic study of a molecular biology laboratory. In R. A. Jones, L. Hargens, and A. Pickering (Eds.), *Knowledge and Society: Studies in the sociology of science past and present,* vol. 8 (pp. 193–217). Greenwich, CT: JAI Press.

Bateson, G. (1972). *Steps to an ecology of mind.* New York: Ballantine Books.

Baxter, L. (1991). Content analysis. In B. Montgomery & S. Duck (Eds.), *Studying interpersonal interaction* (pp. 239–254). New York: Guilford Press.

Blalock, H. M. (1982). *Conceptualization and measurement in the social sciences.* Beverly Hills, CA: Sage Publications.

Brinberg, D., & McGrath, J. E. (1985). *Validity and the research process.* Beverly Hills, CA: Sage Publications.

Buber, M. (1965). *The knowledge of man* (M. Friedman & R. G. Smith, Trans; M. Friedman, Ed.). New York: Harper and Row.

Campbell, D. T. (1981). Comment: Another perspective on a scholarly career. In M. B. Brewer & B. E. Collins (Eds.), *Scientific inquiry and the social sciences* (pp. 454–501). San Francisco: Jossey-Bass.

Campbell, D. T., & Stanley, J. C. (1966). *Experimental and quasi-experimental designs for research.* Chicago: Rand McNally.

Cappella, J. N. (1990). The method of proof by example in interaction analysis. *Communication Monographs, 57,* 236–240.

Cook, T. D., & Campbell, D. T. (1979). *Design and analysis of quasi-experiments for field settings.* Chicago: Rand McNally.

Cronbach, L. J. (1972). *The dependability of behavioral measurement.* New York: John Wiley.

Cronbach, L. J. (1982). *Designing evaluation of educational programs.* San Francisco: Jossey-Bass.

Davidson, D. (1980). Toward a unified theory of meaning and action. *Grazer Philosophische Studien, 2,* 1–12.

Davidson, D. (1983). *Inquiries into truth and interpretation.* Cambridge: Cambridge University Press.

Douglas, W. (1987). Affinity-testing in initial interactions. *Journal of Social and Personal Relationships, 4,* 3–15.

Fisher, W. R. (1987). *Human communication as narration: Toward a philosophy of reason, value, and action.* Columbia: University of South Carolina Press.

Folger, J. P., Hewes, D. E., & Poole, M. S. (1984). Coding social interaction. In B. Dervin & M. J. Voigt (Eds.), *Progress in communication sciences, 4* (pp. 115—162). Norwood, NJ: Ablex.

Folger, J. P., & Poole, M. S. (1982). Relational coding schemes: The question of validity. In M. Burgoon (Ed.), *Communication yearbook 5* (pp. 235–248). New Brunswick, NJ: Transaction Books.

Gadamer, H.-G. (1976). *Philosophical hermeneutics.* (D. Linge, Trans.). Berkeley: University of California Press.

Gadamer, H.-G. (1984). The hermeneutics of suspicion. In *Hermeneutics* (G. Shapiro & A. Sica, Eds.). Amherst: University of Massachusetts Press.

Gadamer, H.-G. (1985). *Philosophical Apprenticeships* (R. R. Sullivan, Trans.). Cambridge, MA: MIT Press.

Gadamer, H.-G. (1989a). *Truth and method* (2nd rev. ed.), (J. Weinsheimer & D. G. Marshall, Trans.). New York: Crossroad Books.

Gadamer, H.-G. (1989b). *Dialogue and deconstruction: The Gadamer-Derrida encounter* (D. P. Michelfelder & R. E. Palmer, Eds.). Albany: State University of New York Press.

Geertz, C. (1973). *The interpretation of cultures.* New York: Basic Books.

Habermas, J. (1970). A review of Gadamer's *Truth and method*. In F. R. Dallmayr & T. A. McCarthy, (Eds.), *Understanding and Social Inquiry* (pp. 335–363). Notre Dame, IN: Notre Dame University Press.

Habermas, J. (1984). *The theory of communicative action*, vol. 1, *Rationality and rationalization*. Boston: Beacon Press.

Habermas, J. (1988). *The theory of communicative action*, vol. 2, *The critique of functionalist reason*. Boston: Beacon Press.

Hirsch, E. D., Jr. (1967). *Validity in interpretation*. New Haven, CN: Yale University Press.

Jackson, S. (1986). Building a case for claims about discourse structure. In D. G. Ellis & W. A. Donohue (Eds.), *Contemporary issues in language and discourse processes* (pp. 129–148). Hillsdale, NJ: Lawrence Erlbaum.

Jackson, S., & Jacobs, S. (1980). Structure of Conversational Argument: Pragmatic bases for the enthymeme. *Quarterly Journal of Speech, 66,* 251–265.

Jacobs, S. (1986). How to make an argument from example in discourse analysis. In D. G. Ellis & W. A. Donohue (Eds.), *Contemporary issues in language and discourse processes* (pp. 149–168). Hillsdale, NJ: Lawrence Erlbaum.

Jacobs, S. (1988). Evidence and inference in conversation analysis. In J. A. Anderson (Ed.), *Communication yearbook 11* (pp. 433–443). Newbury Park, CA: Sage Publications.

Jacobs, S. (1990). On the especially nice fit between qualitative analysis and the known properties of conversation. *Communication Monographs, 57,* 243–249.

Jaspers, K. (1955). *Reason and existenz*. New York: Noonday.

LeCompte, M. D., & Goetz, J. P. (1982). Problems of reliability and validity in ethnographic research. *Review of Educational Research, 52,* 31–60.

Leeds-Hurwitz, W. (1989). *Communication in everyday life: A social interpretation*. Norwood, NJ: Ablex.

Levinas, E. (1969). *Totality and infinity* (A. Lingis, Trans.). Pittsburgh: Duquesne University Press.

Lincoln, Y. S., & Guba, E. G. (1985). *Naturalistic inquiry*. Beverly Hills, CA: Sage Publications.

Lynch, M. (1988). The externalized retina: Selection and mathematization in the visual documentation of objects in the life sciences. *Human Studies, 11,* 201–234.

Marcel, G. (1949). *Being and having* (K. Farrer, Trans.). New York: Harper Books.

Maslow, A. (1970). *Motivation and personality* (2nd ed.). New York: Harper and Row.

McCarthy, T. (1987). General introduction. In K. Baynes, J. Bohman, & T. McCarthy (Eds.), *After philosophy: End or transformation?* (pp. 1-20). Cambridge, MA: MIT Press.

Mead, G. H. (1934). *Mind, self, and society from the standpoint of a social behaviorist.* Chicago: University of Chicago Press.

Mishler, E. G. (1990). Validation in inquiry-guided research: The role of exemplars in narrative studies. *Harvard Educational Review, 60,* 415–442.

Mitroff, I. (1974). *The subjective side of science: A philosopical inquiry into the psychology of the Apollo moon scientists.* Amsterdam: Elsevier.

O'Keefe, D. J. (1982). The concepts of argument and arguing. In J. R. Cox & C. A. Willard (Eds.), *Advances in argumentation theory and research* (pp. 3–23). Carbondale: Southern Illinois University Press.

Palmer, R. P. (1969). *Hermeneutics.* Evanston, IL: Northwestern University Press.

Pomerantz, A. (1990). Conversation analytic claims. *Communication Monographs, 57,* 231–235.

Ricoeur, P. (1981). *Hermeneutics and the human sciences: Essays on language, action, and interpretation* (John Thompson, Trans. and Ed.). Cambridge: Cambridge University Press.

Ricoeur, P. (1984). *Time and Narrative,* (K. McLaughlin & D. Pellauer, Trans.). Chicago: University of Chicago Press.

Rogers, C. (1980). *A way of being.* Boston: Houghton Mifflin.

Rogers, E., & Millar, F. (1982). The question of validity: A pragmatic answer. In M. Burgoon (Ed.), *Communication Yearbook 5* (pp. 249–258). New Brunswick, NJ: Transaction Books.

Rorty, R. (1979). *Philosophy and the mirror of nature.* Princeton, NJ: Princeton University Press.

Rorty, R. (1982) *Consequences of Pragmatism.* Minneapolis: University of Minnesota Press.

Shotter, J. (1984). *Social accountability and selfhood.* Oxford: Basil Blackwell.

Stewart, J. (1991). A postmodern look at traditional communication postulates. *Western Journal of Speech Communication, 55,* 354–379.

Sullivan, H. S. (1953). *The interpersonal theory of psychiatry.* New York: W. W. Norton.

Taylor, C. (1971). Interpretation and the sciences of man. *Review of Metaphysics 25,* 3–51.

Taylor, C. (1985a). *Human agency and language: Philosophical papers,* vol. 1. New York: Cambridge University Press.

Taylor, C. (1985b). *Philosophy and the human sciences: Philosophical papers,* vol. 2. New York: Cambridge University Press.

Taylor, C. (1988). Reply to de Sousa and Davis. *Canadian Journal of Philosophy, 18,* 449–458.

Watzlawick, P., Beavin, J. H., & Jackson, D. D. (1967). *Pragmatics of human communication.* New York: W. W. Norton.

Wittgenstein, L. (1953). *Philosophical Investigations.* Oxford: Basil Blackwell.

Woolgar, S. (1988). Time and documents in researcher interaction: Some ways of making out what is happening in experimental science. *Human Studies, 11,* 171–200.

Specifically, I argue that the key to understanding Hans-Georg Gadamer's contribution to the study of interpersonal understanding is his view of understanding as *communicative*. Speech communication scholars have long recognized that Gadamer's perspective on language offers potential contributions to communication theory (Campbell, 1978; Chen, 1987; Deetz, 1973, 1978; Heinrich, 1989; Hyde & Smith, 1979; Littlejohn, 1989; Scult, 1983; Stewart, 1978, 1981, 1986; Stewart & Philipsen, 1984). Although Gadamer's perspective is not new to the field of interpersonal communication research, I offer one reading of Gadamer that illustrates how particular constructs of his work can provide a means for articulating elements of interpersonal understanding. This chapter attempts to describe Gadamer's relevance to interpersonal communication studies by showing how his hermeneutics points to the necessity of an interpersonal context for articulating the process of human understanding. He argues that understanding is communicative; it is never the consequence of one leaving society and looking at the world (and language) from some "subjective" standpoint. Like many hermeneuticists, Gadamer assumes that language is not simply a tool we use only for expression; it essentially forms our social reality. Consequently, he is primarily interested in how understanding is made possible within the communication experience. Gadamer's hermeneutics illuminates an approach to understanding where interpersonal communication or *conversation* reveals, constitutes, or embodies the *world* between people. His point is that interpersonal understanding does not consist of the transmission of preexistent meanings from one person to another but is a creative or *productive* understanding that occurs *in* conversation.

The shift to the term *understanding* in this chapter is deliberate, implying an approach involving far more than is suggested by such terminology as knowledge, explanation, prediction, control, or science. Brockriede (1982) observes understanding is a construct that invites alternative interpretive perspectives in which one dimension is featured and others, although present and functioning, receive less emphasis. As he states, "Human understanding may be thematized empirically, personally, or linguistically" (Brockriede, 1982, p. 137). Although terms like *knowledge* and *explanation* point to the prominence of the empirical dimension, the hermeneutic approach of this chapter emphasizes the kind of relationship people have with one another when they try to reach an understanding. I recognize that understanding is always about something and is always negotiated within language, but unlike perspectives like semiotics or Derridean deconstruction, this chapter comments on the nature of the dialogue between speakers, on the question of the *self* in understanding, and the kind of relationship persons have with one another with regard to understanding. To put it another way, whereas traditional epistemology describes how interpersonal knowledge is possible, Gadamer's hermeneutics describes how interpersonal understanding is possible, with the reservation that understanding is not reducible to knowledge or explanation. On the contrary, the assumption is that knowledge is best seen as a subdivision of interpersonal understanding.

I begin with the thought of Martin Heidegger as both Gadamer and Derrida acknowledge a debt to Heidegger. I briefly attempt to explicate two specific contributions of Heidegger to our view understanding and its relation to language: (1) his contention that words in living language contain a multiplicity, or a "multivocity" of semantic elements, and (2) that language brings individuals into collective experience. I then proceed to show how these two "pathways" or questions differentiate the works of Derrida and Gadamer and, finally, how they lead to a fuller illumination of Gadamer's contribution to the study of interpersonal understanding. On the other hand, this endeavor is by no means a detailed comparative analysis of Gadamer and Derrida. Although I feel comfortable discussing the significance of Gadamer's philosophical project for the study of interpersonal understanding, I cannot say the same for my discussion of Derrida. To paraphrase Heidegger, I feel at best on the way to Derrida. But in spirit with Gadamer (1989b) who observes that over the years, beginning with Derrida's *Speech and Phenomena* (1973), he has sought to work his way into the world of Derrida's thinking (p. 114), I present the following observations.

HEIDEGGER AND THE COLLECTIVITY OF HUMAN UNDERSTANDING

Martin Heidegger began his intellectual project by claiming that the Western tradition had misdescribed and misinterpreted human being. He clearly challenged the Cartesian subject-object distinction as the central presupposition of modern thought, and his critique of the rational subject—the so-called death of man theme—was first articulated in his *Letter on Humanism* (1977b). There Heidegger argued that human "Being-in-the-world" (in-der-Welt-Sein) is the primary characteristic of human existence. This seems to suggest that the isolated, detached, meaning-giving, knowing subject is complemented by an embodied, meaning-giving, *doing* subject (Dreyfus, 1991, p. 47). Thus, for Heidegger, human understanding is not a goal to be achieved, but an active mode of human being. Heidegger was not interested in how one achieves valid and reliable knowledge, but in the possibilities and limits of the process of understanding that makes a person a person. He shifted the foundation of transcendental philosophy from Decartes's *cogito* and Husserl's "consciousness" to "the more fundamental one of Being-in-the-world" (Bleicher, 1980, p. 100).

One of Heidegger's great services was the *destrucktion* of the traditional language of metaphysics. Addressing the question of language and human existence, Heidegger rediscovered that the classical Greeks did not see language simply as spoken words that represent or designate, but as fundamentally a disclosive medium. By translating the Greek terms for linguistic signs, *semeia* (that which shows), *symbola* (that which holds to each other), and *homoiomata* (that which likens), Heidegger (1971) interpreted the early Greek view of language "consistently in terms of showing, in the sense of bringing about the appearance, which in its turn consists of the prevalence of unconcealment or *aletheia*" (p. 115). By drawing upon a particular etymological rendering of the Greek *aletheia* as a means of explicating the disclosive nature of language, Heidegger argued that it was only later that language as "showing" became transformed into a conventional correspondence between sign and signified.

As Stewart and Philipsen (1984) explain, "Heidegger wants to recover the idea of truth as unconcealment or disclosure, and he sees language as the phenomenon by which this unconcealment is accomplished" (p. 184). At this point, Heidegger's argument that truth has a partial nature becomes beneficial for any understanding of his view of language and its relation to human understanding. For Heidegger, truth has the form of an ongoing process whereby there always remain alternative or *multiple* perspectives that evoke further disclosure. As Caputo (1989) observes.

> There is a point in Heidegger's later writing when he gives up on the word *Wahrheit*, on truth as preserving (*verwahren*), and begins to think the sheer happening or event of *aletheia*, according to which "there is" only the successive unfoldings of the multiple events of Being. (p. 261)

Consequently, language is also associated with the concealing that abides in any unconcealing. Language, as the "house of being," has a polysemous nature. The idea that language is constitutive of human experience, and opens up the possibility of understanding, indicates, for Heidegger, the *alterity* inherent in language and, thus, for understanding. As polysemous, language always surpasses its subjectively intended uses; it is not even precise in its meaning for the speaker. By "listening" to the nonliteral, suppressed, and "unthought" dimensions of words, texts, and linguistic traditions, humans can become attuned to its polysemous and obscure nature and open themselves to multiple interpretive disclosures. Although DiCenso (1990) emphasizes that Heidegger does not pursue the "semantic pluralism [of language], its relationship to interpretive perspectives, and the conflicts of interpretation which this produces" (pp. 54–55), Heidegger did establish the multivocal nature of language and critiqued the certainty underlying ideal interpretations of Being and human understanding.

The argument that words in living language contain a multiplicity or a "multivocity" of semantic elements led Heidegger to a second fundamental recognition: any conception of knowledge must exist within a context of speakers of a mutually constituted linguistic world. Heidegger (1984) observed that the ancient Greek philosophers originally referred to *Logos* as a collectivity, as "the unique gathering of beings" (p. 8). Although Western civilization has variously interpreted the word as *Ratio*, as *Verbum*, as cosmic law, as the logical, as necessity in thought, as meaning, and as reason, Heidegger argued that early Greek thinking defined the concept socially and ontologically. This perspective is developed by Heidegger (1977a) by associating the concept of Logos with the German term *legen:* to lay down and lay before. For Heidegger, *Logos* as speech means to make manifest "what is being talked about" (p. 79), and *Logos*'s connection to "laying before" justified translating the term as denoting a "bringing together" in the sense of a collecting and bringing together human beings (1984, p. 60). Heidegger saw that "human existence is 'infused' not 'with an artificial identity' but rather with an indelible communal character" (Smith & Hyde, 1991, p. 448).

As Heidegger (1962) explained, "so far as Dasein (human being) *is* at all, it has Being-with-one-another as its kind of Being" (p. 163). What an individual is now in life carries with it a history that has "always already" been shaped by the Other. The world of *Dasein* is a *Mitwelt*, a "with world" (DiCenso, 1990, p. 45). Because "the world of Dasein is a *with-world (Mitwelt)*, Being-in [the-world] is *Being-with* Others" (Heidegger, 1962, p. 155). Consequently, the "bringing together" or "gathering" of *Logos* more fundamentally implies relationship patterns historically embedded through language. While *Dasein* is delineated as that mode of Being essentially determined by its being able to speak, *Legein* is the guideline for arriving at the "structure" of Being (Heidegger, 1977a, p. 71). The very constitution of human beings is based upon cultural interaction, and the human self is shaped in relation to others through language. Heidegger's point is not that individuals are characterized by an absence of autonomy, uniqueness, and creativity, but that they are not completely "self-constituted." Heidegger questions the modernist primacy of the isolated, rational subject and suggests that one becomes an individual only in participation within a world not of one's own making.

According to Heidegger, it is impossible to isolate cognitive understanding from development within relational and historical contexts.
Human experience is disclosed through language bringing individuals
into collective experience. Thus the essential role of language in understanding is determined neither by mere vocalization nor by signifying,
but by its relational quality "of the sort that maintains itself in the
abode of mortals" (Heidegger, 1984, p. 68). Language constitutes *the
public* that is the basis of everyday understanding. Human language *is*
the medium of human gathering called *Dasein* and individual existence
is public, that is, it takes place within a space of interpersonal communicative meaning. Consequently, Heidegger also recognized the interpretive constraints embedded within human collectivity and argued that
they are manifested in the very forms of language use in which individuals participate (DiCenso, 1990, p. 47). Heidegger used the term *Gerede*
or "idle talk" to describe that form of language that "falls" prey to the
thrown nature of accepted interpretations, and believe that *Gerede* is
not an isolated tendency but a *general* dimension of language: "In language as a way things have been expressed or spoken out (*Ausgesprochen-
heit*), there is a hidden a way in which the understanding of *Dasein* has
been interpreted" (1962, p. 211).

Ultimately, Heidegger arrived at the philosophical position that
human collectivity or *das Man* represses the potential for an "authentic
self." (DiCenso, 1990, pp. 48–49). But he also opened the way for
seeing that collectivity *"belongs to Dasein's positive constitution"* (1962,
p. 167). Following these two distinct, but related, lines of thought, both
Derrida and Gadamer explore the phenomenon of discourse itself, but
pursue different paths concerning language and its relationship to interpersonal understanding. Whereas Derrida is more interested in showing
how understanding is undermined by language's multiplicity or *différance*,
Gadamer chooses to describe how language is the positive basis for
human understanding. Consequently, the next two sections of this chapter contrast Derrida and Gadamer on these points. But rather than place
their ideas in philosophical opposition, I wish to adhere to the view that
beyond the boundary of their ways of bringing things out, Derrida and
Gadamer can be read as offering complementary observations about the
nature of interpersonal understanding.

DERRIDA AND THE DECONSTRUCTION
OF UNDERSTANDING

Deconstruction is the name for a philosophical view and a method for
handling texts that derive from the work of Jacques Derrida, whose
most influential writing appeared in France in the 1960s and early

1970s. Deconstruction accepts the premise, common to poststructuralist theories of language and culture, that meaning is a function of the relation among signifiers; that is, consciousness is a structure of images, or "texts," of the world, and the images are significant for us because of their place in the structure, not because they represent something outside consciousness. Derridean deconstruction moves beyond this view by rejecting the idea that the structure must have a center, that is, a fundamental, discoverable principle of order. To deconstructionists, a center would mean that constitutive principles of the structure would be "privileged," not a function of relation. Deconstruction attempts to open up a vista of indeterminacy, debunk hierarchies of values, and release the "free play" of signifiers.

Derrida's thought occupies one of the most significant positions in hermeneutic thinking and is central to this discussion of interpersonal understanding; because of its radical critique of the reductionist search for certainty that has historically structured Western thought—a critique that can include Gadamer's approach (Hoy, 1985). In contrast to traditional epistemology, Derrida completely rejects the idea that the consequence of understanding is to supply final meanings or static knowledge. He maintains that meaning is always indeterminate and relational. Derrida arrives at this position by way of his decision to work up from language *toward* Being. By beginning his analysis of understanding and meaning at the level of words. Derrida uncovers the logical necessity for establishing the concept of the coherent "word." Derrida argues that, for any conceptualization of transcendental rationality to exist, there must first exist the ideal word. Derrida directly challenges this particular form of metaphysical presence and begins cutting at the very heart of epistemological "foundationalism" and of all nominalist versions of interpersonal knowledge.

According to Derrida, interpersonal understanding can never involve one mind in perfect immediacy with another. On the contrary, because understanding is a process of signs and mediation, it is beset with confusion and misunderstanding. Specifically, Derrida illustrates the problematic nature of all understanding by arguing the indeterminancy of the meaning in texts. His deconstructive approach uncovers—through structural analysis of the sign—the indeterminate, even contradictory, meanings of a text. Derrida understands texts to represent innumerable possibilities of structures and meanings; how a person assigns meaning to a text is only one possible meaning and rarely corresponds with the alternative meanings of other people or as indicated by the text itself. For example, his *Of Grammatology* "questioned the unity 'word' and all the privileges with which it was credited, especially its nominal form." (Derrida, 1988, p. 4). Drawing from the semiological view of language, Derrida sees the structure and meaning of a text as indeterminate in the ways in which signs delineate something from something else, a relational quality he calls *différance*. According to Derrida (1978), language is nothing more than a differential system of deferred meaning (p. 25). The meaning of any given sign depends solely on its diacritical opposition to other signs. As Madison (1991) explains the position:

> Meaning is thus a wholly intra-linguistic sort of affair: there is no "transendental signified," something outside of the play of signifiers themselves whose function it would be to confer on them their meaning, be this an empirical or ideal state of affairs or a psychological meaning-intention. (p. 126)

Différance is the "unfolding of difference" (Derrida, 1981, p. 10) or the "undoing of logocentrism" (Derrida, 1976, p. 74). The multiplicity of meaning is really located in the factuality of the signs or words themselves. Caputo (1987) notes that "it is *différance* which makes possible the endless linkages of signifiers in an irreducible diversity of combinatorial and associative chains and interweavings" (p. 145). Consequently, it does not advocate a unitary position. Deconstruction and *différance* are plural, open, not an attempt to find essences or centers (Gasche, 1986, pp. 100, 123). One way of understanding what Derrida means by *différance* is by defining "it as that which always escapes" (Hekman, 1990, p. 25), that which is deferred in the attempt to define knowledge as any form of presence. Whereas the focal point of the "metaphysics of presence" is the binary opposition of positive and negative terms, Derrida rejects such binary oppositions. *Différance* is Derrida's response to the failure of Western rationality to give a satisfactory account of the dynamic and relational qualities of human understanding. Although the traditional polarities of Western thinking—mind-body, subject-object, identity-difference, immanence-transcendence—attempt to present a dynamic description of human experience, the dichotomies themselves suggest that understanding can be temporarily disengaged from the processes where life is manifested, and resting spots can be found from the movement. In contrast, *différance* is the relational movement *between* imagined polarities such as subject-object or speech-writing, and symbolizes both sameness and difference. Derrida offers one example of the dynamic character of *différance* by the pointing to the fact that it is impossible to distinguish between *différance* and *différence* in French speech. It is only in reading and writing that the distinction can be made. This stresses the idea that "the movement of *différance*, as that which produces different things, that which differentiates, is the common root of all oppositional concepts that mark our language" (Derrida, 1981, p. 9). For *différance* is neither speech nor writing alone but the quality that permits the articulation of both. It is not the ordinary *presence* of speech nor the mere absence of the speaker in writing, but the condition of possibility for both (Derrida, 1981, pp. 8–9).

According to Derrida, life is not any sort of entity that we can easily categorize or circumscribe by interpretation or meaning. In fact, *différance* is the condition of all possibilities and the condition of the impossibility of any determinant or final understanding (Hekman, 1990, p. 25). *Différance* is primarily in describing human understanding because words make the absent "present" by only presenting a "trace" of that which is excluded. Through their repetition, words form these traces, but never the presence of the things themselves. Despite the claims of phenomenology, the "thing itself" always escapes. Words stand in place of what could be brought to presence but are *never* identical to any one thing. For every word includes *alterity* and indeterminancy within its being, an intrusion of other meanings that contaminates any self-identity of the word. As Derrida (1981) states, "The play of differences supposes, in effect, syntheses and referrals which forbid at any moment, or in any sense, that a simple element be present in and of itself, referring only to itself" (p. 26).

Any discussion of interpersonal understanding can benefit from taking into account the deconstructive idea of *différance*. Derrida argues that any linguistic form of presence, including phenomena like "understanding," are subordinate systems of differences. He argues that it is a mistake to subordinate "the movement of *différance* in favor of the presence—stopping the flux—of a value or a meaning supposedly antecedent to *différance*, more original than it, exceeding and governing it in the last analysis. This is still the presence of . . . the 'transcendental signified'." (Derrida, 1981, p. 29). Like Gadamer, Derrida has pursued a path extending from Heidegger's thought. Derrida wants to do justice to the multivocity of language while striving to overcome the trivial fixation of words and meanings on the basis of discursive sense and intention. Consequently, Derridean deconstruction can be understood as agreeing with a hermeneutical critique of traditional epistemology and nominalist versions of interpersonal knowledge. However, Derrida locates interpersonal understanding in radical undecidability and argues that words have double, contradictory, and undecidable meanings that always derive from their syntax. His approach points to a now common critique of hermeneutics; that is, although hermeneutics may not think of itself as a version of metaphysics, the traditional hermeneutic desire to decipher the univocal meanings of texts may mirror the desire of epistemology for a complete and comprehensive account of the meaning of everything, including interpersonal understanding.

GADAMER AND
COMMUNICATIVE UNDERSTANDING

Gadamer's field of study, *philosophical hermeneutics*, is the exploration of the character and fundamental conditions of all understanding. His discussion of how understanding takes place in conversation with others speaks directly in questions of interpersonal communication scholars. For example, Gadamer's contribution to the study of interpersonal communication is evident in one section of *Dialogue and Deconstruction* (1989b), "Hermeneutics and Logocentricism," where Gadamer responds to Derrida's thought and places understanding primarily in an interpersonal context. There he asks: "Where is the multiplicity of meaning really located? Isn't it found in the constitution of sense that takes place in the concrete give and take of language, and not in the factuality of the signs themselves?" (p. 115). Although Gadamer (1976) views language, like Derrida, as "the real mark of our finitude" (p. 64), his approach moves beyond language as signs by describing understanding as that which emerges in conversation between *persons* in interpersonal communication. He emphasizes that "to speak means to speak *to* someone" (Gadamer, 1976, p. 65). As Gadamer (1989a) argues, "For language is by nature the language of conversation; it fully realizes itself only in the process of coming to an understanding" (p. 446).

In contrast to Derrida, Gadamer chooses to extend Heidegger's concept of *das Man* to emphasize language as a productive mode of human existence and understanding. In one section of *Truth and Method* (1989b), "Language as Horizon of a Hermeneutic Ontology," Gadamer states: "Language is not just one of man's [*sic*] possessions in the world; rather, on it depends the fact that man has a *world* at all. The world as world exists for man as for no other creature that is in the world. But this world is verbal in nature" (p. 443). Throughout his writing, Gadamer (1976) argues that language is much more than simply an instrument or tool that can be picked up and used and then laid aside for future use. "Rather, in all our knowledge of ourselves and in all knowledge of the world, we are always already encompassed by the language that is our own. . . . In truth we are always already at home in language, just as much as we are in the world" (pp. 62–63). Gadamer develops Heidegger's thesis of the linguisticality of understanding and provides a framework for describing interpersonal understanding. He contends that language does not simply represent something outside consciousness (textual "signifiers" that point to extratextual "signified") but that language is *central* to human understanding. The world is presented to us in language.

Virtually all hermeneutic thinkers agree that interpretation can never be divorced from language. Understanding—as communicative—is our mode of being and, as language, is always socially situated. Gadamer rejects understanding as an "objective" process that uncovers truth by a "mirroring of" a distinct and separate reality and argues against the hegemony of such approaches over all forms of rigorous inquiry and reliable knowledge. In place of immutable and ahistorical foundations for scientific objectivity, Gadamer (1986a) focuses on knowledge as a *coping with* reality and defines human understanding as a form of practical understanding (*phronesis*) that is, not so much a technique or method, but a social process of constructing justification (pp. 37-39). Gadamer's view is that human understanding is always situated in communication and is modeled by understanding that emerges between persons in interpersonal communication. His focus on conversation is fundamental for grasping what is distinctive about his contribution to the study of interpersonal understanding. For Gadamer (1989a), what is most characteristic of human understanding is its interpersonal mode of being. Understanding is a process of communication *between* two or more people opening up to each other and understanding a subject matter at hand (p. 385). Consequently, Gadamer cannot conceive human understanding as primarily involving individual intent. Rather it is in the process of communication itself in which understanding develops. Thus, the following theoretical concepts fit within a framework whose central concept is conversation and whose elements explicate Gadamer's view of interpersonal understanding. These concepts can provide a framework for a hermeneutic approach to interpersonal understanding.

Categories and Elements of Gadamer's Conversational Framework

As already noted, Gadamer's personal or communicative approach to understanding springs from the assumption that understanding and knowledge are *socially*, rather than individually, constructed in conversation with others. His *constitutive-dialogic* approach is developed by the following concepts—the dynamic of play (*Spiel*), the structure of question and answer, the concept of prejudice, historically effected consciousness (*wirkungsgeschichtliches Bewusstsein*), the centrality of the subject matter (*die Sache*), and the fusion of horizons (*Horizontverschmelzung*)—which form an intricate relationship and offer a rich framework for making sense of interpersonal understanding.

THE DYNAMIC PLAY   The notion of play is one of the more notable instances of the contrast between Gadamer's hermeneutics and Derrida's deconstruction and can serve as an organizing principle for explaining Gadamer's contribution to the articulation of the process of interpersonal understanding. Derrida's concept of the role of play (*jeu*) in human understanding is that of the free play of signifiers, groundless, without direction or goal. His form of play makes all standards and distinctions meaningless. As Derrida (1978) explains, *jeu* is "the Nietzschean *affirmation*, that is the joyous affirmation of the play of the world of signs without fault, without truth, and without origin which is offered to an active interpretation" (p. 292).

As Stewart and Philipsen (1984) observe, Gadamer sees the fundamental character of the linguisticality that discloses human understanding as the dynamic of *play* (p. 186). According to Gadamer (1989a), play is a "to-and-fro movement that is not tied to any goal which would bring it to an end . . . rather, it renews itself in constant repetition" (p. 103). The point is not that a single game never ends, but that no particular game will ever complete the general activity of game playing. Play is continually renewed by each "playing." But unlike Derrida, Gadamer's path is not marked by an ontological dependence on the concept of the sign. Gadamer (1989b) wants to separate the concept of the word from its grammatical sense and to reveal words as what they are only as spoken discourse (p. 124).

For Gadamer, the place of understanding is not found in Derrida's play (*jeu*) of words, but rather in the play (*Spiel*) of speakers. As Gadamer (1989b) argues, "What is involved here is not the ambiguity of a typeface or of a stock of physical marks, but rather an ambiguity as to what these designate when they are actualized by someone reading [or speaking] them" (p. 118). In contrast to Derrida, Gadamer argues that the decisive characteristic of the to-and-fro movement we call *play* is not words, but *conversation*. Every conversation has an inner infinity and no end. Gadamer (1976) argues that "one breaks it off because it seems that enough has been said or that there is nothing more to say. But every such break has an intrinsic relation to the resumption of dialogue" (p. 67). This is because play has its own dynamic, independent of the consciousness of those who play the game. Gadamer (1989a) contends that it "here the *primacy of play over the consciousness of the player* is fundamentally acknowledged" (p. 104), and it "absorbs the player into itself, and thus frees from him the burden of taking the initiative, which constitutes the actual strain of existence. . . . The player experiences the game as a reality that surpasses him" (pp. 105–109).

Gadamer argues that, whereas understanding is not simply a mentalist activity that an individual intends and in which she or he directs, it does involve submitting to the collective norms and requirements.

Gadamer (1989a) reminds us that "the actual subject of play is obviously not the subjectivity of an individual who, among other activities, also plays but instead the play itself" (p. 104). Rather, when a person communicates, that person too is *caught up* in something larger than his or her immediate intentions or subjective attitudes, that is, the person is caught up in a conversation. Rather than supporting some form of Nietzschean affirmation, Gadamer's definition of play undermines any dependence on discovering objective knowledge in human understanding and focuses researchers on understanding's interpersonal qualities. Conversation is neither subjective or objective, neither totally relative or fixed, but a *structural unity*. The structure comes from the intelligibility of the conversation itself rather than from the internal factors of individuals or the play of words. Play determines that conversation has an ongoing meaning in itself apart from individuals in the way it is able to lead people to constantly new understandings. Consequently, the use of "play," rather than the transmission qualities of subjective or objective factors, allows Gadamer to describe communication as a process without losing its process characteristics. As Deetz (1978) observes, "Gadamer's analysis using the concept of structural unity makes possible a nonsubjective concept of interpretation for communication studies" (p. 21).

THE STRUCTURE OF QUESTION AND ANSWER   Gadamer's conversational concept of play becomes the general context or ground that underlies the other elements or figures of his description of interpersonal understanding. Gadamer argues that human play comes to its true consummation when it is transformed into a conversational structure (*Gebilde*). As Gadamer (1989a) states: "Play is structure—this means that despite its dependence on being played it is a meaningful whole which can be repeatedly presented as such . . . " (p. 117). According to Gadamer, play takes concrete form as *the structure of question and answer* that happens in conversation. Conversation is a transformation of play when something is suddenly and as a whole something else. In the case of human understanding, that something is the individual speakers who no longer exist as subjective determinants of meaning. In conversation, one's understanding of a statement is enhanced by determining the question to which another person's statement responds. Understanding is possible because "nothing that is said [in a conversation] has its truth simply in itself, but refers instead backward and forward to what is unsaid. Every assertion is motivated, that is, one can sensibly ask of everything said. 'Why do you say that?' " (Gadamer, 1976, p. 67). As Gadamer (1989a) explains:

Thus we return to the conclusion that the hermeneutic phenomenon too implies the primacy of dialogue and the structure of question and answer. . . . a person who wants to understand must question what lies behind what is said. He must understand it is an answer to a question. (pp. 369–370)

It is within the conversational process of question and answer that understanding takes its communicative form in Gadamer's view. Conversation is a give and take, a to and fro, a process of understanding a whole through the concrete statements of an interlocutor. This process can be described by the *hermeneutic circle* or the *canon of totality* (Bleicher, 1980). Gadamer (1987) states that "the hermeneutic circle is in fact a contextually fulfilled (*inhaltlich erfüllter*) circle, which joins [conversationalists] into a unity with a processual whole" (p. 87). As a circle of give and take, of question and answer, understanding is necessarily governed by an anticipation of meaning that follows from the context of what has been *said* before. Thus the movement of understanding is constantly from the whole to the part and back to the whole. The task is to expand the unity of the understood meaning by seeing the harmony of all details with the whole as the criterion of correct understanding. Gadamer (1989a) believes that "the failure to achieve this [structural] harmony means that understanding has failed' (p. 291). Interpersonal understanding is not just the consequence of an inquiring subjectivity, but rather the result of the back and forth process of conversational understanding.

THE CONCEPT OF PREJUDICE   For Gadamer, conversational play—responding to questions underlying assertions—requires an effort to bring our own presuppositions and prejudices into "play" with actual human discourse. Conversational play requires the recognition of the role *prejudice* takes in human understanding. In fact, Gadamer argues that human prejudice or preconception is the starting point for all understanding. He observes, "Pure seeing and pure hearing are dogmatic abstractions that artificially reduce phenomena. Perception always includes meaning" (Gadamer, 1989a, p. 92). Gadamer points out that *prejudice* literally means simply "prejudgment": thus, a prejudice can be either confirmed or disconfirmed by conversation. Prejudices can be either positive or negative, and to assume that all prejudices are illegitimate and misleading, as the Enlightenment implies, is in Gadamer's view, simply a "prejudice against prejudice." Any person who is trying to understand is necessarily involved in a process of "projecting" his or her prejudices.

Gadamer (1987) argues that communicative understanding requires

the suspension of one's prejudices, whether this involves another person through whom one learns one's own nature and limits, or an encounter with a work of art, or a text: always something more is demanded than to understand the other, that is to seek and acknowledge the immanent coherence contained within the meaning claim of the other. (p. 87)

To understand, we need to designate self-consciously our opinions and prejudices and qualify them as such so that we can recognize the authentic questions of a different person whose claim to truth must be perceived over and against our own preconceived notions. Claiming to be objective or free of bias is counterproductive. Deetz (1978) observes that "the person who imagines himself free from prejudices not only becomes unconsciously dominated by them but cuts himself off from their positive insight" (p. 18). The positive insight of prejudice is that other people are a source of our ability to understand. Thus, Gadamer's hermeneutic approach to interpersonal understanding attempts to make explicit our presumptions rather than to attempt to determine their veracity from an objective and neutral perspective.

HISTORICALLY EFFECTED CONSCIOUSNESS   Hermeneutic understanding and the play of conversation is concerned with *tradition*. According to Gadamer (1989a), "tradition is a genuine partner in dialogue" (p. 358). He argues that "the historicity of our existence entails that prejudices, in the literal sense of the word, constitute the initial directedness of our whole ability to experience" (Gadamer, 1976, p. 9). With this statement, he points the way to a central tenet: one always communicates experience and understands from the perspective of tradition. Tradition, in his sense, includes our history, our language, and our cultural values. Weinsheimer (1985) emphasizes that it is the vantage point—the fundamental prejudice—that gives us a way of understanding: "History is what prejudices us, and if there is any knowledge produced by history, it is prejudiced knowledge" (p. 170). Littlejohn (1989) observes that understanding is always colored by a linguistic history and community: "In other words, the past operates on us now in the present and affects our conceptions of what is yet to come. At the same time, our present notions of reality affect how we view the past. We cannot exist outside a historical tradition" (p. 140).

Consequently, we always understand within a social tradition, rather than solely with individuals, and within a tradition that is embodied in language. We let tradition "speak" to us, for we cannot understand ourselves or others apart from the prejudices and presuppositions tradition has supplied. Gadamer (1986b) says that it is "in our daily life we proceed constantly through the coexistence of past and futures (p. 10). Only when one appreciates the prejudice of social tradition as a positive force, acknowledges it, and uses it productively, can purely subjective understanding be constrained. When we understand that the power of history prevails over finite human consciousness, we realize that "to be historically means that knowledge of oneself can never be complete" (Gadamer, 1989a, p. 302). Gadamer uses the term *historically effected consciousness* to label the awareness that the act of understanding is not wholly a subjective act, but rather a consequence of history that "acts" upon us and our communication.

Conversation involves recognizing this shared tradition and bringing it to life in its *application* to the speakers' own developments. As Gadamer (1989a) states, "understanding is not a method which the inquiring consciousness applies to an object it chooses and so turns it into objective knowledge; rather, being situated within an event of tradition . . . is a prior condition of understanding (p. 309). Understanding always involves something like the application of a written text to be understood to the present context of a reader. Consequently, there is a danger of a like-mindedness guiding what is really significant and meaningful in tradition. And as we are always situated within traditions, we do not always conceive of what tradition says as something alien or questionable. Gadamer's problem is to recover an understanding that not only requires that we allow ourselves to be *addressed* by tradition, but also uncovers new questions and criticisms. The *"hermeneutical task becomes of itself a questioning of things"* (Gadamer, 1989a, p. 269).

Gadamer's response to charges that his recovery of tradition is a "conservative hermeneutic" (Caputo, 1987, p. 97) is to argue for a hermeneutic disposition that requires a form of understanding that, in our finite, incomplete human situation, "insists that there is no higher principle than continually holding oneself open in a conversation" (Gadamer, 1985, p. 189). To Gadamer, every act of communication becomes an opportunity to "test" all our prejudices and to understand ourselves through the tradition from which we come. Taken from this perspective, understanding never involves an absolute position but is a way of being. By definition, persons with hermeneutical consciousness are people who are "radically undogmatic." Because of the many experiences they have had and the knowledge they have drawn from those experiences, they are particularly well-equipped to have new experiences and to learn from them. As Gadamer (1989a) observes, "The dialectic of experience has its proper fulfillment not in definitive knowledge but in the openness to experience that is made possible by experience itself" (p. 355). Thus, Gadamer's hermeneutic approach to interpersonal understanding would emphasize knowledge as an *openness* to conversation rather than as a product of inference or perception.

THE CENTRALITY OF THE SUBJECT MATTER   Gadamer (1989a) states: "To conduct a conversation means to allow oneself to be conducted by the subject matter to which the partners in the dialogue are oriented" (p. 367). Historically effected consciousness always involves the primacy of play and openness in the process of being questioned by a *subject matter*. Warnke (1987) concludes that any conversation guided by historically effected consciousness is one in which each partner to the conversation is concerned entirely with the subject matter and with arriving at the "truth" with regard to it (p. 100). Although understanding is dependent on one person's immediate participation with another perspective, it is not based on transposing oneself into another person. As Gadamer (1989a) argues. "To understand what a person says is, as we saw, to come to an understanding about the subject matter, not to get inside another person and relive his experiences" (p. 383).

Hence, understanding the subject matter means that a common language must be worked out in a conversation. Warnke (1987) argues that for Gadamer, "understanding is primarily agreement" (p. 102); it is essentially a process of reaching consensus. This agreement does not mean consensus on every issue but sometimes simply agreement to converse. Gadamer does not argue against conflict and disagreement over content. The unity he is concerned with is not the result of one partner's imposing his or her views on another. Rather, when conversational partners come to an understanding of the subject matter, their understandings are not the original property of any one person, but represent a new understanding of the subject matter. Gadamer (1989a) argues "that is why understanding is not merely a reproductive, but always a productive activity as well" (p. 296). Gadamer's subject matter orientation is that of a Socratic dialectic in which the position to which Socrates and his interlocutors come at the end represents a significant advance over the position each maintained at the beginning. As Warnke (1987) concludes, "the process, then, is one of integration and appropriation" (p. 101). Therefore, Gadamer does not mean that interpersonal knowledge is the direct product of a consensus about a common conversational topic. Rather, it is the consequence of what Gadamer calls a *fusion of horizons.*

THE FUSION OF HORIZONS   Because the focus of conversation is the subject matter at issue, Gadamer views understanding as always a *fusion of horizons* of the conversational partners. If the participants are ready, they will be able to weigh counterarguments while still holding on to their own arguments. This willingness to understand requires that each partner take seriously the claims of the other, defining and testing one's prejudices against these claims and coming to a new understanding of the subject matter. Weinsheimer (1985) observes that Gadamerian understanding occurs as a mediation of the horizons of the participants—the situation of understanding being our horizon (p. 182). Hermeneutic conversation reflects communicative understanding: one that reflects a fusion or transformation of the initial positions of all the discussion participants. As understanding involves the fusion of one's own horizon of meanings and assumptions with the horizon of another person, it remains based on the prejudices that one brings with him or her. Because prejudices continue to constitute the larger horizon of the particular present, understanding requires that persons test all their prejudices again and again. Thus Gadamer (1989a) argues that "the hermeneutic task consists in not covering up this tension by attempting a naive assimilation of the two but in consciously bringing it out" (p. 306). Although two different horizons are always involved in understanding, one for each speaker, this does not mean that they remain alienated from each other.

Gadamerian Postulates of Interpersonal Understanding

The elements of Gadamer's conversational view of understanding just described represent an analogy for visualizing interpersonal understanding and for judging Gadamer's relevance for investigations of interpersonal understanding and knowledge. In the following section, I propose some theoretical postulates of interpersonal understanding based on my reading of Gadamer's conversational approach. They help relate the elements of Gadamer's thinking, clarify his constitutive-dialogic assumptions, and suggest implications for interpersonal communication research.

INTERPERSONAL COMMUNICATION CONSTITUTES HUMAN UNDERSTANDING   Gadamer believes that speech reveals or *constitutes* our understanding of the world rather than merely represents it. Understanding is inherently communicative. People are born into and communicate within a tradition that is already laden with values inherent in our language. However, Gadamer (1987) says that "it is a grave misunderstanding to assume that emphasis on the essential factor of tradition which enters into all understanding implies an uncritical acceptance of tradition and sociopolitical conservatism" (p. 87). As begins in a historical and *living* process, we are not solely constituted by the values of others; we also contribute to the tradition. Gadamer (1989b) acknowledges that "Derrida is right to insist on this essential 'difference' [*Differenz*], and I myself recognize it fully" (p. 118). Gadamer (1989a) insists that we help constitute tradition by communicating from our unique lived experiences and interpretations because "it is enough to say that we understand in a *different* way, *if we understand at all*" (p. 297). "What can we make of the fact that one and the same message transmitted by tradition will be grasped differently on every occasion, that it is only understood relative to the concrete historical situation of its recipient?" (Gadamer, 1987, p. 115). In other words, Gadamerian communication does not require the blind acceptance of the interpreted claims of other people, just the continuing transformation of tradition and individual understandings.

CONVERSATION IS THE PRIMARY EVENT OF HUMAN UNDER-STANDING   According to Gadamer (1989a), conversation is *the* primary event of human understanding. Language is not simply a tool that produces understanding; "being that can be understood is language" (p. xxxiv). We cannot separate our understanding from language, or separate it from interpersonal communication. Understanding is always twofold: constitutive of our existence and a moment of conversation. Understanding is language bound and person bound. Therefore, understanding *is* language in practice. Gadamer (1989a) observes that understanding is *application* (p. 341), always the application of individual meanings, prejudices, and presuppositions to our concrete communication experiences. Gadamer (1978) recognizes that "in hermeneutics . . . application is a constitutive moment" (p. 125). He contends that meanings, prejudices, and presuppositions—the starting points for understanding—are continually applied to specific situations for understanding to occur.

Warnke (1987) recognizes that Gadamer's emphasis on application seems to be an emphasis on the contextuality of interpretation and on the way interpretations will necessarily differ depending on the situation (p. 98). However, although Gadamer does claim that all understanding is prejudiced, at the same time he denies that the situatedness of understanding makes it completely a matter of subjective opinion. Gadamer argues that application is communicative, a type of *intersubjective* process that denies any subjective-objective split. Gadamer (1989a) sees understanding as requiring shared meanings (p. 292). He argues that "the true locus of hermeneutics is this in-between" (p. 295), and "this process of attaining and communicating understanding always takes place entirely in the medium of one person's *speaking* with another" (1980, pp. 104–105). Unlike other perspectives that concentrate on individual speakers' choices or assume that the primary goal of understanding is to reproduce another's intent, Gadamer's emphasis on application explores how understanding *happens* in the play between people in a process of interpersonal conversation.

INTERPERSONAL UNDERSTANDING IS A DIALOGICAL PRO-
CESS   In contrast to Derrida, Gadamer (1989a) argues that meaning
does not belong to words (or individuals) but to dialogue, and he cannot conceive of human understanding as completely subjective or a
mere act of psychological transposition (p. 388). Conversation as the
medium of language makes it all possible. Gadamer (1989a) sees conversation as "a process of coming to an understanding" (p. 385). Understanding is *dialogical* and happens when another person addresses
us. Only when it is possible for two people to make themselves understood through dialogue can the problem of understanding even be raised.
As Gadamer (1981) states, "The communality of all understanding as
grounded in its intrinsically linguistic quality seems to me to be an
essential point in hermeneutical experience" (p. 110). His view of dialogue as constitutive of understanding centralizes interpersonal communication as the fundamental context that underlies all other forms of
understanding.

Communication, not individual interpretation, encompasses things
and experience and brings meaning to people. Deetz (1973) observes
that Gadamer's dialogical approach shows that "language makes possible the meaningfulness of things by disclosing the life-world and by
developing the projective stance from which the subject matter's implications arise or are revealed" (p. 48). Understanding requires *openness*
to the possible truth of another person's claim and an openness to the
possible challenge these claims present to one's prejudices. Gadamer
(1989a) explains, "it belongs to any true conversation that each person
opens himself up to the other, truly accepts his point of view as valid
and transposes himself into the other to such an extent that he understands not the particular individual but what he says" (p. 385), for "it is
the tyranny of hidden prejudices that makes us deaf to what speaks to
us in tradition" (p. 270). Open dialogue with another person is the
possibility of distinguishing legitimate from illegitimate prejudices. As
Gadamer (1989a) states, "[dialogue] does not mean that when we listen
to someone or read a book we must forget all our foremeanings concerning the content and all our own ideas. All that is asked is that we
remain open to the meaning of the other person or text" (p. 268).

Thus Gadamer defines rationality communicatively. Warnke (1987)
argues that "the awareness that one's knowledge is always open to
refutation or modification from the vantage point of another perspective is not the basis for suspending confidence in the idea of reason but
rather represents the very possibility of 'rational progress' " (p. 173).
Gadamer's dialogical view of understanding is centered on the conversation, not on objective thought. Warnke (1987) sees that what is at issue
for Gadamer "is not the intention behind a person's saying what that

person says but its possible truth" (p. 100). In dialogue, meanings are applied to concrete communication experiences in a mutual process of equality and active reciprocity. Rationality and understanding are subverted whenever one speaker concentrates on the other speaker rather than on the subject matter, that is, when a speaker is not open to the dialectic of conversation.

INTERPERSONAL UNDERSTANDING IS A DIALECTICAL PROCESS   As his discussion of dialogue and rationality suggests, Gadamer believes that the particular character of understanding is reflected most accurately in a *dialectical* structure of question and answer. According to Gadamer (1989a):

> As the art of asking questions, dialectic proves its value because only the person who knows how to ask questions is able to persist in his questioning, which involves being able to preserve his orientation toward openness. The art of questioning is the art of questioning even further—i.e., the art of thinking. It is called dialectic because it is the art of conducting a real dialogue. (p. 367)

As dialectical, understanding involves a type of questioning that does not involve simply interrogating the conversational partner but allows him or her to interrogate back. Each speaker in a dialectical conversation calls the other's horizon into question, serves a *negative* role that transforms the other's understanding of the subject matter. Acknowledging a debt to Hegel, Gadamer (1989a) argues that all experience has the structure of "historically effected consciousness," a continual reversal of consciousness. "Only through negative instances do we acquire new experiences. . . . Every experience worthy of the name thwarts an expectation" (p. 356). Understanding takes place as a continually negative process of false generalizations or presuppositions being refuted and new understandings being created. Therefore, Gadamer (1989a) explains, "The dialectic of experience has its proper fulfillment not in definitive knowledge but in the openness to experience that is made possible by experience itself" (p. 355). Understanding is intrinsically *speculative*. Or as Palmer (1969) observes, "[it] is not fixed and dogmatically certain, but because it is always in process as event of disclosure, it is ever moving, shifting, fulfilling its mission of bringing a thing to understanding" (p. 209). Understanding involves the kind of dialectical and speculative communication with another person that allows new possible relationships to speak to us and address our understanding. The negativity that Gadamer (1989a) speaks of is alive to new disclosures of being as a continuing antidote to dogmatism: "A speculative person is someone who does not abandon himself directly to the tangibility of appearances or to the fixed determinateness of the meant" (p. 466).

INTERPERSONAL UNDERSTANDING IS A TRANSFORMATIONAL PROCESS   Gadamer's reference to the dialectical nature of understanding supports the claim that understanding does not occur either when one conversational partner imposes his or her views on another or when one simply assents to the views of another; rather, as Warnke (1987) observes, that understanding "is not the original property of one or the other but represents a new understanding of the subject matter at issue" (pp. 100–101). Understanding reflects a dialogue with another person and a transformation of the initial positions of all the discussion partners. Gadamer (1989a) argues that "in genuine dialogue, something emerges that is contained in neither of the partners by himself" (p. 419). In other words conversation is *transformational* in that understanding always exceeds that which was originally understood by either partner. Not only occasionally, but always, the meaning of a conversation goes beyond its participants. As DiCenso (1990) observes, conversation "discloses perspectives and insights in a creative and transformative manner through dialogue and interaction" (p. 101). Both speakers in a conversation are called forward to a new understanding as it unfolds in interpersonal communication. Both find implications in the conversation that neither saw prior to the interaction.

Transformational conversations are those where both speakers focus less on reproducing the meanings of others and concentrate more on the subject matter at hand and on the knowledge that arises. They create insights, ideas, and solutions to problems that none of the conversational partners could have anticipated or generated alone. According to Gadamer (1981), this transformational process is illustrated by successful conversations:

> We are continually shaping a common perspective when we speak a common language and so are active participants in the communality of our experience in the world. Experiences of resistance or opposition bear witness to this, for example, in discussion. Discussion bears fruit when a common language is found. Then the participants part from one another as changed beings. The individual perspectives with which they entered upon discussion have been transformed, and so they are transformed themselves. This, then, is a kind of progress—not the progress proper to research in regard to

which one cannot fall behind but a progress that always must be renewed in the effort of our living. (pp. 110–111)

Thus interpersonal understanding is a transformational "fusing of horizons" of speakers, an opening that is beyond any individual. Or as Gadamer (1989a) summarizes the idea, "To reach an understanding in a dialogue is not merely a matter of putting oneself forward and successfully asserting one's own point of view, but being transformed into a communion in which we do not remain what we were" (p. 379).

The Question of Meaning in Interpersonal Understanding

As the previous elements and postulates make clear, Gadamer believes that understanding cannot be defined by one party. Understanding happens in dialogical and dialectical conversation with another person. Although some communication theorists have modeled the understanding process through an explication of both intra- and interpersonal communication, Gadamer's approach attempts to overcome this distinction. To Gadamer, understanding is always an intersubjective activity. As Gadamer (1989a) argues.

> This dialogue, in doubt and objection, is a constant going beyond oneself and a return to oneself, one's own opinions and one's own points of view. . . . It is in this experience of language—in our growing up in the midst of this interior conversation with ourselves, which is always simultaneously the anticipation of conversation with others and the introduction of others into the conversation with ourselves—that the world begins to open up and achieve order in all the domains of experience. (p. 543)

Clearly, the theory of knowledge (epistemology) and the theory of understanding (hermeneutics) have traditionally been preoccupied with different paradigms. Although epistemology has presupposed rational subjectivity as the guarantee of certainty, perception as the case model, and atemporal truths as the goal of understanding, Gadamer's hermeneutics proposes no uniquely privileged standpoint for understanding, offers conversation as the exemplar model, and argues that understanding constantly changes. Gadamer's form of intersubjective understanding locates the subject of meaning not in the play of an isolated consciousness or in the play of signs, but in the play of conversation. Unlike deconstruction's critique of "logocentrism," the "metaphysics of presence," and the rationalist tradition of occidental thought,

Gadamer's constitutive-dialogic theory of understanding addresses the question of meaning and the role of subjectivity in understanding. Although there can be no concept at all of subjectivity in Derrida's "free play of signifiers." (Smith, 1988, pp. 46–47), "hermeneutics maintains that there is always the possibility of meaning, but, in contrast to logocentism, it maintains that it is never possible to arrive at a final meaning" (Madison, 1991, p. 131).

First, Gadamer contends that *language and tradition* encompass the entire conversation between persons understanding. In contrast to more individualistic models of understanding that privilege rational subjectivity as the locus of meaning, Gadamer's approach illustrates social meaning resulting from the speakers' mutual existence within and dependence on a shared language and tradition. The term *horizon* suggests itself as a prime example because speakers are not completely discrete individuals who use language as a tool simply to represent their original thoughts and to reproduce the thoughts of others. Gadamer (1989a) says that the term *horizons* expresses "the superior breadth of vision that the person who is trying to understand must have. To acquire a horizon means that one learns to look beyond what is close at hand—not in order to look away from it but to see it better, within a larger whole and in truer proportion" (p. 305). As all-encompassing, language "speaks" persons as much as persons speak language, focusing their thinking and highlighting certain aspects of their environment while hiding other features. Thus Hekman (1986) concludes that "horizons are *particular* vantage points which, although they encompass a range, are exclusive as well" (p. 105).

Second, Gadamer believes *conversation* is the paradigm case of understanding, not a traditional approach that cites perception as a one-way instrument for discovering another speaker's intentions or meanings. Understanding is not treated as simply a process where skillful communicators take turns preparing and delivering messages to each other, watching for significant reactions and responding. Instead, the subject matter of the conversation, like a third participant, also "directs" understanding, leading persons in some directions and not others. In other words, conversational partners are continually transformed by *what* they are talking about. According to Gadamer, interpersonal understanding also involves a concrete link with a subject matter that has *the structure of question and answer*. Persons are not only continually questioned by each other's particular slant on a topic, but by the nature of the subject matter itself. In the play of the subject matter, both horizons *project* their meanings in the structure of questions to the other, *anticipate* the other's questions through the vantage point of their own prejudices, *integrate* the questions raised by the subject matter and the other into their own questions, and in turn, *appropriate* other points of views.

Consequently, neither speaker's intention controls the outcome of the conversation. Warnke (1987) observes that "Gadamer's model here is that of a Socratic dialogue in which the position to which Socrates and his interlocutors come at the end represents a significant advance over the position each maintained at the beginning" (p. 101). The ongoing conversation between persons is again transformational; it involves the endless production of new meanings. Thus the essence of Gadamer's (1989a) conversational view of interpersonal understanding is the opening up of possibilities (p. 299). The subject matter is neither entirely within individuals (subjective) nor entirely outside of the individuals (objective), but describes the process of understanding as a communicative interplay of *prejudices* and *openness*. As presented by Gadamer, understanding is based on the prejudices the speakers bring to the event. Prejudices constitute their particular horizons. Consequently, genuine questioning within a process of projection, anticipation, integration, and appropriation requires that speakers designate self-consciously their opinions and prejudices and recognize the authentic questions of another person. Their goal becomes openness to this process and to the possible truth of the other's claim. "Suspension" of prejudices and openness to possibilities then become an opportunity to distinguish legitimate prejudices from illegitimate ones.

Third, Gadamer argues that understanding has a *temporal* quality. As Gadamer believes that we cannot separate ourselves from our temporality (*Bedeutsamkeit*), whether as part of the past, in the present, or anticipating the future, understanding is not presented as an ahistorical "action" in a timeless vacuum. Neither is it seen as determined entirely by either communicator's choice or intent. Rather, it has the character of an *event* in history. As a movement in time, understanding is always twofold: an immediate experience and a developing meaning. Whereas communication with another about a subject matter supplies the immediate content, time influences its meanings and effects by performing a filtering process by which persons will eventually distinguish legitimate prejudices from illegitimate ones. In other words, time is the condition within which meanings always change and develop. As part of an hermeneutical circle, persons communicate and understand in terms of the context of time. Gadamer (1989a) argues that "it is a circular relationship in both cases. The anticipation of meaning in which the whole is envisaged becomes actual understanding when the parts that are determined by the whole themselves also determine this whole" (p. 291). Every separate event of communicative understanding is deepened by the whole of time.

To Gadamer, the *fusion of horizons* symbolizes the temporal quality of all communicative understanding between speakers. Understanding is an event of two persons communicating with each other. It results primarily from their consciousness of the hermeneutical situation, of their finitude, and of the extent to which all understanding is historically mediated. Historically effected consciousness reflects a unity of the conversationalists that recognizes their prejudices and realizes that both speakers accept some things that are against him or her even though no one else forces them to do so. Gadamer (1989a) sees this event of understanding as "parallel to the hermeneutical experience. I must allow tradition's claim to validity, not in the sense of simply acknowledging the past in its otherness, but in such a way that it has something to say to me" (p. 361). In other words, some presuppositions *always* remain hidden and historically effected reflection can never be completely achieved. In summary, a Gadamerian approach to interpersonal understanding stresses persons understanding through an appreciation that their historical situations mean that understanding can never be complete. Because Gadamer views understanding as constitutive, dialogical, dialectical, and transformational, he is fully aware that prejudices may be false and opinions of the subject matter may be wrong. They are always changing and always open to the challenge of other beliefs within a community of discourse.

Although persons understand from different standpoints, this does not mean that understanding cannot take place. Language, for Gadamer, is not, as it is for Derrida, "a kind of self-enclosed, self-subsisting entity" (Madison, 1991, p. 133), and meaning is not determined by a system of forces that is not personal. Application is the central problem of hermeneutics (Gadamer, 1989a, p. 315), and "understanding here is always application" (p. 309). To Gadamer, meaning is always "applicable meaning," because understanding always involved *applying* the experiences to be understood to a person's present situation. Consequently, Gadamer does not maintain, as Derrida seems to do, that there are nothing but signs. On the other hand, he does not speak of some final interpretant. Gadamer's work confronts the two traditional ways of relating to the world—by way of observation and by way of action—by attempting to end up neither in a self-sufficient mind nor in an independent world. Madison (1991) argues that this is an important distinction between Gadamer's and Derrida's approaches:

> Derrida quite simply omits to take into account in his theorizing (if it can be called that) the fact that texts [or conversations] have readers [or speakers]. And these readers [or

speakers] are always *particular individuals* existing in *particular situations*, in the light of which and by application to which the text [or conversation] assumes, by means of what Gadamer calls a "fusion of horizons," a particular, decidable meaning. (p. 130)

Gadamer's particular spin on the concept of meaning is what I identify as *functional meanings* or *functional truths*. The phrases suggest that there is no fundamental distinction between what words mean and how they are applied in concrete situations. Understanding is not a subjectless process in all essential ways given over to the forces of *truth* or language. Instead, Gadamer proposes a conception of "the subject" that is limited, but that allows space for the subject or person to take responsibility. Whereas Derrida ends up privileging the discursive apparatus of understanding, Gadamer allows persons a moment of appropriation. Meanings "function" to allow persons to take some responsibility and to act, because they do not aim at the ultimate truth of things. A Supreme Court decision is an apt analogy. Even such monumental decisions that allow our society to function in such fundamental ways are in no way final. They are always vulnerable to reexamination and being overturned. But they are the locus of responsibility for our collective decisions and permit citizens to guide their actions by those decisions, even if the decisions are temporary—what Caputo (1987) calls *fictions*— and constantly open to change.

Gadamer's concept of play, unlike Derrida's, rejects neither the collective norms of tradition nor the responsibility of individuals to arrive at meanings. By thematizing the interpersonal dimension of understanding, Gadamer actually puts the spotlight on a less "subjectivistic" sense of self that allows us to rethink conceptions of subjectivity through his description of communicative understanding. Gadamer clearly argues that his mediating view of human understanding and meaning has got to do something with living and acting persons. It is persons who encounter each other in communication, who continually confront their tradition, and who participate in changing their social world within the bounds of interpersonal communication. Not totally at the mercy of either ideal reason or the free-floating play of language, the form of human subjectivity that Gadamer offers is similar to Levin's (1991) description of the "postmodern self," a concept of self that is "formed and informed, tries to live life without getting caught in any fixed form, structure, or identity" (p. 110). Ultimately, although valuing the proliferation of differences, Gadamer's constitutive-dialogic approach brings articulation to the process of interpersonal understanding without retarding its movement or binding it to any discursive form.

CONCLUSION

In this chapter, I have been able only to sketch some distinctive features of various sensitizing and heuristic categories and concepts—play, question and answer, prejudice, the centrality of the subject matter, historically effected consciousness, fusion of horizons—that outline a Gadamerian approach to interpersonal understanding. A fuller form of this endeavor would include a more historically developed and thorough description of where Gadamer and Derrida contrast with the thought of each other and of Martin Heidegger, who laid the groundwork for a constitutive-dialogic approach to language and being (Stewart, 1986, p. 69). The implied contention of this chapter is that, unlike Derrida, Gadamer effectively responds to Heidegger's tendencies to posit *Being* as a suprahistorical and original source of truth by more fully explicating the concrete nature of ontological understanding as communicative.

Gadamer argues that interpersonal communication warrants study because it is the location of the emergence of human being. He not only supplies a rationale for the study of interpersonal understanding, but offers a rich perspective for describing it. This chapter has given interpersonal communication scholars a way to evaluate Gadamer's thought and its relation to our field. More specific implications of Gadamer's approach for interpersonal communication research deserve attention, but I leave that for future discussions. This chapter raises questions about one productive direction for thinking about interpersonal understanding; namely, Gadamer's constitutive-dialogic perspective. Unlike Derrida's deconstruction, Gadamer's hermeneutics argues that there is always the possibility of understanding, but in contrast to logocentrism that both Derrida and Gadamer critique, it contends that it is never possible to arrive at a final understanding. Gadamer's approach illustrates that understanding as communicative never ends: no particular conversation will ever complete the general activity of understanding. Understanding is continually renewed by each conversation.

REFERENCES

Berger, C. R., & Bradac, J. J. (1982). *Language and social knowledge: Uncertainty in interpersonal relationships.* London: Edward Arnold.

Berger, C. R., & Calabrese, R. J. (1975). Some explorations in initial interaction and beyond: Toward a developmental theory of interpersonal communication. *Human Communication Research, 1,* 99–112.

Berger, C. R., & Douglas, W. (1982). Thought and talk: Excuse me, but have I been talking to myself. In F. E. X. Dance (Ed.), *Human Communication Theory* (pp. 42–60), New York: Harper and Row.

Berger, C. R., Gardner, R. R., Parks, M. R., Schulman, L., & Miller, G. R. (1976). Interpersonal epistemology and interpersonal communication. In G. R. Miller (Ed.), *Explorations in Interpersonal Communication* (pp. 149–171). Beverly Hills, CA: Sage Publications.

Bleicher, J. (Ed.). (1980). *Contemporary hermeneutics: Hermeneutics as method, philosophy and critique.* New York: Routledge and Kegan Paul.

Brockriede, W. (1982). Arguing about human understanding. *Communication Monographs, 49,* 137–147.

Campbell, J. A. (1978). Hans-Georg Gadamer's Truth and Method. *Quarterly Journal of Speech, 64,* 101–122.

Caputo, J. D. (1987). *Radical hermeneutics: Repetition, deconstruction, and the hermeneutic project.* Bloomington: Indiana University Press.

Caputo, J. D. (1989). Gadamer's closet essentialism: A Derridean critique. In D. P. Michelfelder and R. E. Palmer (Eds.), *Dialogue and deconstruction: The Gadamer-Derrida debate* (pp. 258–262). Albany: State University of New York Press.

Chen, K.-H. (1987). Beyond Truth and Method: On misreading Gadamer's praxial hermeneutics. *Quarterly Journal of Speech, 73,* 183–199.

Deetz, S. (1973). Words without things: Toward a social phenomenology of language. *Quarterly Journal of Speech, 59,* 40–51.

Deetz, S. (1978). Conceptualizing human understanding: Gadamer's hermeneutics and American communication studies. *Communication Quarterly, 26,* 12–23.

Derrida, J. (1970). Structure, sign and play in the discourse of the human sciences. In R. Macksey & E. Donato (Eds.), *The Structuralist Controversy* (pp. 246–272). Baltimore: Johns Hopkins University Press.

Derrida, J. (1973). *Speech and phenomena* (D. Allison, Trans.). Evanston, IL: Northwestern University Press.

Derrida, J. (1976). *Of grammatology* (G. Spivak, Trans.). Baltimore: Johns Hopkins University Press.

Derrida, J. (1978). *Writing and difference* (A. Bass, Trans.). Chicago: University of Chicago Press.

Derrida, J. (1981). *Positions* (A. Bass, Trans.). Chicago: University of Chicago Press.

Derrida, J. (1988). Letter to a Japanese friend. In D. Wood & R. Bernasconi (Eds.), *Derrida and difference* (pp. 1–5). Evanston, IL: Northwestern University Press.

Desilet, G. (1991). Heidegger and Derrida: The conflict between hermeneutics and deconstruction in the context of rhetorical and communication theory. *Quarterly Journal of Speech, 77*(2), 152–175.

DiCenso, J. J. (1990). *Hermeneutics and the disclosure of truth: A study in the work of Heidegger, Gadamer, and Ricoeur.* Charlottesville: University Press of Virginia Press.

Dreyfus, H. L. (1991). *Being-in-the-world: A commentary on Heidegger's Being and Time, division 1.* Cambridge, MA: MIT Press.

Gadamer, H.-G. (1976). *Philosophical hermeneutics* (D. E. Linge, Trans.). Berkeley: University of California Press.

Gadamer, H.-G. (1980). *Dialogue and dialectic: Eight hermeneutical studies of Plato* (P. C. Smith, Trans.). London: Yale University Press.

Gadamer, H.-G. (1981). *Reason in the age of science* (F. G. Lawrence, Trans.). Cambridge, MA: MIT Press.

Gadamer, H.-G. (1985). *Philosophical apprenticeships* (R. R. Sullian, Trans.). Cambridge, MA: MIT Press.

Gadamer, H.-G. (1986a). *The idea of the good in Platonic-Aristotelian philosophy* (P. C. Smith, Trans.). London: Yale University Press.

Gadamer, H.-G. (1986b). *The relevance of the beautiful and other essays* (N. Walker, Trans.). New York: Cambridge University Press.

Gadamer, H.-G. (1987). The problem of historical consciousness (J. L. Close, Trans.). In P. Rabinow & W. M. Sullian (Eds.), *Interpretive social science: A second look* (pp. 83–140). Berkeley: University of California Press.

Gadamer, H.-G. (1989a). *Truth and method* (J. Weinsheimer & D. G. Marshall, Trans.). New York: Crossroad.

Gadamer, H.-G. (1989b). Hermeneutics and logocentrism (R. Palmer & D. Michelfelder, Trans.). In D. P. Michelfelder and R. E. Palmer (Eds.), *Dialogue and Deconstruction: The Gadamer-Derrida Debate* (pp. 114–125). Albany: State University of New York Press.

Gasche, R. (1986). *The tain of the mirror: Derrida and the philosophy of reflection.* Cambridge, MA.: Harvard University Press.

Heidegger, M. (1962). *Being and time* (J. Macquarrie & E. Robinson, Trans.). New York: Harper and Row.

Heidegger, M. (1971). *On the way to language* (P. D. Hertz, Trans.). New York: Harper and Row.

Heidegger, M. (1977a). Being and time: Introduction (J. Macquarrie & E. Robinson, Trans.). In D. F. Krell (Ed.), *Martin Heidegger: Basic writings* (pp. 41–89). New York: Harper and Row.

Heidegger, M. (1977b). Letter on humanism (F. A. Capuzzi, Trans.). In D. F. Krell (Ed.), *Martin Heidegger: Basic Writings* (pp. 193–242). New York: Harper and Row.

Heidegger, M. (1984). *Early Greek thinking: The dawn of Western philosophy* (D. F. Krell & F. A. Capuzzi, Trans.). New York: Harper and Row.

Heinrich, J. A. (1989). *Communication as productive understanding: Toward a new story.* Unpublished doctoral dissertation, University of Washington, Seattle.

Hekman, S. J. (1986). *Hermeneutics and the sociology of knowledge.* Notre Dame. IN: University of Notre Dame Press.

Hekman, S. J. (1990). *Gender and knowledge: Elements of a postmodern feminism.* Boston: Northeastern University Press.

Hoy, D. (1985). Jacques Derrida. In Q. Skinner (Ed.), *The return of grand theory in the human sciences* (pp. 41–64), Cambridge, Ma: Cambridge University Press.

Hyde, M. J., & Smith, C. R. (1979). Hermeneutics and rhetoric: A seen but unobserved relationship. *Quarterly Journal of Speech, 65,* 347–363.

Levin, D. M. (1991). Phenomenology in America. *Philosophy and Social Criticism, 17*(2), 103–119.

Littlejohn, S. W. (1989). *Theories of human communication.* Belmont, CA: Wadsworth.

Madison, G. B. (1991). Beyond seriousness and frivolity: A Gadamerian response to deconstruction. In H. J. Silverman (Ed.), *Gadamer and hermeneutics* (pp. 119–135). New York: Routledge.

Palmer, R. E. (1969). *Hermeneutics: Interpretation in Schleiermacher, Dilthey, Heidegger, and Gadamer.* Evanston, IL: Northwestern University Press.

Scult, A. (1983). Rhetoric and hermeneutics reconsidered. *Central States Speech Journal, 34,* 221–228.

Smith, C. R., & Hyde, M. J. (1991). Rethinking "the public": The role of emotion in being-with-others. *Quarterly Journal of Speech, 77*(4), 446–466.

Smith, P. (1988). *Discerning the subject.* Minneapolis: University of Minnesota Press.

Stewart, J. (1978). Foundations of dialogic communication. *Quarterly Journal of Speech, 64,* 183–201.

Stewart, J. (1981). Philosophy of qualitative inquiry: Hermeneutic phenomenology and communication research. *Quarterly Journal of Speech, 67,* 109–124.

Stewart, J. (1986). Speech and human being: A complement to semiotics. *Quarterly Journal of Speech, 72,* 55–73.

Stewart, J., & Philipsen, G. (1984). Communication as situated accomplishment: The cases of hermeneutics and ethnography. In B. Devin & M. J. Voigt (Eds.), *Progress in Communication Sciences,* vol. 5 (pp. 177–217). Norwood, NJ: Ablex.

Warnke, G. (1987). *Gadamer: Hermeneutics, tradition and reason.* Stanford, CA: Stanford University Press.

Weinsheimer, J. C. (1985). *Gadamer's hermeneutics: A reading of Truth and method.* New Haven, CT: Yale University Press.

4

Dialectic of Difference: A Thematic Analysis of Intimates' Meanings for Differences

JULIA T. WOOD, LISA L. DENDY, EILEEN DORDEK, MEG GERMANY, AND SHARON M. VARALLO

FOLK WISDOM CLAIMS, on the one hand, that "birds of a feather flock together" and, on the other, that "opposites attract." Yet the former idea has received considerably more attention and support from researchers than the later. This is surprising, given clinicians' recurrent observation that recognizing distinction from a partner is routine in healthy intimacy (Karpel, 1976; Lidz, 1976; Sager, 1976; Wexler & Steidl, 1978). Further, partners who comfortably recognize their differences are unlikely to become excessively interdependent (Sager, 1976; Scarf, 1987). To date, however, a paucity of research has examined differences between intimates and how these may affect close relationships. Consequently, we have an impoverished understanding of the meaning and role of differences in intimacy, and specifically, we have little insight into the positive contributions differences may make to enduring relationships.

This study investigates the ways individuals define and make sense of differences between themselves and their partners. It thus participates in the interpretive tradition that views relationships as cultures within which individuals symbolically construct and sustain meanings for themselves and their activities.

INTERPRETIVE STUDY OF CLOSE RELATIONSHIPS

Recent scholarship increasingly reflects interpretive understandings of close relationships as mini-cultures, an approach that partakes of a rich tradition of theorizing in both the humanities and social sciences (Berger & Kellner, 1975; Lewis, 1972). In 1982 I introduced the concept of relational culture, defining it as "a privately transacted system of understandings that coordinates attitudes, actions, and identities of participants in a relationship" (Wood, 1982, p. 76). "Like any culture," I argued "a relational culture consists not of objective things and cognitions, but rather of the interpretive orientation to them. It is the forms and definitions of experience that people have in mind, their models for perceiving and acting" (p. 76). Studying relationships as cultures assumes that the essence of a relationship is the meanings partners discursively constitute for it and the activities, feelings, and events composing it. Further, this approach assumes, as Conville (1988) has noted, that "the textual nature of human action is a given" (p. 428); that is, it is a coherent narrative ordered by deep structures of meaning that guide action and interaction (see also Delia & Grossberg, 1977).

Situating her research within interpretive traditions, Baxter (1987) amends Langer's classic statement to argue that "relationships can be regarded as webs of significance" spun by partners' communication (p. 262). Then, drawing on Geertz (1973, p. 9), Baxter defines the task for cultural analysts of relationships as " 'sorting out the structures of signification' . . . which constitute symbolic articulation of the culture" (p. 262).

Owen's work on relational themes has particularly advanced understanding of relationships as symbolically constructed and maintained cultures (1984, 1985). In a 1984 study he adapted the established concept of family theme to introduce relational theme, which he defined as a "patterned semantic issue or locus of concern around which interaction of a couple centers" (p. 274). Elaborating this, Owen defined a theme as "a limited range of *interpretations* [italics added] used to conceive and constitute relationships" (p. 274). By highlighting the interpretive nature of relational themes, Owen drew attention to partners' active roles in creating the reality of their relationships through symbolic activities that define the meanings of events and interactions within them. Thematic analysis is doubly interpretive because it not only probes symbolic constructions, but also relies on discursive accounts as the primary data that reveal the meanings partners generate for their activities.

The present study contributes to understanding relationship cultures by inquiring into one facet common to all close relationships: the ways in which partners define the meaning of their differences. Additionally, this investigation extends Owen's heuristic work on thematic analysis. Whereas he studied themes to identify how participants make sense of their overall relationships, we explored how themes reveal partners' efforts to make sense specifically of their differences. Finally, this study participates in what has been called the *discursive turn* infusing scholarship in numerous disciplines by focusing on language as particularly capable of illuminating how we constitute and sustain the realities by which we live.

THE DIALECTIC OF INTIMACY

Research on close relationships consistently reveals two basic phenomena—variously described as differentiation and integration, autonomy and connection, intimacy and individuality, commonality and difference, and closeness and distance—that alternately and simultaneously characterize intimate interaction. Among others, Baxter (1990), Goldsmith (1990), and I (Wood, in press) have shown how these seemingly contradictory tendencies operate in many relationships. Their mutual presence in close relationships gives credence to the wisdom of oxymoronic folklore proclaiming the attractiveness of both difference and likeness.

According to many scholars of interpersonal communication, satisfying intimacies variously accommodate the twin dynamics of closeness and distance, both of which are normal, enduring, and healthy human tendencies. Scharf's 1987 book, *Intimate Partners,* identifies satisfying needs for autonomy and intimacy as an ongoing process in close relationships. "The question of how to be one's own self (autonomous) and yet remain close to the marital partner (intimate) is the major marital dilemma . . . and must be addressed and readdressed continually" (p. 22).

Initial efforts to conceptualize these twin processes were grounded in equilibrium models, which emphasize maintaining balance in relationships. An early report by Argyle and Dean (1965), who launched equilibrium models, as well as elaborative work by Patterson (1976, 1984), demonstrated that if one aspect of a relationship is altered to create greater intimacy than has been standard for a couple, there will be a compensatory shift to create distance elsewhere within the relationship in order to restore normative equilibrium. More recent evaluations of equilibrium models conclude its emphasis on homeostasis misrepresents the highly complex and developmental dynamics encumbent in adequately satisfying needs for both autonomy and closeness.

Arguing it offers a conceptually sophisticated representation of the dynamics of intimacy, Baxter (1990) has strongly endorsed a dialectical perspective for the study of relationships. As central to this conception, Baxter (1990), following Cornforth (1968), identifies the root concepts of *progress* and *contradiction*. Process implies a concern with development and focuses researchers' attention on how tension between contradictory dynamics produces changes in relationships. Contradiction exists when two dynamics are both interdependent and reciprocally negating (Baxter, 1990, p. 70) and invites researchers to discover how needs for autonomy and closeness interact.

Several recent studies shed light on the dialectic of autonomy and connection. Investigating relational maintenance and repair, Baxter and Dindia (1987) identified both autonomy enhancing and intimacy enhancing strategies as useful in sustaining relationships. Lloyd and Cate (1985) also reported that critical to the development of closeness is finding ways to satisfy both autonomy and intimacy needs.

Particularly persuasive support for a dialectical understanding of autonomy and closeness dynamics comes from Owen's (1984) study of how partners make sense of their relationships. Identifying "involvement in the relationship" as a frequently employed theme that focuses on "the quality and quantity of talk, time spent together, and the perception of sharing in a relationship" (p. 279), Owen reported that none of his respondents used this theme when intimacy and distance needs were satisfied, but did invoke it when they perceived too much or too little intimacy. Only spouses reported too little involvement and only live-in partners noted too much involvement, which Owen interpreted as revealing the respective difficulty of maintaining togetherness and independence (p. 280) for the two types of relationships.

Finally, consider how Fitzpatrick and Best's (1979) pivotal study of relational types informs appreciation of differences between intimate partners. Their measures of relationships included autonomy as one of eight dimensions; two other dimensions, sharing and undifferentiated space, also tap autonomy by converse measure. Fitzpatrick and Best used the tension between autonomy and interdependence as one key criterion for distinguishing among relational types. Notably, the type labeled *independents* demonstrated a high degree of autonomy, which did "not seem to impair the cohesiveness" (p. 178) although it was associated with lower satisfaction. The import of Fitzpatrick and Best's study for the present research is that autonomy (and closeness) is an issue in all relationships; what differs is how various couples interpret and respond to the tension between desires for autonomy and togetherness.

ATTENDING TO DIFFERENCES

Despite convincing empirical evidence and clinical judgment that distancing is part of healthy, enduring relationships, it has received considerably less positive evaluation than its dialectical mate, closeness. This may reflect the strong emphasis on togetherness evident in interpersonal research in general and developmental models in particular. Bonding, regarded as the stage of commitment, is typically presented as the penultimate goal in relational development; Knapp's (1978) visual model depicts bonding as the literal height of relational evolution. Further, terms used to describe "growth" stages—*invitational, explorational, integrating, intensifying*—have positive connotations whereas terms depicting "decay" stages—*differentiating, disintegrating, stagnation, termination*—have negative ones (Knapp, 1978; Phillips & Wood, 1983).

Discussions of distancing behaviors are generally pejorative. Knapp, for example, defines differentiating communication as "mainly a process of disengaging or uncoupling" (1978, p. 23). The content and vocabulary of developmental models imply that increasing intimacy is at odds with distance and difference (Wood, 1993). Inherent in championing closeness and devaluing distance is an assumption that the two exist in a locked and ungenerative antagonism, rather than that their antithetical tendencies might actuate useful changes in an ongoing relationship. The play between these dialectical dynamics merits further consideration if we are to understand the complexities of how human relationships evolve over time.

Inadequate attention to differences between intimates has not gone unnoticed. In reviewing prior work on relationships to chart an agenda for the 1990s, Duck called attention to the importance of studying small and large differences and how partners deal with them as central to understanding the ongoing business of close relationships. Emphasizing the open-ended, processual nature of intimacy, Duck (1990) suggests "that we consider the inherent tensions of relationships that prompt continual balancing" (p. 9). An important aspect of this ongoing process is how partners define and deal with the tension between needs for closeness and difference.

Differences, of course, have no inherent, universal significance. As with other social and personal phenomena, the meanings of differences depend largely on how partners interpret and negotiate them. A difference that one person construes as "a problem," another may see as "an opportunity." Differences themselves, then, are of less interest than how partners define them.

The present study investigates the meanings intimate partners attribute to their differences. The research question guiding this inquiry was, Do individuals use themes to make sense of differences with intimate partners, and if so, what are those themes? Consistent with the social reality tradition of theorizing, we sought to illuminate partners' own interpretations of differences they recognized in their relationships. Our inquiry, then, required methods that would minimize researcher imposition on participants and maximize insight into individuals' perceptual words and vocabularies of motive and meaning.

METHODOLOGY

As Acitelli and Duck (1989) have pointed out, there are often discrepancies between insider and outsider views of relational phenomena, so researchers must make methodological and philosophical choices consistent with their conceptual goals. Our interest in meanings for differences called for a methodology that would emphasize participants' perspectives. In making this choice we did not assume that insiders' perspectives are more "objective" or "accurate" than those of outsiders. We did, however, assume that partners' meanings for difference influence their attitudes and actions more than those of external observers (Baxter, 1990; Olson, 1977). This approach responds to Duck's (1990) advice to "explore the underlying philosophies at work on relationships and to challenge the 'objective' stance that is often presumed for an observer" (p. 9).

Pilot Study

Prior to conducting the study reported here, preliminary interviews were done to develop questions that would yield insight into how intimate partners conceive differences. Over one year's time the senior researcher interviewed 12 individuals about their differences with partners. Additionally, respondents were invited to comment on the interview questions. These pilot responses guided development of the final interview protocol.

Respondents

Respondents were partners in eight couples (16 individuals) who agreed to be interviewed about their relationships. All participants defined themselves as in established, enduring commitments; three couples were cohabiting, three were married, and two were committed without sharing living quarters. Respondents ranged from 23 to 42 years old; 14 were employed and 2 were in graduate school. All were white and heterosexual. We reasoned that people out of college and in long-term commitments should have relatively stable views of their intimacies.[1]

Data Collection

Over a period of five months three extensive interviews were conducted. At the outset of each interview, participants were guaranteed confidentiality and encouraged not to discuss anything they considered private or were uncomfortable revealing. Each partner was interviewed separately using a standard interview protocol that included seven questions, each with follow-up probes.[2] Interviews with individual partners ranged from 38 to 90 minutes in length. Following preliminary analysis of data, interviewers met with couples to discuss initial interpretations and to invite them to amend and elaborate tentative readings.[3] Couple interviews lasted 25 to 53 minutes. A total of 401 pages of transcripts was produced from tapes, ranging from 24 to 68 pages per couple. At the end of the study participants were offered the only copy of the tape of their interviews.

Analysis

Thematic interpretation was the method of analysis. Following Owen (1984), a theme was identified in respondents' discourse when three criteria were present: (1) recurrence, defined as a meaning that recurs at different points in an interview; (2) repetition, defined as repetition of words at different junctures in interviews; and (3) forcefulness, identified by vocal inflection, volume, or nonverbal cues indicating special emphasis on certain words or ideas.

FINDINGS

Six themes emerged to describe respondents' meanings for differences between them and their partners: (1) broadens perspective, (2) enhances relational integrity and safety, (3) ensures autonomy, (4) energizes relationships, (5) creates division, and (6) disconfirms self. Although each of these themes was expressed by several respondents, specific content varied. Table 4.1 summarizes the frequency of each theme's occurrence and shows how broadly it was employed among individuals. The descriptive statistics in Table 4.1 are used to summarize data, not to suggest generalizations.

Each theme will be discussed by first defining its conceptual nature. Following that, we present and comment on excerpts from interviews to reveal in respondents' own language various ways they employed themes to make sense of differences. All excerpts are from interviews with individual partners.

Broadens Perspective

Broadens perspective is a prevalent theme for interpreting differences with a partner. Surfacing 76 separate times in interviews, this theme reflects individuals' perceptions that differences prompt desirable changes in self. Thirteen of 16 respondents mentioned ways in which differences

Table 4.1. Summary of Responses by Person and Frequency

	Broaden	Integrity	Autonomy	Energize	Divide	Disconfirm
Louise	10	2	8	3	0	4
Charles	6	10	6	12	0	0
Laura	8	0	0	0	7	3
Lloyd	0	0	9	0	9	0
Iris	2	0	2	2	0	0
Stanley	4	4	0	0	0	0
Kate	4	12	0	0	2	0
Matt	2	6	0	0	6	0
Erica	0	6	3	0	0	0
Ken	4	6	0	0	0	0
Fran	1	0	3	0	0	0
Martin	0	5	13	0	0	0
Jane	6	4	0	0	0	0
Scott	11	5	4	6	0	0
Michelle	10	6	6	8	0	0
Lee	8	10	0	0	4	0
Totals:						
Mentions	76	76	54	31	28	7
Individuals	13	12	9	5	5	2

with partners changed their perspectives, and consistently respondents indicated this "improved" them personally. For 42-year-old Lloyd, differences were an impetus for enhancing his perspective:

> She's taught me—not just about us, but about relationships in general. So I am a broader person, have a broader understanding of people. . . . she's broadened my perspective, my perspective on life. She introduces angles and perspectives on things that wouldn't occur to me, so I have a larger, a broader perspective. I myself am larger, broader..

Lloyd's account reveals all three indicators of themes. First, the idea of growth recurs in different phrasings throughout his comments as he notes what he has learned: how he is "larger," and how he understands more because his partner has a different perspective. Second, repetition is most obvious in his repeated use of two words, *perspective* and *broad*, along with derivations of the later. Finally, there is evidence of forcefulness in Lloyd's tendency to underline words meaning "broadened" with appositive phrases: "*a broader person, a broader understanding*," "*a larger, a broader*," and "*larger, broader.*"

A second example of this theme comes from Ken:

> She makes my life bigger. Choosing a mate, I think, has to do with choosing the way—one of the primary ways to augment your own perspective. . . . She augments my perspective. I bring to her a perspective that would be very hard for her to fill in. And she does that for me.

Again, Ken's account illustrates both recurrence and repetition through repeated references to the positive effects on his perspective of a partner who sees things differently.

The theme of broadens perspective assumes a different form in responses from two women, both of whom described themselves as recipients but not grantors of broadened understandings. Laura and Louise perceive differences with partners as indicative of their own impoverished understandings and opportunities for them to become more informed:

> [Laura] I learn from him. When we have differences of opinion, then I learn why he thinks what he does and I can then understand the issue better and what I ought to believe. He knows a lot more than I do, so I learn from him. . . . Lloyd's views are well thought-out, not like mine, so I can pay attention to them and revise mine accordingly. . . . I learn from what he says, and I get more perspective, better perspective.

> [Louise] He tells me things I don't know, so I'm a bigger person. . . . Usually if we disagree it's because I don't understand something, I don't know something Charles does. So I learn and then change my opinion. . . . He helps me understand stuff so I have more perspective. . . . I didn't understand about this war strategy thing, so he told me how it worked, and then I understood, and then I agreed with his opinion. So when we have differences of opinion I get better informed.

Broadens perspective appears to be a theme that might endure in relationships because it reflects not just appreciation of particular views a partner offers, but general respect for a partner's capacity to expand one's own perspective. Yet although all respondents who use broadens perspective as a theme define it as a positive means to personal expansion, an outside critic might well raise questions about the degree of deference and power imbalance reflected in some respondents' interpretations of differences. This possibility highlights a limitation inherent in insider perspectives.

Enhances Relational Integrity and Safety

Rivaling broadens perspective for the most frequent theme is enhances relational integrity and safety, which appears in 12 of 16 respondents' accounts and garners 76 separate references in interviews. This is a complex theme, entailing three interrelated issues: communication, honesty, and safety. These three intertwined ideas coalesce into the belief that having and expressing differences is one means to relational integrity and security. Illustrative of how these facets weave together to form a coherent theme is Erica's discourse:

> I would have to place an emphasis on the honesty . . . being honest about how we feel instead of trying to be the person that we think the other person wants. . . . I'd have to go back to this honesty thing. Faith in honesty . . . in his being honest. Honesty and feeling safe expressing ourselves. . . . When I have a problem with something that's going on I need to feel like it's safe, safe telling him . . . feeling safe to be honest . . . need to feel safe telling him how I feel no matter how bad it is.

This theme also pervades the comments of Erica's partner, Ken:

> Honesty, certainly. In a sense less discriminate honesty than you sometimes get. I mean I've paid lip service to honesty for years, but she's said things that one part of me really didn't want to hear, but that had to be said. . . . We disagreed about what it [an issue] meant, but at least we talked about it. We really need honesty. . . . Honesty certainly. . . . honesty and integrity to one another. . . . Erica makes me feel safe to say how I feel. . . . Honesty in the sense of communicativeness.

The dominance of references to honesty throughout Ken and Erica's interviews and the ways in which each of them link it to feeling safe indicate they converge in believing differences and the expression of them enhances the quality of their relationship. Kate's use of the theme clarifies the link between communication and relational security:

Communication [not to] play games. That's one of the big things that we've always said, like, if you have a problem come to me with it, I want to know. . . . Communication is of the utmost importance in a relationship, communication. . . . I really trust that if there's something that he needs to communicate to me that he's not going to hold back and he'll tell me. . . . Number 1 is to be totally honest.

The centrality of this theme is evident in Kate's emphasis on honesty even when it provokes conflict as well as her repetition of key words (*communication, honesty*) and recurrent associations between security and honesty about feelings. Illustrating coordination between partner's themes, Kate's interpretation of relational integrity is echoed by her partner, Matt:

Honesty. Total honesty no matter what. It may hurt me a little or a lot now, but better now than later. . . . If you're upset about something, talk. Talk . . . just talk . . . I think we're getting better all the time with confronting each other. I don't think that there are a lot of games. We could have played a lot of games, but I can think of specific times when both of us made moves to keep the other from playing games by just confronting.

The connection between relational security and confrontation about differences is crystallized by an incident both Kate and Matt emphasized in separate interviews as one that shaped their relationship. Early in their dating history they had an argument while shopping. When they did not easily resolve their difference, Matt left Kate at the store. She returned to her home, called Matt, and told him "you're a jerk." According to Matt, he learned that walking out is "a wrong way to resolve our conflicts." His response to her call, related by Kate, was to say "I'm glad you called me to talk about it. It made me build trust in you that you would call me to talk about it rather than just getting mad and blowing me off." Kate then assured Matt that "I'll always talk about it." The clash of opinions in this incident led to an interaction that generated a rule for their relationship—an agreement that they would always discuss conflicts. Thus, the existence of conflicts and willingness to talk about them serves to assure Matt and Kate that their relationship is meeting their standards for integrity.

The prevalence of this theme among respondents suggests one result of tension between differences and closeness may be to give rise to a new dialectic in which differences, whose expression is interpreted as evidence of security and a safeguard against future problems, is interdependent with relational health and closeness. A dialectical perspective's emphasis on process, in fact, inclines researchers to look for developments such as the generation of new dynamics because, as Baxter (1990) points out, "to a dialectical thinker, the presence of paired opposites, or contradictions, is essential to change and growth" (p. 70).

Ensures Autonomy

Complementing foregoing themes is a third one that emphasizes the importance of autonomous identities. This theme defines differences as key evidence that partners remain distinct individuals and have not melded into a couple identity. Striking about this theme is the value attributed to proof of differences with partners. Iris exemplifies how this theme was used to understand differences:

> Like who I am—as an individual—is much clearer to me because I see how different we are. Like I'm very interested in investments, and Stanley could care less. He asks questions that are really naive, which show me how different I am from him in this area, how individual. . . . shows me we're not the same, we're different, you know, like two really distinct individuals.

Like Iris, Martin describes differences with his partner as reassurance that he is distinct from her:

> We don't feel the need to be carbon copies of each other, so she can have a different opinion than I can. . . . It shows that she's an independently thinking person, not just an addendum to me. *That's a must.* We both need to be people, we can't be just, ah, half a couple . . . individual people. . . . We're two people and we both have our own goals and our own personalities. We're both very comfortable expressing ourselves as individuals within the unit.

By repeatedly emphasizing individuality and juxtaposing it against being "just half a couple," Martin reveals differences function as evidence that his individuality is secure.

Similarly, Michelle interpreted differences as clarifying her unique personality and preventing too much couple merger:

> I need to know he sees me as an individual, so it's sometimes good that we disagree. . . . When we differ, it makes it real clear that we're distinct people, individuals, you know, that we haven't melded into some conglomerate personality. . . . I'm

not Lee, and I don't want to be, and so we differ on some things. I think that's good because it reminds us we're not always alike, not you know, the Bobbsey Twins, we're separate individuals; we're a couple, but we're separate, we're individuals too.

A different slant on this theme departs from the implied equality between partners evident in the foregoing interpretations. One respondent, Lloyd, regards differences as evidence he is not only distinct from, but superior to his partner:

I know a lot more about things, you know events, politics, business, things that she does, so we're really different that way. . . . I take a lot of pride in knowing about things, knowing more than most people do about what's happening. . . . Most of our disagreements come about because she doesn't know what I do. . . . It's [when we differ] a chance to educate her, to inform her about things. . . . We're real different in what we know and that's real clear when we disagree.

The ensures autonomy theme emerges as an important way partners make sense of differences. Because all respondents using this theme described it positively, we inferred they perceive differences and intimacy as compatible and perhaps as mutually supportive. It may well be that evidence of autonomy makes closeness more comfortable. We underline, however, that we are reporting respondents' *perceptions*. It could be argued that despite partners' belief in their individuality, they are, in fact, enmeshed in highly complementary bonds in which the differences actually serve to sustain enmeshment. This certainly occurs as one plausible interpretation of Lloyd and Laura's relationship, which can be seen as a highly traditional, even stereotypical, connection in which power is defined and enacted in gender-stratified ways.

Energizes Relationship

A fourth theme is differences energize relationships by creating novelty and challenge. This supports Baxter's (1990) positing of predictability-novelty as one of three contradictions forming dialectical dynamics in close relationships. Emerging in five respondents' descriptions of what differences mean, this theme was expressed 31 times in the course of interviews. Most often energizes relationship reflects definitions of differences and even conflict as stimulating the bond and allaying the potential for boredom; in other cases it represents a constructive challenge to oneself and current norms of the relationship.

Iris, a 39-year-old writer, provides a good example of how this theme makes sense of differences:

I count on our differences to, you know, to charge our relationship, to put life in it. If we agreed all the time, it would
be dead, there'd be no charge, no electricity to generate
us. . . . When we clash, there's a real spark, a charge. . . . It's
exciting, energizing.

In repeatedly using the word *charge* and synonyms such as *electricity,*
spark, and *energizing,* Iris's comments demonstrate both recurrence and
repetitiveness to express her definition of differences as energizing.

Martin, a 24-year-old professional, supplements Iris's ideas by defining differences as fun:

If we agreed on everything I'd get real bored . . . I'll have an
argument with her . . . because I think that's fun. . . .
[Arguments] keep the pot stirred, the brain cells move . . . a
playful sparring match, a verbal sparring match and . . . this
[is] very attractive.

Thirty-three-year-old Michelle, a full-time homemaker, also views
differences as positive in their power to energize her relationship:

I goad him into arguments, drive him to disagree just to feel
the energy between us . . . like I want to fight to feel that
intensity, that energy between us . . . I . . . set up an argument, pick a topic I know will cause discord just to generate
something intense, some energy between us. . . . Energy is really important to me, so I make it happen.

A variation in this theme involves defining differences as providing
positive challenges or insights into oneself. Consider the following accounts from Ken and Scott:

[Ken] I can be maddening . . . can forget why the hell I'm on
the side I'm on just for the sheer pleasure of making the
argument. . . . She has the good sense to recognize
that. . . . [She] checks my perspective.

[Scott] It's scary sometimes to find out about yourself. . . . I've
had to learn. I'm learning more about myself. . . . [From our
differences I] learned about myself, and I learned . . . learn more
about yourself . . . I've learned and I think it's helped me.

With slightly different emphases, both Ken and Scott demonstrate that
they make sense of differences with their partners by defining them as
encouraging self-knowledge and growth. Energizes relationship is a theme
that interprets differences as creating constructive, welcome tension that
mitigates against staleness.

Create Division

Less pronounced, yet still notable is a view that differences create division between partners. This theme has two distinct forms: positive and negative.

Four of the five respondents who understood differences as creating division found this undesirable. Laura, for instance, understood differences as revealing or forecasting separation:

> It pulls us apart. . . . Sometimes I fantasize that if we argue he'll just leave and not come back. [Conflict] makes me feel really distant from him, like we're apart, apart, not together like couples should be. . . . I feel separated, not together.

Laura's language reveals that differences threaten her security in the relationship and challenge her idealized model of relationships as harmonious and close. Thus, she feels separated, apart, not together, and distant, all formulations that reflect the thematic meaning of difference as undesirable division. Laura's partner, Lloyd, voices a consistent view of differences:

> They make things unpleasant, make us comfortable with each other. When we disagree there's this wedge between us, drives a wedge between us . . . we can't be close if we disagree. [Having differences is] not the way a marriage should be— should be close, not divided by that wedge of difference.

Employing the metaphor of wedge, Lloyd articulates a dramatic view of differences as driving a couple apart. His account also suggests he shares Laura's idealized view of marriage as consistently harmonious. Further, their congruent view of marriage could be regarded as additional support for an interpretation of them as enmeshed in a stereotypically complementary relationship.

Interviews with Matt and Kate provided further examples of interpreting differences as threats to continuation. Viewing differences as irreconcilable, Matt interprets them as reasons not to invest further:

> We have religious differences . . . I don't think people can work around that and have as fulfilling a relationship as marriage should be. . . . I don't think it's ultimately satisfying in a marriage. Differences that would affect a long-term relationship like marriage. . . . I'm sort of doing nothing towards it [resolving differences]. . . . I've tried to force myself at times consciously and I think subconsciously not to get as involved or as committed. . . . I'm afraid to invest, invest, invest. . . . I'm scared to death to say "let's go for it."

Kate, too, seems to define some differences as irreconcilable and not improved by talk. Revealing her interpretation of differences as divisions that cannot be addressed, Kate avoids them:

> I'm sick of him getting mad, so . . . I don't want to know every time he gets mad. . . . I'd rather not know. . . . Just let it go. . . . I don't see any reason to rehash it over and over.

A third delineation of creates division surfaces in the comments of Lee, a 36-year-old professional, who thought desirable results accrued from the divisiveness difference generates:

> I hate scenes, disagreements with her. It makes me feel separated, apart from her, not close. I don't like the distance our differences create, don't like fighting. . . . Some of our most important discoveries about each other come out of fights, disagreements. We've learned what *really* matters or how each other sees things—just discoveries about each other that make it a lot easier to be close. . . . When we argue we often discover important stuff that doesn't come out in our more pleasant moments. Maybe you have to have distance, you have to be separate to discover what's really what.

Although Lee clearly interprets differences as divisive, he does not interpret division as necessarily or exclusively destructive. His own reflections suggest difference, division, and discovery interact in how he makes sense of moments of tension. Thus, his interpretations further support the dialectical perspective's premise that contradictions can prompt change and growth.

The theme of creates division has distinct variations. It may provoke insecurity about a relationship's continuity, inform choices to not commit or to avoid discussion, or be linked to discovering important insights. Thus, it seems that division may be understood as a barrier or a facilitator of closeness. Both interpretations appear related to the relational theme of relationships as fragile, which Owen (1984) reported may be used to justify increasing or decreasing investments in intimacy.

Disconfirms Self

A final theme punctuates accounts offered by two women respondents. Disconfirms self involves seeing differences as evidence that one is wrong, uniformed, or otherwise inadequate in relation to a partner. Louise and Laura both understand differences as matters of being right or wrong, and they interpret differences as revealing their ideas were wrong:

[Laura] Often I feel like I must be wrong if we disagree. Like he's right, so I must be wrong. . . . I don't think he's wrong so I must be, because we can't both be right when we disagree. . . . I figure what I believe must be wrong.

[Louise] Sometimes I feel really stupid about stuff after the argument, because I was just ignorant, stupid, and Charles was right. . . . It [brewing disagreement] makes me feel like I'm going to be wrong, stupid, you know, because he always knows what he's talking about, or at least that's how I feel when we disagree, you know, stupid. . . . When we disagree I'm always wrong because he's smarter.

Because Laura and Louise understand differences as matters of right and wrong and view themselves as less knowledgeable than partners, they define differences as proof of their "stupidity." Although this theme shares broadens perspective's view of differences as affecting perspective, the valence of the two is distinctive. Broadens perspective is cast in a decidedly favorable light, whereas disconfirms self entails undesirable feelings.

This theme may reflect larger cultural trends that devalue women and encourage them to dismiss their own insights and knowledge and to consider themselves inferior to others, particularly men (Belenky, Clinchy, Goldberger, & Tarule, 1986). If so, disconfirms self might be more prevalent in accounts from women less educated and professionally involved than the respondents in the present study.

The six themes that emerged from our analysis provide insight into a range of ways individuals make sense of differences with partners. These diverse understandings of difference surely affect how partners feel about themselves, their relationships, and the inevitable tensions that punctuate them.

SUMMARY

Two major findings emerge from this research. First, we identified six discrete themes by which people make sense of differences with intimate partners. Second, we found thematic analysis useful as a means of understanding how individuals symbolically construe one important dynamic in close relationships.

Our first finding responds to our research question, which asked whether individuals use themes to make sense of differences with intimate partners and, if so, what those themes are. We found six thematic ways partners interpret differences in close relationships: broadens perspective, enhances relational integrity and safety, ensures autonomy, energizes relationship, creates division, and disconfirms self.

This investigation neither attempted nor makes claims to comprehensive identification of ways intimates interpret differences. Further research might uncover additional themes by which people make sense of their disagreements. More important than the particular themes identified in this study is the finding that individuals do interpret differences thematically, and their discourse reveals the understandings they hold.

Our second finding concerns thematic analysis as a method of illuminating actors' perspectives on relationships. Focusing on themes proved useful in revealing how intimate partners make sense of differences between them. In relying on discourse as primary data, this method is particularly sensitive to participants' own voices and ways of conceiving their lives. We thus agree with Owen that thematic analysis illuminates "the discursive process of relational construction" (1985, p. 2). Yet, insider perspectives are not the only valid and useful ones.

This study, in particular Laura and Lloyd's narrations of their marriage, suggests the value of research that combines attention to partners' perceptions with perspectives from outside the relationship. Although focus on actors' understandings does illuminate how individuals perceive their relationships, alone it is a problematic basis for describing relationships or assessing their health. In enmeshed relationships, for example, the very dynamics that create enmeshment often also seal off partners' awareness of those dynamics and their outcomes. Thus, partners' perceptions are distorted in ways both systematic and systemic.

Enmeshment, as well as other patterns and meanings not visible from within a relationship, are most likely perceived when outsiders' perspectives are also voiced. Researchers, who are not caught up in the inner logic of relationships and who are informed by theoretical and conceptual matters, have the capacity to situate local lives within larger settings whose structures and processes infuse particular partnerships. In other words, a distinct contribution of researchers to interpretations of communication in relationships is their ability to locate specific embodiments within larger social and institutional contexts that establish normative personal and interpersonal meanings (Wood & Cox, in press).

This study suggests several avenues for future research. To extend the work reported here, researchers might investigate *how* thematic understandings of difference actually emerge in interaction as well as how they are—or are not—coordinated between partners to construct common meanings. Mindful of Duck's (1990) advice to study not just thoughts about interaction but also actual conduct (pp. 20 ff.), a logical extension of this research would be to explore how themes are manifest in interaction itself. Relatedly, forthcoming studies might trace the impact of themes on relational satisfaction and endurance of themes individuals and couples develop to define their differences.

This study also invites investigation of connections between themes and other phenomena. Existing scholarship on gender, for instance, would suggest the theme of enhances relational integrity and safety might be more important to women, given their demonstrated greater focus on relationships. Ensures autonomy too might differ in salience between genders, yet the direction of difference is less predictable: it might be more salient to women, given the historical embeddedness of their identity in relationships, or to men, who conventionally prize independence. Phenomena other than gender could also be examined for their association with themes identified here. For example, is honest communication particularly important to individuals who are insecure or who have been betrayed in previous relationships?

A third avenue for future work is to explore the coherence of partners' themes for differences. This study's intent to identify themes individuals use to make sense of differences would be complemented by insight into the significance of consensus and complementary between themes two partners employ.

A final suggestion for ongoing inquiry into how differences are enacted and perceived is to extend research to other groups of people. For instance, scholars might identify themes for interpreting differences used by lesbians, gays, older individuals, people of color, disabled partners, and so forth. Because what happens within particular relationships is influenced by partners' identities and by broad social definitions of people, we might well expect to see distinctive kinds of themes surfacing in relationships consisting of people culturally defined as marginal.

This study furthers understanding of the dialectic between autonomy and closeness by illuminating ways in which differences are interpreted, kinds of growth that may be promoted by tension, and the positive contributions differences are seen as making to intimacy. Additional study of differences promises to refine our understanding of how couples make sense of their relationships and how dialectical dynamics operate to create change and growth in enduring relationships.

NOTES

1. We do not here imply partners achieve static understandings. Instead, we agree with Duck (1990) that relationships are constantly in process and whatever resolutions of particular issues are achieved at any given time only presage new negotiations, new areas of discrepant opinion or feeling that may then become issues for which resolution is attempted.

Individuals in established relationships are nonetheless more likely to have tentatively stable understandings than are neophyte partners.

2. The interview questions follow: (1) How would you describe your relationship with X so that I could understand it? (2) Why do you two fit well as a good couple; why does your relationships work? (3) Can you think of understandings, like private rules, you and X go by? (4) Tell me about important values and goals you and X share about your relationship. (5) Explain how you and X arrived at these understandings, moments or events when they came into being for your relationship. (6) Tell me about "essentials" or "absolutes" in your relationship—qualities or understandings that you consider centrally important. (7) If you and X talk about your relationship, what kinds of things do you discuss? Each question was accompanied by a series of probes that encouraged respondents to offer specific examples and elaborate on responses.

3. We chose to discuss our initial interpretations of data with participants because we did not want to presume we had correctly represented their thinking and their meanings. Insightful essays by Alcoff (1991) and Borland (1991) have instructed us in the dangers of "speaking for the other." At the same time, Alcoff and Borland's arguments create a space for outsiders' voices, that is, those of researchers and do not presume there is or should necessarily be convergence between the interpretations of participants and observers. What is critical is that scholars recognize that insider and outsider views have distinctive contributions to make to the conversational process of conducting research.

REFERENCES

Acitelli, L., & Duck, S. (1989). Intimacy as the proverbial elephant. In D. Perlman & S. Duck (Eds.), *Intimate relationships: Development, dynamics and deterioration* (pp. 239–253). Newbury Park, CA: Sage Publications.

Alcoff, L. (1991). The problem of speaking for others. *Cultural Critique, Winter,* 5–32.

Argyle, M., & Dean, J. (1965). Eye-contact, distance and affiliation. *Sociometry, 28,* 289–304.

Baxter, L. A. (1987). Symbols of relational identity in relational cultures. *Journal of Social and Personal Relationships, 4,* 261–280.

Baxter, L. A. (1990). Dialectical contradictions in relationship development. *Journal of Social and Personal Relationships, 7,* 69-88.

Baxter, L. A., & Dindia, K. (1987). Strategies for maintaining and repairing marital relationships. *Journal of Social and Personal Relationships, 4,* 143–158.

Belenky, M., Clinchy, B., Goldberger, N., & Tarule, J. (1986). *Women's ways of knowing: The development of self, voice, and mind.* New York: Basic Books.

Berger, P., & Kellner, H. (1975). Marriage and the construction of reality. In D. Brissett & C. Edgely (Eds.), *Life as theatre* (pp. 219–233). Chicago: Aldine Press.

Borland, K. (1991). "That's not what I said!": Interpretive conflict in oral narrative research. In S. B. Gluck & D. Patai (Eds.), *Women's words* (pp. 63–76). New York: Routledge.

Conville, R. (1988). Relational transitions: An inquiry into their structure and function. *Journal of Social and Personal Relationships, 5,* 423–437.

Cornforth, M. (1968). *Materialism and the dialectical method.* New York: International Publishers.

Delia, J., & Grossberg, L. (1977). Interpretation and evidence. *Western Journal of Speech Communication, 41,* 32–42.

Duck, S. (1990). Relationships as unfinished business: Out of the frying pan and into the 1990s. *Journal of Social and Personal Relationships, 7,* 5–28.

Fitzpatrick, M. A., & Best, P. B. (1979). Dyadic adjustment in relational types: Consensus, cohesion, affectional expression and satisfaction in enduring relationships. *Communication Monographs, 46,* 167–178.

Geertz, C. (1973). *The interpretation of cultures.* New York: Basic Books.

Goldsmith, D. (1990). A dialectic perspective on the expression of autonomy and connection in romantic relationships. *Western Journal of Speech Communication, 54,* 537–556.

Karpel, M. (1976). Individuation: From fusion to dialogue. *Family Process, 15,* 65–82.

Knapp, M. (1978). *Social intercourse: From greeting to goodbye.* Boston: Allyn and Bacon.

Lewis, R. A. (1972). A developmental framework for the analysis of premarital dyadic formation. *Family Process, 1,* 17–48.

Lidz, T. (1976). *The person: His and her development throughout the life cycle* (rev. ed.). New York: Basic Books.

Lloyd, S. A., & Cate, R. M. (1985). The developmental course of conflict in dissolution of premarital relationships. *Journal of Social and Personal Relationships, 2,* 179–194.

Olson, D. H. (1977). Insiders' and outsiders' views of relationships: Research studies. In G. Levinger & H. L. Rausch (Eds.), *Close relationships: Perspectives on the meaning of intimacy* (pp. 115–135). Amherst: University of Massachusetts Press.

Owen, W. F. (1984). Interpretive themes in relational communication. *Quarterly Journal of Speech, 70,* 274–287.

Owen, W. F. (1985). Thematic metaphors in relational communication: A conceptual framework. *Western Journal of Speech Communication, 49,* 1–13.

Patterson, M. L. (1976). An arousal model of interpersonal intimacy. *Psychological Review, 83,* 235–245.

Patterson, M. L. (1984). Intimacy, social control, and nonverbal involvement: A functional approach. In V. J. Derlega (Ed.), *Communication, intimacy and close relationships* (pp. 105–132). Orlando, FL: Academic Press.

Phillips, G. M., & Wood, J. T. (1983). *Communication and human relationships: The study of interpersonal communication.* New York: Macmillan.

Sager, C. (1976). *Marriage contracts and couple therapy: Hidden forces in intimate relationships.* New York: Brunner/Mazel.

Scarf, Maggie. (1987). *Intimate partners.* New York: Random House.

Wexler, J., & Steidl, J. (1978). Marriage and the capacity to be alone. *Psychiatry, 41,* 72–82.

Wood, J. T. (1982). Communication and relational culture: Bases for the study of human relationships. *Communication Quarterly, 30,* 75–84.

Wood, J. T. (1993). Enlarging conceptual boundaries: A critique of research in interpersonal communication. In S. Bowen & N. Wyatt (Eds.), *Transforming visions: Feminist critiques in communication studies* (pp. 19–49). Cresskill, NJ: Hampton Press.

Wood, J. T. (In press). Engendered relations: Interaction, caring, power, and responsibility in close relationships. In S. W. Duck (Ed.), *Understanding relationship processes,* vol. 4. Newbury Park, CA: Sage Publications.

Wood, J. T., & Cox, R. (In press). Rethinking critical voice: Materiality and situated knowledges. *Western Journal of Communication.*

5

On Interpersonal Competence

CARINA P. SASS

WHAT DOES THE INTERPRETIVIST SAY about communication competence? Should anything be said at all? When asked to speak on interpersonal competence, the first question raised could be, "Why?" As these questions are considered, it should be easy to reach the conclusion that competence is a central and significant component of interpersonal communication. As interpretivists, we consider social interaction as the means for the construction of reality. The centrality of communication in the social order and process suggests that how *well* interactants communicate (or how well they perceive they communicate) would be of significant interest to the communication researcher. The perceived quality (competence) of interaction certainly has an impact on the construction of social reality. Interpretivists, however, are just recently taking an interest in interpersonal communication as a field of study. Most notable is a discussion presented by Bochner (1985), as well as a two-issue forum in *Communication Theory* (Leeds-Hurwitz, 1992a, 1992b). This book provides another example of this increased interest.

The model proposed in this chapter is offered as an additional perspective from which to study interpersonal communication competence. It is not being proposed as the answer to studying communication competence, but rather as an idea with which to explore competence in new ways. This symbolic interactionist model of communication competence may develop into a leading model of communication competence. A more realistic goal, however, is for this chapter to initiate dialogue and encourage the exploration of interpersonal communication competence from an interpretive stance.

This chapter presents a model of competence based on the philosophical and theoretical assumptions of symbolic interactionism (as well as social constructionism and ethnomethodology) as a way in which interpretive scholars might consider communication competence. It is my hope that this model will yield insights into the symbolic and social construction of competent interpersonal relationships. To reach this goal, I will present a cursory review of the direction traditional interpersonal communication competence research has taken, as well as provide the philosophical context and foundations for an interpretive model of competence. An overview of symbolic interactionism, the primary foundation for the model, is followed by a discussion of major assumptions upon which the model is based. Concluding this chapter is a discussion of the weaknesses as well as the potential of this model to provide new insights into relational interaction and development.

TRADITIONAL APPROACHES TO COMMUNICATION COMPETENCE

Communication competence research programs, although varying widely in conceptualizations and definitions of competence (Parks, 1985; Spitzberg, 1983, 1991), are rooted primarily in positivistic, social scientific perspectives. To propose a model of interpersonal competence, it is important to relate such a model to existing research models and their goals. It is not the purpose of this section to provide a comprehensive review of competence research (see Spitzberg & Cupach, 1984, for such a review), but rather to provide a general context in which to place the proposed model.

Bochner and Kelly (1974) and Wiemann (1977) provide models of competence that share significant similarities with one another. Bochner and Kelly (1974) base their model on psychological, social psychological, and psychiatric theories, whereas Wiemann (1977) integrates approaches based on psychological theory, social psychological, and sociological theory. Both models focus on effectiveness as the primary characteristic of competent communication.

Interpersonal communication competence has been viewed as an individual trait, a disposition, a set of skills, knowledge about communication, or an evaluation made by an observer (Onyekwere, Rubin, & Infante, 1991; Pavitt & Haight, 1985, 1986; Spitzberg & Cupach, 1984). Skills or traits are emphasized in a number of competence models. Skills such as empathy and behavioral flexibility are identified by both Bochner and Kelly (1974) and Wiemann (1977). Other competent skills include self-disclosure, owned feelings and thoughts, and descriptiveness (Bochner & Kelly, 1974), and affiliation/support, social relaxation, and interaction management skills (Wiemann, 1977).

Hart and his colleagues have developed a model of interpersonal communication competence that identifies individuals as one of three types of communicators: the *noble self*, the *rhetorical reflector*, and the *rhetorically sensitive individual* (Hart & Burks, 1972; Hart, Carlson, & Eadie, 1980; Ward, Bluman, & Dauria, 1982). Each of these models focuses on competence as a characteristic or behavior that can be identified and judged by an observer.

Pavitt (1981) advocates an inferential approach to competence. He argues that individuals hold conceptions, or prototypes, of the characteristics of the "ideal communicator," which are used to make inferences regarding an individual's degree of communicative competence (Pavitt, 1981; Pavitt & Haight, 1985, 1986). The prototype of the communicatively competent person "functions as an 'implicit theory' about trait and behavioral associations from which impressions of specific communication are inferred" (Pavitt & Haight, 1986, p. 223). Once the observer forms an impression of the person communicating (based on this "implicit theory"), then an evaluation is made based on how closely this impression matches the prototypical competent communicator (Pavitt, 1990). Pavitt takes a different perspective than the others mentioned in this review. Bochner and Kelly (1974), Hart and Burks (1972), and Wiemann (1977) all focus on the behaviors of the competent (or incompetent) communicator. Pavitt's focus, however, is on the perceptions of the observer in evaluating a competent (or incompetent) communicator's behavior.

All of the preceding conceptualizations focus on competence as a trait or skill possessed by an individual. Bochner and Kelly (1974), Pavitt (1981), and Wiemann (1977) all assert that one's competence can be evaluated by others based upon one's behavioral choices. In Pavitt's (1981) model, these behaviors are not determined in an a priori fashion, but rather are more subjective than the clearly defined behavioral skills of Bochner and Kelly (1974) and Wiemann (1977).

Unlike previous models, Brian Spitzberg and his associates have developed a unified conceptualization of communication competence that focuses, not on the individual, but on the relationship (Spitzberg, 1983; Spitzberg & Cupach, 1984; Spitzberg & Hecht, 1984). Their analysis of competence research culminates in a model of communication competence that is considered by many to be the definitive statement on communication competence (Duran & Zakahi, 1987; Onyekwere, Rubin, & Infante, 1991). Their model is utilized in a broad range of research, including conflict strategies (Canary & Spitzberg, 1987, 1989, 1990), and communication education (Spitzberg & Hurt, 1987).

In the relational approach *competence* is defined in part as "a dyadic or interpersonal impression and must include the perspective of both interactants" (Spitzberg & Hecht, 1984, p. 576). Competence is located in the interpersonal interaction, or "between" the interactants. The model focuses on both the appropriateness and effectiveness of communication. Other competence models tend to emphasize effectiveness as a primary consideration (e.g., Bochner & Kelly, 1974; Wiemann, 1977). In the relational model, competence is viewed as having the potential to change over time. Competence is also viewed as highly contextual. These assumptions are interrelated. As the situation, or context, changes, the perception of competence may change. In addition, interactants' perception of a given interaction may change over time, thus affecting their conclusions regarding the degree to which that interaction is considered competent (Spitzberg & Cupach, 1984).

Finally, according to the relational model, competent communicators must be motivated to communicate, have some knowledge about communicating and possess the skills to communicate well, be aware of the desired outcomes (the communicator's goals), and be sensitive to the particular context (Spitzberg & Cupach, 1984). These five components are central to studying competence from this perspective.

Communication research develops out of at least two perspectives. Most lines of competence research assume a positivistic approach. This way of thinking, also called a *received view* (Bochner, 1985 or *rational-world paradigm* (Fisher, 1978; Pearce, 1977), is based on objectivity and rationality. It is founded in scientific thought, emphasizing the existence of objective truth or knowledge, and adhering to behavioristic, social scientific methods (Fisher, 1978; Pearce, 1977; Putnam, 1983b). Early models of competence tend to utilize a molecular unit of analysis, focusing on the individual as opposed to the relationship and seeking to generalize to the larger population rather than focusing on individual differences. Further, models generally take a mechanistic approach to behavior: competent behavior occurs because competence is an innate characteristic or an ability that individuals either do or do not possess. Finally, competence research from such a perspective seeks prediction of behavior.

A second perspective is known by a variety of names, including the *naturalistic paradigm* (Lincoln & Guba, 1985; Putnam, 1983a) or the *interpretive approach* (Leeds-Hurwitz, 1992a, 1992b; Putnam, 1983a). Such a perspective is meaning centered and assumes (1) a symbolically constructed reality (of society as well as of self); (2) that the researcher is inextricably engaged with his or her subject (and therefore unable to attain complete "objectivity"); (3) the goal of research is to describe particulars rather than produce broad generalizations; (4) research cannot establish causality; and (5) research is inherently value laden (Lincoln & Guba, 1985).

The various models of communication competence just reviewed play an important role in gaining an understanding of communication competence. These approaches, however, are more useful to the positivist than to the interpretivist. A model that responds to the questions and seeks to meet the goals of interpretivist research must be described in the vocabulary of interpretivism and set within the framework of interpretivism.

ON SYMBOLIC INTERACTIONISM

I have taken a rather eclectic approach to developing such an interpretive model of communication competence, drawing upon several related lines of thought. All of the ideas that inform the model being developed fall under a single "paradigm," identified by sociologist George Ritzer (1992) as the "social-definition paradigm" (p. 526). The primary focus of the model will be on symbolic interactionism, drawing heavily from the ideas of George Herbert Mead. A general overview of symbolic interactionism provides a basis for understanding the development of the proposed model.

Symbolic interactionism has its foundations in the social philosophies of George Herbert Mead (1934) and Herbert Blumer (1969). For the symbolic interactionist, symbols are central to all social behavior. Society develops through the use of symbols and continued interaction. Also, a perception of one's self emerges through ongoing interaction. Further, symbolic interactionists argue that through our ability to use symbols and hold a shared meaning of those symbols we are enabled to hold "internal conversations" that allow us to create meaning and choose behavioral responses to others' actions (Craib, 1984; Meltzer, Petras, & Reynolds, 1975; Mead, 1934).

Mead (1934) delineates three main concepts of society, self, and mind. According to Mead, *society* is created through the continuing process of human interaction. Through interaction individuals create a shared understanding of symbols, or shared meanings. These *significant symbols* provide the basis of the cooperative activity known as *society* (Craib, 1984; Meltzer, 1972; Mead, 1934). Society is characterized as a process rather than a structure, being likened to a conversation, with "The same qualities of flow, development, creativity and change as we would experience in a conversation around the dinner table" (Craib, 1984, p. 72). Societies provide a valuable "framework" for individuals to understand the world, themselves, and to make behavioral choices.

The development of the *self* is a second aspect of social interaction. Through interaction with others an individual is able to experience the view of others and to reflect upon that view in relation to his or her actions. The self is a product of the ongoing interaction between an individual and others. The individual responds to both internal and external (social) stimuli, each moderating and modifying the other (Meltzer, Petras, & Reynolds, 1975). This external stimuli is a composite of all "others" into one *generalized other.* We understand our selves through the perceptions of others and our ability to see ourselves as we perceive others to see us. We respond to what we perceive to be the others' intentions (Meltzer, 1972; Meltzer, Petras, & Reynolds, 1975; Mead, 1934).

The shared meaning of symbols and the ability to take the role of the generalized other also strengthen Mead's concept of mind. *Mind* refers to the capability of inner dialogue or conversation with oneself. Through this self-conversation meanings can be attributed to the behavior of others (Craib, 1984; Meltzer, Petras & Reynolds, 1975). Humans are also able to rehearse behavioral choices in their minds prior to enacting the behavior. This allows the individual to choose the most appropriate behavior (Meltzer, 1972).

Mead's discussion of the "I" and the "me" illustrates the manner in which this conversation occurs. The "I" refers to the spontaneous impulses of an individual, and the "me" to the internalized representation of the "other." Conversation between the impulsive "I" and the socialized "me" provides the opportunity for the self to work out appropriate behavioral responses (Meltzer, 1972; Meltzer & Petras, 1972; Meltzer, Petras, & Reynolds, 1975; Mead, 1934).

For the symbolic interactionist, symbols, and the meaning attributed to them, are central to the creation of the social self, relationships with others, and society in general. The centrality of the interaction to the development of the self necessitates a focus on what occurs *between* interactants rather than a focus on each individual. This *between* is the result of the interaction of two individuals, a creation of something (the relationship) that goes beyond the sum of what each brings into the interaction. This creation requires an ongoing, ever-developing dialogue.

A MODEL OF INTERPERSONAL COMPETENCE

Symbolic interaction furnishes us with an interpretive framework to approach the study of interpersonal competence. The model that follows is an attempt to reach the "between" of interactions—the relationship that develops out of the social interaction of the individuals. It allows us to examine and identify the symbolic construction of the interpersonal relationship.

To present my definition and model of communication competence, I must first delineate a number of significant assumptions of my perspective. These assumptions spring forth from the basic tenets of symbolic interactionism, ethnomethodology, and social constructionism, as well as from the thinking of Kenneth Burke and the philosophy of Martin Buber. Both Buber and Burke, although not traditionally considered symbolic interactionists, can philosophically fall under such a rubric (Pfuetze, 1961). These factors direct the creation of this model. The assumptions will be followed by a definition of communication competence and a discussion of the components of that definition.

Assumptions

REFLEXIVE NATURE OF INTERPERSONAL COMMUNICATION The first assumption I present is that interpersonal relationships are reflexive and interdependent. This is based on Mead's (1934) concept that an individual's "self" is a product and process of interaction with other individuals and the greater social group. The individual responds not only to the other individual, but also to a *generalized other* that is a composite of all "others" in that person's social community. In other words, an individual develops, through continued interaction, a general "picture" of what others in his or her social group believe. This picture of the *generalized other* provides the individual with an external, "objective" view of oneself.

We understand ourselves through the perceptions of others. One's identity as an individual is dependent on the ability to be able to take the perspective of the "other" and reflect on oneself. It is through the eyes of the other that we define our "selves." Buber (1970) similarly views "self" as emerging through an intersubjective interaction with another. This concept of self suggests that an individual's identity is not only a product of social interaction, but is also inseparable from the interaction. According to Buber (1970) and Mead (1934), one cannot have a sense of "self" apart from others.

The implications of this reflexive relationship described by Buber (1970) and Mead (1934) include (a) that an individual's concept of self, as well as any individual goals, needs, or objectives brought into a relationship, are subject to influence from the relational interaction; (b) the nature of the relationship will be defined through the relational interaction and will include the development of any relational rules or norms, needs, goals, or objectives; and (c) definition through relational interaction suggests a dynamic quality of the relationship and the self. The dynamic, reflexive quality of relational interaction affects perceptions of relational competence through the perceptions of how well individual and relational goals were met and rules or norms maintained.

CONTEXTUAL NATURE OF INTERPERSONAL COMMUNICATION
Another assumption that emerges from symbolic interactionism is the highly contextual nature of interpersonal communication and, more specifically, competent communication. This contextuality includes the social and historical context—both of the relationship and the individuals, as well as the immediate context. Several characteristics of symbolic interactionism support this assumption.

First, the proactive nature of human beings allows for behavioral choices to be made based on previous social interactions, a socially derived view of self, and the shared meaning of the immediate interactants (Craib, 1984). This is further elucidated in Mead's concept of "emergence" (Meltzer, Petras, & Reynolds, 1975). The process of emergence refers to the influence the past has upon the present and how subsequent events influence one's perception or interpretation of the past. Here Mead is not only recognizing the proactive, or indeterminate, nature of humans, but also the socially reactive or determinate nature of humans (Meltzer & Petras, 1972; Meltzer, Petras, & Reynolds, 1975). *Context* refers not only to the immediate context, but also to the historical context and the interaction of the two.

Second, social acts as reflexive process suggest a contextual nature. In any interaction, each individual influences and is influenced by the other, resulting in new "objects" (the relationship and symbols relevant to it). This form of influence is not easily predicted. From the perspective of Mead's concept of "I" and "me," the "I" provides the unknown quantity in the interaction. Whereas the "me" responds to societal expectations and is therefore fairly predictable, the "I" reflects the individual's impulses (Mead, 1934). With the "I" involved in social interactions, it is difficult for general expectations to exist across contexts.

Finally, the centrality of interaction to social development and its dynamic nature require the recognition of the dialogical influence between society, self, and our interaction with others. Just as one's self-concept is created and formed through interacting with others, so also are relationships with other individuals and the larger societal structure. Self-concept, relationships, and society concurrently influence and affect one's interactional choices. Competence is dependent on what occurs in the relationship. As the relationship develops over time and as the situation surrounding the interaction changes, so do the "rules" for competent communication. The degree to which context influences competent communication varies depending on the type of relationship, the psychological states of the participants, the physical as well as sociocultural environment, as well as the communicative history of the interactants (with each other as well as with others).

UNIFYING NATURE OF INTERPERSONAL COMMUNICATION
A third assumption of symbolic interactionism is that interpersonal relationships unify the participants. Symbolic interactionism illustrates how shared meaning and the ability to take the role of the other are necessary for the formation and continued existence of society. Society is based on mutual understanding and cooperation (Meltzer, Petras, & Reynolds, 1975). This is also valid at the interpersonal level.

In Mead's conceptualization of society and self, social interaction is the medium for the development of self (as one becomes able to take the perspective of the *generalized other* or greater society), as well as for societal change (through the influence of the individual and the interaction). Interpersonal communication is unifying by its very centrality in the development of self. Our very selves exist because we are able to see ourselves as others see us, "from the particular standpoints of other individual members of the same social group, or from the generalized standpoint of the social group as a whole" (Mead, 1934, p. 138). That ability comes about only through interaction with others.

Others not directly identified with symbolic interactionism, but sharing the assumption of the symbolic construction of reality, further support the assumption of the unifying nature of communication. In his definition of humankind, Kenneth Burke (1966) describes humans as naturally divided, both physically and mentally, as separate beings. We can experience our own thoughts, emotions, and physical sensations, but we are separated from the thoughts, emotions, and physical sensations of others. We must rely on our ability to communicate those experiences symbolically to understand the experiences of the other. This very problem of division serves as a motivation toward communication and increased *identification* with one another. Burke (1950) argues that only through symbolic action, a sharing of meaning, can individuals achieve a greater degree of identification, or unity, with one another.

Buber (1970, 1973) also expresses the necessity to develop and maintain unity and uniqueness in relationships through symbolic interaction. Individuals make choices when interacting. One might choose to seek to achieve personal goals without regard to the other (seeing the other as an object), or one might choose to seek to know and appreciate the other as a unique human being, striving to understand the experiences of the other. The first is identified by Buber (1970) as an *I-It* relationship. The second is referred to as an *I-Thou* relationship.

Buber's (1970) *I-Thou* relationship and Burke's (1950) concept of identification both refer to ideals that interactants strive for but can never completely attain. Theorists have addressed this issue of the unattainable ideal in discussions on symbolic interactionism (Fisher, 1978), naturalistic research (Poole & McPhee, 1983; Putnam, 1983b), and intercultural empathy (Broome, 1991). A common theme in these discussions is to deemphasize *accuracy* (one can never share in another's experiences or understanding with complete accuracy), and to emphasize the *degree* of shared belief or perception of understanding.

Although based on hermeneutic phenomenology, Broome (1991) presents a conceptualization of relational empathy that is consistent with symbolic interactionism. Relational empathy is described as "the creation of *shared meaning* during the interpersonal encounter" (Broome, 1991, p. 241). Shared meaning is never complete; it is provisional, dynamic, and highly contextual (Broome, 1991). Interactants are continually molding and reworking their understanding of one another, their selves, and their relationships, always in the process of creation and re-creation, never completing this process. This relational dynamic can be likened to a dialogical dance: the dance is both separate from and a part of the interactants—it ceases to exist when one stops moving, yet while each individual moves, the dance itself takes on an identity of its own.

Broome's (1991) concept of relational empathy reflects symbolic interactionism's emphasis on shared meaning developed through social interaction, its focus on the relationship and the dynamic quality of relationships, as well as the contextual basis of meaning (Broome, 1991; Buber, 1970; Mead, 1934). The concept of relational empathy also reflects a striving for that *I-Thou* relationship, the continual development of understanding and respect for the other as a unique, authentic individual.

These three assumptions of interpersonal communication and relationships as reflexive, contextual, and unifying can serve as a foundation for the further development of models of interpersonal communication. From this point, there are many directions one may choose. I have chosen a direction that I believe is central to the study of interpersonal communication and will use these assumptions as a foundation for a definition and model of interpersonal communication competence.

Definition

From a symbolic interactionist perspective, *communication competence* may be defined as "the relational participant's perception of the degree to which their interaction serves to meet relational and individual needs, while maintaining the authentic quality of their relationship."

COMPETENCE AS RELATIONAL   First, there is a relational, rather than an individual, focus. In symbolic interactionism, the individual is inseparable from the relationship due to the reflexive nature of discourse. Just as the individual is defined through social interaction, so too is the relationship. The relationship cannot be divided, and a focus on the individuals apart from the relationship cannot be "summed up" to reflect the nature of the relationship. Gergen (1985) similarly identifies the relationship as the "locus of human action" (p. 12) and directs social constructionists to seek understanding at the relational level.

This relational focus is, to date, uncommon in the study of competence. Competence research has been focusing largely on the individual. The research of Bochner and Kelly (1974) and Wiemann (1977) focus on the individual, each identifying skills or behaviors of the individual that they consider "competent." Hart and Burks (1972) also focus on the individual, identifying three basic types of communicators characterized by the proportion to which each type focuses on "self" or "other." Another model that has the individual as the locus of study is the prototype conceptualization of competence (Pavitt, 1981; Pavitt & Haight 1985, 1986). Unlike most other competence researchers, Spitzberg and his associates present a dyadic, or relational, perspective on competence (Spitzberg, 1983, Spitzberg & Cupach, 1984; Spitzberg & Hecht, 1984).

The primary difference between the model presented in this chapter and that of Spitzberg is in regard to the basic philosophical assumptions undergirding each approach, as well as the form research would take from the respective approaches. Spitzberg's model, relying on positivistic, social scientific methods, answers those research questions associated with social scientific inquiry and seeks generalizable findings, resulting in explanation and prediction. A symbolic interactionist model asks much different questions, seeks description and understanding, and approaches the subject of study from much different perspectives.

COMPETENCE AS SHARED PERCEPTION   Second, communication competence is based on both participants' perceptions regarding the interaction. *Identification* (Burke, 1950) refers to the degree to which individuals share an understanding of the meaning of their interaction and relationship. This concept is further developed in Davis and Roberts (1985) discussion on the *I-Thou* relationship. In a social constructionism application of Buber, Davis and Roberts (1985) describe competent *I-Thou* relationships as those in which the relationship is mutually negotiated and defined. Specifically, there is a mutual acceptance of status, and differences are negotiated and acknowledged. "In shared worlds, each may be said to understand how things count for each other, including how atypical, as well as conventional, expressions of the relationship are to be taken" (Davis & Roberts, 1985, p. 147).

Mutual perception is an integral aspect of a symbolic interaction approach to interpersonal communication (Fisher, 1978). This requires that communication competence be considered at that level. Communication competence, therefore, is based on the degree to which interactants share an understanding of and satisfaction with their communication encounters.

The focus on identification or "sharedness" and the celebration of the other's uniqueness as described by Buber (1970) further strengthens the idea of interdependence. As it is through symbols (specifically the symbolic interaction between participants) that the participants and their relationship are defined, it is also through such interaction that communication competence is evaluated. Further, as the interactants' identity in relation to one another is defined symbolically (and reflexively), evaluations are necessarily subjective perceptions of the interaction.

COMPETENCE AS MUTUALLY SATISFACTORY   The relational characteristic of communication competence implies that communication must be satisfactory in some degree to both participants. An individual is seen as bringing into a relationship a concept of self, as well as individual goals, needs, or objectives. These are subject to influence from the relational interaction, which in turn defines the relationship, including the development of any relational rules or norms, needs, goals, or objectives. Relational and individual goals and needs are so interrelated that satisfaction of one participant's goals cannot come about without affecting the other and the relationship. Satisfaction is related to the degree of shared understanding or congruence of the participants' perception of their relational interaction. The degree to which the interactants share a perception that their relational needs and goals are being met reflects the degree to which they consider their communication to be competent.

COMPETENCE AS AUTHENTIC   This component of the model suggests the involvement of motives and values. Interpersonal communication requires that the participants not only approach the other person with respect as a unique individual, but the individuals must also come into the relationship honestly and authentically. Authenticity and spontaneity are considered significant results of the *I-Thou* relationship (Davis & Roberts, 1985). Authenticity involves higher levels of interpersonal communication (such as "gut level" and "peak" communication, described by John Powell, 1969, pp. 57–61).

The authenticity that participants exhibit in the relationship is a necessary consideration of communication competence, as is the degree of empathy. Authenticity does not equate to complete self-disclosure. Rather, authentic communication relates to the *I-Thou* communication described by Buber (1970) and Davis and Roberts (1985), and the dynamic, creative dialogue of Broome's (1991) relational empathy. Authenticity requires taking the responsibility to seek shared understanding of each other. It is a relational process that requires participation by both members. To approach an *I-Thou* relationship, it is important to present one's self authentically to the other as well as seek to experience and understand the authentic self of the other participant (Buber, 1970).

Mead (1934) provides a related description in his discussion of sympathy. He identifies sympathy with a cooperative social process and the ability to "(arouse) in one's self the attitude of the other" (p. 299). This idea, as does Buber's (1970) *I-Thou*, suggests a degree of selflessness and valuing of the relationship (and the other as part of that relationship).

I would dare take this idea of authenticity one step further into the realm of the moral. I suggest that individuals, interpersonal relationships, and the larger social group have a mutual responsibility to one another. Again, hearkening back to the reflexive nature of relationships and the mutual influencing of self and society, the individual self exists only in relation to the larger social group (through social interaction), and the social group exists through the interaction of its individual members. This interdependence cannot be considered apart from mutual responsibility. Mead (1934) addresses this in his essay on ethics: "On the one side stands the society which makes the self possible, and on the other side stands the self that makes a highly organized society possible. The two answer to each other in moral conduct" (pp. 385–386).

The term *authenticity* is not a completely adequate representation of this complex concept. Competent communication requires a relating-to-the-other that serves the best interests of the relationship. It is an honest representation of oneself; it is taking on the attitude, emotions, and perspective of the other.

The presentation of this model of interpersonal competence is incomplete without a discussion of its application as a foundation for research. How should the study of interpersonal competence be approached from an interpretivist perspective? Research methods traditionally utilized in the study of competence are inappropriate for an interpretivist perspective. Research must take a naturalistic form, and the researcher must be prepared to confront and engage the subject. Critical issues and concerns are presented for the prospective competence researcher to consider.

Research Approach

The goal of interpersonal competence research is to develop an understanding of how the relational participants perceive the competence of their relational interactions. Researchers seek to understand the way interactants negotiate and define acceptable, competent communication within that relationship. This goal is reached through "thick description," which is described by Geertz (1973) as "setting down the particular meaning particular social actions have for the actors whose actions they are" (p. 27). Thick description is utilized to identify how the actual relational members make sense and meaning of their actions. This requires the researcher to confront the complexities of a personal relationship and seek to identify the connections, rules, roles, and subtle nuances of meaning in that relationship. To do so, the researcher must seek to take the perspective of the actors, to get "inside the actor's world and . . . see the world as the actor sees it" (Meltzer, Petras, & Reynolds, 1975, p. 57). Charles H. Cooley, whose work in sociology predates the birth of symbolic interactionism, identifies this methodology as "sympathetic introspection" (Meltzer, Petras, & Reynolds, 1975, p. 10).

The complex and continually emerging nature of personal relationships requires significant, in-depth attention from the researcher. Lincoln and Guba (1985) stress "prolonged engagement" and "persistent observation" as necessary to accurately account for the processes and constructions of the focus of study. Unique rules, norms, and expectations that develop in relationships are not always apparent nor, when apparent, are they always as they appear to an initial observer. In addition, the relationship changes and develops through present and past interactions, and the perceptions of past interactions change as the relationship moves from one "present" to another. Interpretive researchers, therefore, must take a longitudinal approach to the study of interpersonal communication competence.

It is important for a researcher to begin a study with some type of theoretical structure. Geertz (1973) emphasizes that one's initial foray into the context of study, which he refers to as *finding one's feet* (p. 27), must be undertaken with some theoretical basis. Such research is an ongoing clarification, extension, and refinement of related studies. Theory provides the foundation for a tentative hypothesis from which research occurs. This hypothesis should be continually assessed and revised "until it accounts for *all known cases without exception*" (Lincoln & Guba, 1985, p. 309).

The symbolic interactionist perspective suggests certain methodological approaches to succeed at getting "inside" the actor's reality. This includes the utilization of "sensitizing concepts" (Meltzer, Petras,

& Reynolds, 1975, p. 60) to identify the assumptions or issues considered significant by the subjects of study (Craib, 1984; Fisher, 1978). This would also determine the general characteristics of behaviors that might be evaluated by interactants in various situations (Fisher, 1978; Pacanowsky & O'Donnell-Trujillo, 1982). In the process of becoming sensitized to the subjects, it is also important for the researcher to become sensitized to his or her own predispositions and biases. Recognizing how the researcher's perceptions influence research is something that is often given insufficient attention.

Subsequent research might involve an ethnographic approach, developing "thick description" of the relationships under study. Such research requires a multilevel approach consisting of such methods as observation, participant observation, as well as nondirective interviews and conversations, letters, diaries, and other personal documents (Denzin, 1972; Meltzer, Petras, & Reynolds, 1975). This provides the researcher with various opportunities to "get at" the meanings underlying relational interactions. The use of multiple methods (known as triangulation) also strengthens the credibility of the research (Lincoln & Guba, 1985).

Because competence is a relational concept, it is important to identify the shared perception of that relationship. Such a description would incorporate the researcher's observations, the reports of the participants, as well as descriptions of the process. Another type of triangulation would include obtaining data from multiple sources, including members of the relationships under study and the researcher himself or herself (Lincoln & Guba, 1985). Ideally, research would take place over a long period of time, with the researcher becoming a member of the living community.

From this description of shared perceptions, processes and patterns will begin to emerge. Through the identification of shared perceptions and meanings, significant issues will be highlighted. It will also provide an understanding of the manner in which relational participants develop a competent relationship. At this point particularly, the researcher can be likened to a literary critic (Geertz, 1973), "sorting out the structures of significance" (p. 9). The analysis, or interpretation, of the description is significant in that it identifies a structure or order to the relationship that provides a deeper understanding of that relationship. This provides opportunity to revise the researcher's original hypothesis (known as "negative case analysis" by Lincoln & Guba, 1985, p. 309), which further strengthens the quality of the research.

The results provide a basis for subsequent related studies that probe further into the issue of competence in similar relationships. These are not generalizable results, nor are they meant to be. Rather, they are an in-depth look at a particular type of relationship, which will become a part of a cluster of particular, in-depth studies of similar relationships. It is, according to Lincoln and Guba (1985), the responsibility of subsequent researchers to determine the transferability of findings to another context.

DISCUSSION

This model of communication competence provides the theoretical basis for an interpretive perspective of competence research. The foundations of the model, based in symbolic interactionism, include assumptions of symbolic interaction as a means of constructing social reality and the reflexive, highly contextual, and unifying nature of interpersonal communication.

From this, competence is then seen as a relational concept that is negotiated by the participants. In other words, the relational interactants have a shared understanding regarding what is competent within their relationship. Given that participants have a shared perception of competence, it would follow that the relationship would be considered mutually satisfactory, or meeting both interactants relational needs. And finally, with the nature of interpersonal communication being unifying, competent communication would require the interactants' to approach the relationship authentically and empathically.

Developing and utilizing an interpretive model such as this has several implications for interpersonal communication research. First, the goals of this approach provide a much deeper, richer view of the interpersonal communication in a given relationship than other, primarily quantitative, types of research. Whereas many researchers focus on specific behaviors (variables) and seek to generalize findings to the larger population, this model focuses on particular relationships, taking a more integrative perspective on the relational communication. Such a focus allows the researcher not only to come to understand particular behaviors within a relationship, but also to see the interrelationships of various behaviors within the relationship. Additionally, the processual-developmental nature of relationships can be explored more fully than with many other types of research.

A second implication is in regard to the relationship between individuals and the society in which they live. The model recognizes the dynamic interrelationship and interdependence of individuals and society. Emphasis on such an interrelationship allows the researcher a greater focus on the context in which individuals interact (familial, social, and work relationships, as well as in the society at large). This focus is much deeper than when context or culture is considered simply another variable. The dynamic nature of this individual-societal interconnection requires the recognition of the processual nature of human interaction.

Communication competence is generally considered in terms of effectiveness and appropriateness (Spitzberg & Cupach, 1984). A final implication of this model is the consideration of an ethical dimension of interpersonal communication. Individuals are considered by the symbolic interactionist as having a high degree of interdependence, and their relationships are considered highly reflexive. As mentioned earlier, individuals may choose either to objectify or personalize the other individual. In competent communication, interactants strive in their relationship to attain something akin to Buber's (1970) *I-Thou* relationship.

This ethical dimension, identified as *authenticity* in the model, emphasizes the interdependence and resulting responsibility individuals have to others, to themselves, and to society at large. It is a general recognition of human worth and respect for others, for one's own worth, as well as a recognition of mutual relational responsibility.

ACKNOWLEDGMENTS

I would like to acknowledge and thank Dan Canary, Ed Hinck, and Rich Wiseman for their encouragement and constructive criticism on earlier versions of this chapter. In addition, I would like to thank Jim Sass for reviewing and providing feedback throughout this project.

REFERENCES

Blumer, H. (1969). *Symbolic interactionism: Perspective and method.* Englewood Cliffs, NJ: Prentice-Hall.

Bochner, A. P. (1985). Perspectives on inquiry: Representation, conversation, and reflection. In M. L. Knapp & G. R. Miller (Eds.), *Handbook of interpersonal communication* (pp. 27–58). Beverly Hills, CA: Sage Publications.

Bochner, A. P., & Kelly C. W. (1974). Interpersonal competence: Rationale, philosophy, and implementation of a conceptual framework. *Speech Teacher, 23,* 279–301.

Broome, B. J. (1991). Building shared meaning: Implications of a relational approach to empathy for teaching intercultural communication. *Communication Education, 40,* 235–249.

Buber, M. (1970). *I and Thou* (W. Kaufman, Trans.). New York: Scribner (original work published 1923).

Buber, M. (1973). Elements of the interhuman. In J. Stewart (Ed.), *Bridges, not walls: A book about interpersonal communication* (pp. 288–302). Menlo Park, CA: Addison-Wesley Publishing Company (reprinted from M. Buber *The knowledge of man,* 1965).

Burke, K. (1950). *A rhetoric of motives.* New York: Prentice-Hall.

Burke, K. (1966). *Language as symbolic action: Essays on life, literature, and method.* Berkeley: University of California Press.

Canary, D. J., & Spitzberg, B. H. (1987). Appropriateness and effectiveness perceptions of conflict strategies. *Human Communication Research, 14,* 93–118.

Canary, D. J., & Spitzberg, B. H. (1989). A model of the perceived competence of conflict strategies. *Human Communication Research, 15,* 630–649.

Canary, D. J., & Spitzberg, B. H. (1990). Attribution biases and associations between conflict strategies and competence outcomes. *Communication Monographs, 57,* 139–151.

Craib, I. (1984). *Modern social theory: From Parsons to Habermas.* Brighton, Sussex: Wheatsheaf Books.

Davis, K. E., & Roberts, M. K. (1985). Relationships in the real world: The descriptive psychology approach to personal relationships. In K. J. Gergen & K. E. Davis (Eds.), *The social construction of the person* (pp. 145–166). New York: Springer-Verlag.

Denzin, N. K. (1972). The research act. In J. G. Manis & B. N. Meltzer (Eds.), *Symbolic interaction: A reader in social psychology* (2nd ed.; pp. 76–91). Boston: Allyn and Bacon.

Duran, R. L., & Zakahi, W. R. (1987). Communication performance and communication satisfaction: What do we teach our students? *Communication Education, 36,* 13–22.

Duran, R. L., & Zakahi, W. R. (1988). The influence of communicative competence upon roommate satisfaction. *Western Journal of Speech Communication, 52,* 135–146.

Fisher, B. A. (1978). *Perspectives on human communication.* New York: MacMillan.

Geertz, C. (1973). *The interpretation of cultures: Selected essays.* New York: Basic Books.

Gergen, K. J. (1985). Social constructionist inquiry: Context and implications. In K. J. Gergen & K. E. Davis (Eds.), *The social construction of the person* (pp. 3–18). New York: Springer-Verlag.

Hart, R. P., & Burks, D. M. (1972). Rhetorical sensitivity and social interaction. *Speech Monographs, 39,* 75–91.

Hart, R. P., Carlson, R. E., & Eadie, W. F. (1980). Attitudes toward communication and the assessment of rhetorical sensitivity. *Communication Monographs, 47,* 1–22.

Leeds-Hurwitz, W. (1992a). Forum continuation: Social approaches to interpersonal communication. *Communication Theory, 2,* 329.

Leeds-Hurwitz, W. (1992b). Forum introduction: Social approaches to interpersonal communication. *Communication Theory, 2,* 131–138.

Lincoln, Y. S., & Guba, E. G. (1985). *Naturalistic inquiry.* Newbury Park, CA: Sage Publications.

Mead, G. H. (1934). *Mind, self, and society: From the standpoint of a social behaviorist.* Chicago: University of Chicago Press.

Meltzer, B. N. (1972). Mead's social psychology. In J. G. Manis & B. N. Meltzer (Eds.), *Symbolic interaction: A reader in social psychology* (2nd ed.; pp. 4–22). Boston: Allyn and Bacon.

Meltzer, B. N., & Petras, J. W. (1972). The Chicago and Iowa schools of symbolic interactionism. In J. G. Manis & B. N. Meltzer (Eds.), *Symbolic interaction: A reader in social psychology* (2nd ed.; pp. 43–56). Boston: Allyn and Bacon.

Meltzer, B. N., Petras, J. W., & Reynolds, L. T. (1975). *Symbolic interactionism: Genesis, varieties and criticism.* Boston: Routledge & Kegan Paul.

Onyekwere, E. O., Rubin, R. B., & Infante, D. A. (1991). Interpersonal perception and communication satisfaction as a function of argumentativeness and ego-involvement. *Communication Quarterly, 39,* 35–47.

Pacanowsky, M. E., & O'Donnell-Trujillo, N. (1982). Communication and organizational cultures. *Western Journal of Speech Communication, 46,* 115–130.

Parks, M. R. (1985). Interpersonal communication and the quest for personal competence. In M. L. Knapp & G. R. Miller (Eds.), *Handbook of interpersonal communication* (pp. 171–204). Beverly Hills, CA: Sage Publications.

Pavitt, C. (1981). Preliminaries to a theory of communication: A system for the cognitive representation of person and object based information. In M. Burgoon (Ed.), *Communication yearbook 5* (pp. 211–232). New Brunswick, NJ: Transaction.

Pavitt, C. (1990). A controlled test of some "complicating factors" relevant to the inferential model for evaluations of communicative competence. *Western Journal of Speech Communication, 54,* 575–592.

Pavitt, C., & Haight, L. (1985). The "competent communicator" as a cognitive prototype. *Human Communication Research, 12,* 225–242.

Pavitt, C., & Haight, L. (1986). Implicit theories of communicative competence: Situational and competence level differences in judgments of prototype and target. *Communication Monographs, 53,* 221–235.

Pearce, W. B. (1977). Metatheoretical concerns in communication. *Communication Quarterly, 25,* 3–6.

Pfuetze, P. E. (1961). *Self, society, existence: Human nature and dialogue in the thought of George Herbert Mead and Martin Buber.* New York: Harper and Brothers.

Poole, M. S., & McPhee, R. D. (1983). A structurational analysis of organizational climate. In L. L. Putnam & M. E. Pacanowsky (Eds.), *Communication and organizations: An interpretive approach.* (pp. 195–219). Beverly Hills, CA: Sage Publications.

Powell, J. (1969). *Why am I afraid to tell you who I am?* Niles, IL: Argus Communications.

Putnam, L. L. (1983a). Preface. In L. L. Putnam & M. E. Pacanowsky (Eds.), *Communication and organizations: An interpretive approach* (pp. 7–11). Beverly Hills, CA: Sage Publications.

Putnam, L. L. (1983b). The interpretive perspective: An alternative to functionalism. In L. L. Putnam & M. E. Pacanowsky (Eds.), *Communication and organizations: An interpretive approach* (pp. 31–54). Beverly Hills, CA: Sage Publications.

Ritzer, G. (1992). *Contemporary sociological theory* (3rd ed.). New York: McGraw-Hill.

Spitzberg, B. H. (1983). Communication competence as knowledge, skill, and impression. *Communication Education, 32,* 323–329.

Spitzberg, B. H. (1991). An examination of trait measures of interpersonal competence. *Communication Reports, 4,* 22–29.

Spitzberg, B. H., & Cupach, W. R. (1984). *Interpersonal communication competence.* Beverly Hills, CA: Sage Publications.

Spitzberg, B. H., & Hecht, M. L. (1984). A component model of relational competence. *Human Communication Research, 10,* 575–599.

Spitzberg, B. H., & Hurt, H. T. (1987). The measurement of interpersonal skills in instructional contexts. *Communication Education, 36,* 28–45.

Ward, S. A., Bluman, D. L., & Dauria, A. F. (1982). Rhetorical sensitivity recast: Theoretical assumptions of an informal interpersonal rhetoric. *Communication Quarterly, 30,* 189–195.

Wiemann, J. M. (1977). Explication and test of a model of communicative competence. *Human Communication Research, 3,* 195–213.

6

Discourse Without Rules

KELLY COYLE

Verbal behavior has many favorable characteristics as an object to study. It is usually easily observed (if it were not, it would be ineffective as verbal behavior); there has never been any shortage of material ([people] talk and listen a great deal); the facts are substantial (careful observers will generally agree as to what is said in any given instance); and the development of the practical art of writing has provided a ready-made system of notation for reporting verbal behavior... —B. F. Skinner, *Verbal Behavior*

IN BORGES'S (1962) "LIBRARY OF BABEL," the librarians—for whom the library is the entire world—are confronted by a profusion of chaos. The library consists of an apparently infinite number of hexagonal rooms, all alike, each containing a like number of nominally identical books:

> There are five shelves for each of the hexagon's walls; each shelf contains thirty-five books of uniform format; each book is of four hundred and ten pages; each page of forty lines, each line, of some eighty letters which are black in color. (p. 52)

The content of the books is mysterious: the letters on the spine of the books "do not indicate or prefigure what the pages will say"; the interiors of the books are no less enigmatic.

> One which my father saw in a hexagon on circuit fifteen ninety-four was made up of the letters MCV, perversely repeated from the first line to the last. Another (very much consulted in this area) is a mere labyrinth of letters, but the next-to-last page says *Oh time thy pyramids*. This much is

already known: for every sensible line of straightforward statement, there are leagues of senseless cacophonies, verbal jumbles and incoherences. (p. 53)

In Borges's narrative the puzzle of the vast incoherent library is solved. But rather than providing a path to self-reflective meaning for the librarians, knowledge of the solution produces melancholy and despair. Once the rules governing the manifest structure of the library are known, there remains no reason to live within it—particularly as a librarian—yet there is no "outside" providing hope for escape.

Two facts are known about the library. First, the symbols that appear in the books number 25, including the comma, period, and space. Second, "in the vast library there are no two identical books" (p. 54). From this it is deduced that

the Library is total and that its shelves register all the possible combinations of the twenty-odd orthographical symbols (a number which, though extremely vast, is not infinite): in other words, all that it is given to express, in all languages. Everything: the minutely detailed history of the future, the archangels' autobiographies, the faithful catalogue of the Library, thousands and thousands of false catalogues, the demonstration of the fallacy of those catalogues, the demonstration of the fallacy of the true catalogue, the Gnostic gospel of Basilides, the commentary on that gospel, the true story of your death, the translation of every book in all languages, the interpolation of every book in all books. (p. 54)

Anything that can be written already exists somewhere in the library. However, the saturation of all discursive space renders this, and any communication (as Borges makes clear), useless.

It will be fairly easy, I think, for any reader to object to analogies between Borges's library and language in use (which I will call "discourse"), even though "everyone knows" that language is rule governed as the library is rule governed. First, discourse is not constrained to any delimited set of orthographic (or other sorts of) symbols. Second, discursive space is never saturated; discursive acts are always contextually bound and strategically employed. There are probably other such objections. But rather than dismissing such an analogy out of hand, I request that you suspend the objections to see it played out. Although it may be that this stance cannot be maintained, we may still learn something from the exercise.

DISCOURSE RULES

Several kinds of rules are used to account for discursive behavior. The rules sometimes presented in so-called "rules theories" (e.g., Pearce, 1976) that are "emergent" and "negotiated" within relationships, or those presented within the "ethnography of communication" (e.g., Hymes, 1962; Philipsen, 1989), which govern the sorts of behavior appropriate to a speech event, are not the sorts of rules that will be treated here. Such rules are binding only to the extent that the community in question enforces them through social sanctions. These rules are constantly bent, broken, unevenly enforced, and suspended in the course of normal social activity. (It should be noted that my construction here is more narrow than the usual use of "regulative rule." I wish to exclude only the rules that are established in communities to control behavior as in "we don't talk politics at the dinner table.")

A second type is the sort of rule that defines the discursive game-in-play, usually called a *constitutive rule*. These rules determine that a request is a request, not an objection or a proposal. To be able to request something, one must be able to formulate a line of action recognizable as a request, which means that both speaker and hearer must share a set of rules that define valid requesting. These are more interesting for the argument at hand because failure to understand the rules results in failure at meaningful communication. Searle (1969) explores this in great detail.

Finally, there's the kind of "rule" that pertains to the autonomous structure of language or discourse. These rules can be described as grammars, and have been employed in terms of syntax (e.g., Chomsky, 1965) and connected discourse (which seems to me to be an adequate description of conversation analysis; see Sharock & Anderson, 1986, for discussion; Goodwin, 1989, for an example). Violation of *these* rules results in gibberish or incoherence, and these rules most resemble the rules of Borges's library.

Thus we have at least three kinds of rules. The first kind is socially contingent, used within communities to regulate members' behavior. The second kind is definitional and provides a basis for undertaking social action through discursive acts. The third kind concerns the autonomous structure of language independent of use or purpose. These categories are murky—perhaps we should envision rules as a continuum ranging from social to structural—but this should suffice to give the flavor of the various approaches.

Regardless of the type employed, the conception of "rules" as a fundamental structural element in discourse is ubiquitous. Taylor and

Cameron (1987) review the major paradigms of discourse analysis—social psychology, speech act theory, conversation analysis, functional approaches, pragmatics, ethnomethodology[1]—to find that every available model of discourse "assumes conversation to consist in certain types of units, the production of which is governed by rules" (p. 159). Reading this, one (correctly) infers that they wish to place rules into question; however, they have nothing to replace them with. Indeed, to abandon "rule" as an explanatory construct is to gaze suddenly at the abyss: no more genres of functional procedures that allow conventional effects to be realized; no more appeals to intersubjective frameworks to account for meaning. Not only is the question of how people manage to communicate reopened—it becomes a matter of conjecture *that* people communicate, at least in the sense of sharing meaning.

For Taylor and Cameron, the precipitating event in the collapse of rules as a useful construct was Marga Kreckel's study of the discourses presented in a BBC documentary. But I believe that Kreckel's work is best developed as an elaboration of Quine's notion of "radical translation," so it is to Quine that we will turn first.

"RADICAL TRANSLATION" AND THE PROBLEMS OF INTERSUBJECTIVITY

Quine (1960) asks us to consider the problem of an anthropologist attempting to learn a previously unknown language. To begin, he or she must segment the stream of conversational sound into units of meaning, then observe the correlations between their occurrence and conditions in the surrounding environment. Thus (from Quine's for example), if the utterance "gavangi" occurs repeatedly in the presence of rabbits, or if when prompted by the linguist's "gavangi" in the presence of rabbits the native speakers express their assent, the linguist may conclude that "gavangi" means "rabbit." Operating in this fashion, he or she can build a repertoire of utterances, culminating (in principle) with a dictionary of all "stimulus" statements in the language. However, this procedure is fraught with interpretive peril: such translation is predicated on a set of "analytic hypotheses" that constitute the translation itself. The possibility thus exists that some *other* set of analytic hypotheses could result in an altogether different interpretation, a "radical translation," conflicting substantially with the first but nonetheless also correlating with the empirical utterances perfectly well.

Of course, Quine does not mean to limit "the indeterminacy of radical translation" to cross-cultural communication. Radical translation is meant to apply to any intrapsychic discourses (see Dennett,

1987); that is, any inferences ("translations") directed toward meaning, intent, belief, desire, and so forth. Because the mental states actually held by others are fundamentally unavailable, one can never know (in principle) if the states one attributes to others are those that actually obtain. (Unlike Skinner, Quine does not maintain that these internal states are *unimportant,* merely that they cannot be reliably assessed.)

Dennett (1987, p. 104) reports that Quine has often been challenged to provide a plausible real-world example of radical translation, but has not been able to. Kreckel's (1981) *Communicative Acts and Shared Knowledge in Natural Discourse* can, perhaps, be seen as motion in that direction. She observes that naive speakers are generally optimistic that "they are able to understand what they are listening to and get across what they want to" (p. 3), and that, generally, discourse analysts (and others concerned with the structure of language) share that optimism. She writes that these scholars

> maintain that different language users arrive at very similar semantic intuitions about their language, since "they are prepared, both by heredity and by previous experience, to induce certain rules and not others. That is simply how the human mind works." Adherents to this position set their hopes on the day we shall have reached a consensus on sets of transformational rules, constitutive rules, or semantic components in order to establish "how the semantic system of the speaker-hearer is used." (p. 3, citations deleted)

At the other philosophic pole are behaviorists like Quine or Skinner who maintain that contingencies of reinforcement can account for coordinated activity and thus that it cannot be determined whether interactants who seem to understand one another do so due to shared rules or otherwise. Kreckel's move, more or less (it is an immensely intricate study), is to follow the semioticians (like Eco) and pose this issue as a question rather than in terms of an axiom. That is, Kreckel attempts to ask, "To what degree must interactants participate in the same experimental world (i.e., share the same rule systems) in order to interact?"

Interestingly, she mostly fails at this, observing that families *seem* to share generic categories of speech acts within themselves, but that there *seem* to be "noteworthy differences" between families in the kinds of speech acts they recognize and in terms of understanding what is being done in any particular event. These differences, however, do not seem to endanger individuals' abilities to make sense of discursive events. Her hesitance in making conclusions stems from a recognition of her inability to know if she is understanding the rules systems of these families any better than they understand each others'.

For Taylor and Cameron (1987), this finding raises serious, perhaps fatal, objections to the entire notion of *communication* as long as communication is understood to be "a means of bringing participants . . . to a mutual awareness, a common perception, of an idea, an emotion, a [cognitive] representation, a governing structure and so on" (p. 161):

> Kreckel's findings indicate that the vast majority of interactions (those which do not take place between family members or other intimates) entail major differences of interpretation between the participants. Must we therefore say that communication does not actually occur in such interactions? (p. 58)

This leaves us in a peculiar bind. The entire concept of *communication* is bound to the idea of transmission. We speak of the transmission of meanings, of course, but transmission is invoked in other uses of *communication*. Derrida (1988) observes

> that one can, for instance, *communicate a movement* or that a tremor, a shock, a displacement of force can be communicated—that is, propagated, transmitted. We also speak of different or remote places communicating with each other by means of a passage or opening. (p. 1)

Can we strip the commonsense notion *communication* of its association with transmission? If we do, do we still have something to talk about?

The wall we face here is an old one. Rather than assaulting it, or, conversely, granting it omnipotence, let us just name it and see where it leaves us. In my classes I call it the "existential problem," and I described it earlier in this chapter: "the mental states of others are fundamentally unavailable." Philosophers, like Dennett, talk about this issue in terms of the difficulties it provides for theories of "knowledge" and "reality." More interesting to those of us in the now-problematically-named field of "communication" is to pose the existential problem as one that individuals must routinely solve. Given that we are always, fundamentally, cut off from the subjectivities of others, and vice versa, how is it that we manage to coordinate our activities? How is it that we manage to attain at least the appearance of shared meaning? How do we account for *our sense of*, at least in some situations at some times, participating in shared experiential worlds with others?

To be sure, it is just this problem that the rules approach to discourse analysis is directed to solve in the first place (see Parsons, 1968, for an explicit statement). Through indoctrination into a speech community one learns the basic actions available through communication, the conventional formulae for invoking those actions, the appropriate occasions for their invocation, and so forth. As speech communities become more and more distant, the potential for misfires and misunderstandings becomes greater, but for communication to be possible at all there must be *some* shared community, however distant. Language "works" through the rule-governed application of shared codes.

Even if we ignore Kreckel (and Taylor and Cameron) for a moment, there seems to be something odd about this formulation. Consider: we had just gotten to the point of considering how individuals solve the existential problem when the "rules" answer reappears. But the rules answer is no answer at all—it attempts to account for the accomplishment of shared meaning through reference to implicit shared meanings. In other words, the rules approach hides the very thing that is interesting and problematic about interaction, even as it pretends to "account" for it.

WRITING AND ITERATION

The notion of communication as transmission, as Derrida (1988) describes it, has the quality of metaphor. Insofar as the mechanical uses of *communication* concern the transmission of forces through some medium, the semiotic *communication* can be seen as the transmission of meanings through the vector of a sign. How, he asks, do we know which sense of *communication* is literal? Thus, for example, Searle's (1969, p. 47) definition of *communication* as the transmission of intention ("we succeed in doing what we are trying to do by getting our audience to recognize what we are trying to do") can be understood as metaphor—one strikes the sign to produce a corresponding recognition in the other.

Under this regime, it follows that the ideal sign machinery is the most efficient, the one that produces the most faithful echo of meaning. (Are you thinking of the communication textbook's "linear model"? Certainly Derrida's observation applies here, but just as well to many of the other models that underlie the work of communication researchers.) Such thinking, in turn, construes communication as a hierarchy of contexts according to the extent that each encourages fidelity in transmission (see Fish, 1982); in particular, for Derrida (1974, 1988) it is in this manner of thinking that the hierarchical relation between "speech" and "writing" is established.

In what could be called the "standard account" of communication, writing is seen as an extension, through space and time, of speech. Speech occurs within a relatively delimited field of sight and sound, of "presence," but writing relaxes those limitations (as do other media) allowing the field of communicative action a larger scope. With the disruption of presence, the absence of audience for sender (and vice versa), participants lose access to an immediately shared context for the determination of meaning. In general, communicative media (for which "writing" is emblematic) *supplant* presence, substituting their self-created contexts ("representations") for the real contexts that ground speech. Such extensions make communication more vulnerable to corruption because there need be (in principle) no access to any "external" information to regulate interpretation.

The assumptions of most normative discourse analytic positions can be reconstructed from this stance. Benvéniste (1971; cf. Ricoeur, 1971) offers a distinction between "discourse" and "text" based on the temporal presentness, referentiality, and transmission of messages pertaining to the former. Linguistic pragmatics (Grice, 1975, 1978; Levinson, 1983; Sperber & Wilson, 1986) is devoted to the relations between an utterance and its context of performance, specifically the way in which context regulates inference making and, hence, transfer of meaning. In *How to Do Things with Words,* Austin (1962) excludes written language from consideration "for simplicity"; without a context to appeal to, the felicity of speech acts cannot be readily judged: "The total speech act in the total speech situation is the *only actual* phenomenon which, in the last resort, we are engaged in elucidating" (p. 148).

In this standard account, then, writing has several qualities that distinguish it from speech (Derrida, 1988, pp. 9–10). First, writing survives its inscription and can thus extend the scope of communicative action beyond the horizons of speech to persons distant in space and time. This provides a text that can be encountered multiple times; writing is not exhausted in its utterance. (Derrida refers to this quality as "iterability.") Second, following from the first, writing functions (at some level) in contexts other than the one in which it is first inscribed:

> the sign possesses the characteristic of being readable even if the moment of its production is irrevocably lost and even if I do not know what is alleged author-scriptor consciously intended to say at the moment [he or she] wrote it, i.e. abandoned it to its essential drift. (Derrida, 1988, p. 9)

Finally (and in sum), writing develops its meaning through the relation of the elements that constitute it, rather than through reference to a (perhaps unavailable) context. We could say that in writing an utterance inscribes its own context, but that is only partly right because a text can suffer various kinds of dismemberment (like my preceding quotation of Derrida) and retain *some* meaning if not the "original" one. Better, perhaps, to say that the concept of "utterance" becomes compromised in writing, because an author cannot control the "disengagement and graft" of the future text, or where and how it will be read.

So speech (or discourse) is present, mannerly, determinate, self-evident; writing (or text) is absent, unruly, indeterminate, mysterious. Discourse occurs in friendly, well-lit *meaningful* environs; text looks like an intrusion from beyond. The question is, Can the comfortable notion of "discourse" be protected from infection by text? If it can, *should* it be?

Relatively few scholars have used this moment—these questions—as starting points for theory. But two lines of argument seems to have developed along this frontier. Following Derrida (also Frank and Ricoeur), the problems that textuality poses *for theorists* can be explored. Or, following Goffman or Garfinkel, one can consider the way that textual concerns are manifest in everyday action.

Theorist's World

Ricoeur (1971) offers a consideration of the differences between discourse and text that follows the standard account just described. However, in his view the distinction between text and discourse is useful only in theories of performance. In performance the qualities ascribed to discourse make themselves felt: the disappearance of the event, the fixing of indexical reference, the shared circumstances of speaker and hearer, the exchange of meaning. When attention is turned to the problems of understanding social events, however, applying the idea of context-bound "discourse" becomes abusive. To *understand* discourse requires that we translate the instance of discourse into something less fleeting. That is, we must learn to write. However, writing does not preserve the entirety of the discursive event but merely "the 'said' of speaking." Any attempt to preserve the event introduces textuality into it. In discourse, "What do you mean?" and "What does that mean?" ask the same question. But as soon as that discourse is captured in text the careers of these questions diverge.

Likewise, Frank (1985) argues that the business of sociology is not to understand discourses, but to understand the reading and writing of the texts in which discourses are reconstituted by theory: the problems of what aspects of discourse to "fix" in text and the problems of which competing interpretations of that text to sanction become the problems of a fully reflexive sociology. To "study" any sort of social activity we must first textualize it so that it becomes available to our interpretive techniques. The theorist runs up against the existential problem just as the social actor does. Our notions of what actors "know," what "rules" they follow, what "mental states" drive their activities cannot provide the basis for subsequent "understanding" of those activities because it is our interpretations of the text of those activities that constitute (within our theories) actors' "knowing," "rule-following," or "social cognition" in the first place.

This is why Kreckel (1981) cannot satisfactorily resolve the issue of the degree to which shared knowledge is required for interaction. Because the families she investigated *do* manage to coordinate their interactions, one could doubtless "discover" a set of rules that regulate those interactions. (A similar argument is made by Sanders, 1983, regarding the "rules" regulating conversational coherence.) In other words, the coordination itself displays a regularity that can (doubtless) be captured in rules. But those rules are the *result* of a reading strategy applied to the text of the event and do not necessarily reveal anything about the principles that the actors use to generate their behavior and understanding.

Thus, when Kreckel asked the respective families about the meaning and use of various speech acts, she found "noteworthy differences." Does this reveal discontinuous knowledges, or just differing ways of talking about language? This is an unanswerable question.

Interactant's World

Discourse-oriented theories consider interactants to be participating in activities according to shared knowledge about what behaviors constitute those activities, and research is directed toward revealing that tacit knowledge or describing rational play within the structure of the "language game." Jacobs and Jackson (1983, p. 52) offer an analogy to chess:

> As with any game, a perfectly satisfying type of explanation comes from a description of the primary rules and elements that define the game and a demonstration of how those rules are applied to the players' goals to produce moves appropriate to the point of the game. This is the sort of explanation that can be found in any chess handbook, and we think that an adequate theory of conversational coherence will be a formalized equivalent of such accounts.

Players need to share, it seems, an understanding of the games available (both in terms of their constitution and their desired outcomes) and some notions about what "rational play" would entail.

Garfinkel's (1967) *Studies in Ethnomethodology* begins with a rejection of just this assumption *Ethnomethodology* can be defined as the study of (-*ology*) the practices by which (-*method*-) participants in a social setting (*ethno*-) make their activities "accountable," as in "able to be accounted for." In Garfinkel's words,

When I speak of accountable my interests are directed to such matters as the following. I mean observable-and-report-able, *i.e.* available to members as situated practices of look-ing-and-telling. I mean, too, that such practices consist of an endless, ongoing, contingent accomplishment; that they are carried on under the auspices of, and are made to happen as events in, the same ordinary affairs that in organizing they describe; that the practices are done by parties to those set-tings whose skill with, knowledge, of, and entitlement to the detailed work of that accomplishment—whose competence—they obstinately depend upon, recognize, use, and take for granted; and *that* they take their competence for granted itself furnishes parties with a setting's distinguishing and par-ticular features, and of course it furnishes them as well as resources, troubles, projects, and the rest. (p. 1–2)

What on earth could he mean by this?

Just this: "Just this" is one of Garfinkel's characteristic locutions[2] by which he means for his auditors to take the sense of what he's about to say in its most literal fashion. By issuing such an "instruction for interpretation," he attempts to exert control over what can be interpre-tatively "done" with whatever it is he is about to say. In other words, he makes the predicate to "just this" *knowable* in the sense of being able to be known. In other words, he produces a context within which his audience is able to "get" his drift, and he relies on their ability to employ such instructions as they formulate their responses. In other words, ethnomethodology considers the apparent order of social situa-tions (that order which discursive approaches take for granted) to be the accomplishment of participants' production of the features that make those situations orderly. In other words, from an ethnomethodological stance the "rules" that are discovered by observers are not "there" because they represent the principles that participants use (like recipes) to order their behavior, but instead are "there" because the participants are working to give their behavior the appearance of order.

Sharrock and Anderson (1986) develop ethnomethodology as a reaction to Parsons's (1968) "action theory." For Parsons, actors are presumed to share a culture that allows them to coorient in a fashion that permits meaningful social behavior. By observing mutually held rules actors are able to coordinate their lines of action. Rather than presuming that such rules are intrinsic to social systems (i.e., known, implicit, embedded), Garfinkel makes problematic the manner in which public behavior is made to seem rational, sensible, or "accountable" by participants. In particular, he discards two central assumptions from the writings of Parsons:

> The assumption of shared meaning is set aside first for the actors themselves. We no longer presume a shared culture. Second, we drop the presumption of the community of observer and subject, i.e. the assumption that they automatically make sense to each other. The net result of the move is, then, that whatever sense we might then find activities to have would be to produced for them. (Sharrock & Anderson, 1986, pp. 28–29)

In Parsons's account, and in general from the discursive orientation, the production of coordinated activity is seen as an automatic outcome of the application of generic, rational, and strategic knowledge by participants. In Garfinkel's universe the world is a hostile, incomprehensible, *alien* place, and social actors struggle to maintain the fragile semblance of rationality. In general, ethnomethodology views the notion of intersubjectivity as hiding what is most interesting about interaction: the way in which its apparent order is accomplished.

Ethnomethodology is often characterized as a phenomenological (or "interpretive" or "subjective") sociology (for discussion and refutation, see Peyrot, 1982; Sharrock & Anderson, 1986), by which it is meant that ethnomethodology is concerned with penetrating participants' meanings in interactions. And, indeed, the terms in which ethnomethodological analyses are presented seem to support such a view: participants are seen to engage in "interpretation," "understanding," "meaning-making," "reality construction, "accounting," "rule-following," and the rest. However, taking this vocabulary in its usual interpretive sense misconstrues ethnomethodology and in fact is incompatible with it. When a participant engages in "interpretation," he or she engages in a public act of assigning meaning to some other social act. Therefore, to exclaim "you have insulted me!" in response to a remark by an other, or merely to "act insulted" in affective display, is to "interpret" the remark as an insult. Likewise with *understanding*:

> When first thinking about this word, we are probably tempted to view it as a description of some private or inner experience. However, when we look closely at the way this word is actually used this view seems less convincing. Ryle has pointed out that this term is often used to mark a claim to success, the sort of situation where one might say "I have been working at the problem and I think I understand it now." However, merely having a moment of insight or a feeling of having cracked the problem is not sufficient. If a person with the feeling of comprehension tries to apply their ideas and finds they do not work, they will know that they were mistaken in the belief that they understood.

Furthermore, if *other people* assess the understanding gained, they may decide that the person only *thinks* they understand—they do not *really* understand. The general point is that although cognitive processes are clearly going on, and people without a brain clearly do not understand, this is not a sufficient condition for understanding. Understanding is assessed by *public criteria* and *practical tests*. The term understanding is properly used when these criteria can be, or have been, satisfied, not merely when people have a certain experience. (Potter & Wetherell, 1987, pp. 179–180)

The rest of the terms undergo similar transformation. So, although it is proper to say that ethnomethodology is concerned with "participant meanings," it is meaning understood in this peculiar way: as a public accomplishment through the coordinated activities of those present. Or, if you will, meaning becomes evident in the *text* of the ongoing social action.

Goffman (1959, 1974) begins his program from a similar position, directed toward understanding the play of information within a social setting. The acquisition of information about interactants is valuable insofar as it allows the holders of such information to form expectations, understand the definition of the situation, and formulate their own lines of action. At the same time, controlling the information that an other receives provides an interactant with a measure of control over those expectations, definitions, and activities.

During the period in which the individual is in the immediate presence of the others, few events may occur which directly provide the others with the conclusive information they will need if they are to direct wisely their activities. Many crucial facts lie beyond the time and place of interaction or lie concealed within it. For example, the "true" or "real" attitudes, beliefs, and emotions of the individual can be ascertained only indirectly, through [his or her] avowals or through what appears to be involuntary expressive behavior. (Goffman, 1959, pp. 1–2)

For Goffman, individuals enter into interaction with mutually opposed (in principle) aims: on the one hand, they are engaged in attempting to acquire knowledge of the true motives, feelings, and so forth, of their partners; at the same time, they attempt to produce suitable indicators of the motives, feelings, and so forth appropriate to their line of activity for consumption by those partners.

Now, certainly, all situations do not involve such mutual deceptions. However, this hostile configuration is not mitigated in those more "honest" circumstances. Even in cases where what one claims to be doing is in fact what one believes oneself to be doing, and where one's feelings and motivations are appropriate to the activity at hand, *still* the actor must take care to provide the public indicators of those states or risk being misinterpreted as having "ulterior motives." Thus Goffman's perspective in some ways mirrors Garfinkel's: to be perceived in a specific way in a social structure, one must produce behaviors that encourage the desired perception and discourage competing perceptions.

However similar to ethnomethodology is its outline, Goffman's approach positions the "locus of analysis" quite differently. Garfinkel insists upon what could be called a "third-person" analysis, which considers participant activities *from the outside,* as if watching the action on a stage or screen. In other words, he is interested in the ways that participants make the order of their activities apparent to an observer. Goffman, conversely, tends to take a "first-person" stance, attempting to assess the problem of order *as it comes to* the individual actor in terms of the constraints and opportunities that it provides. This leads to two (somewhat) separate inquiries: one can consider the qualities of information available to actors in the ways that such information influences the available lines of action (which mostly characterizes *Frame Analysis;* Goffman, 1974); or one can consider the tools that actors have available to them to control that information in the first place (which mostly characterizes *The Presentation of Self in Everyday Life;* Goffman, 1959). In either case, Goffman's central concern is in the strategic manipulation of social information by actors in support of their lines of activity.

CONCLUSION: UNRULY DISCOURSE

So now we can return to Babel to consider what makes its library so frustrating. The story is presented to us as a last message from a dying universe, but we do not know who it is from, except as the author describes himself or herself. Encountering the text, the reader imagines an author, living in this strange universe, leaving this letter that has somehow found its way to us. Or, the reader imagines an author ("Borges") writing a story in which he presents an author in this universe, and so forth.

Faced with this, Goffman (1974) might describe the lamination of multiple "frameworks" of experience. In one framing, the reader assumes that the text *refers* and constructs a world from those references (see Fish, 1982); we might call this framing (in this example) "fictional" because within this framework one can discuss the problems of the librarians and their library. In another framing, the reader (critic?) sees the text as the construction of Borges and as a work of *fiction*; within this framework one can discuss the (real) author's strategies or craft. Goffman would probably call this the "primary" frame because it describes what is "literally," "actually," "really" happening. If asked, "What is going on?" at some point in the story, you may answer that the librarian has just explained the structure of the library, or that Borges has just had the character of the librarian explain the structure of the library. The second seems more fundamental, somehow; closer to the "presence" of an intentional author.

However, Borges's story is interesting in that it draws our attention to another aspect of experience, which Goffman describes (variously) as "out of frame," "below frame," or as "negative experience." Under the rules of the library, we do not even know *that* this text was authored, as the (let us say) document is itself aware: "This wordy and useless epistle already exists in one of the thirty volumes of the five shelves of one of the innumerable hexagons" (Borges, 1962, p. 57). Rather than a letter from the librarian, or a story by Borges, we could consider the text merely as a selection from one of the strange books. There is nothing in the text itself that favors any of these interpretations. Instead, it becomes a matter of the reading strategy one chooses to adopt. The text claims (in the first case) to be authored by a librarian of Babel; it is presented to us (in the second case) in the context of other "fictions," with an author's signature on the binding, and a critical introduction that claims to have been written by an academic; but ultimately it comes to us as an arbitrary collection of marks on a page, from which the rest is constructed through interpretive action.

If we shift to social texts—conversations and local actions—"rules," "shared knowledge," "intersubjectivity," "cognition" and the rest must be seen as the result of the particular reading strategies that produce them. This seems to be something known to all players, at some level, but acknowledged and forgotten so they can settle down to do the work of theory. For example, Skinner (1957, p. 6) objects (as do I) to cognitive accounts of language use because they explain the manifest behaviors in terms of something going on "inside of the organism":

> The difficulty is that the ideas for which sounds are said to stand as signs cannot be independently observed. . . . When we say a remark is confusing because the idea is unclear, we seem to be talking about two levels of observation although there is, in fact, only one. It is the *remark* which is unclear.

Yet his construct of "reinforcement" is no more tangible, but simply the application of a different reading strategy. As we have seen, Taylor and Cameron (1987) see Kreckel's study as challenging the "language rules" paradigm as if those rules were *really* thought to be the way interactants got things done, and not merely analysts' constructs. They argue that the notion of intersubjectivity must be abandoned because those constructs are not validated in naive metacommunication, so that we can find out how language "really" works. But all we can do is apply different reading strategies to our texts.

Therefore I cannot argue that constructing discourse as the result of the application of shared intersubjective knowledge is wrong, per se. Instead, I must suggest that as a reading strategy it obscures certain aspects of discursive events that ought not be obscure. First, as the ethnomethodologists observe, assuming shared knowledge hides the way that participants accomplish shared meaning. Shared meaning should be viewed as a problem interactants must solve in action, not a precondition to that action. Second, the rules approach "normalizes" discourse in the sense of declaring some discursive acts central and others (by implication) deviant. When we seen an example of "incoherent" activity (that is, lying outside our rules systems), will we pronounce it dysfunctional, or do we attempt to ascertain what the speaker was trying to accomplish? Troemel-Ploetz (1991), in a critique of Tannen's *You Just Don't Understand,* suggests that when a speaker is male, or middleclass, or white, we tend to read an act as rule-following, but otherwise it *breaks* rules—and we probably have evidence of this rule-breaking in the way that other, more dominant participants, negatively sanction the act. Third, by talking about what the participants in interaction must know, the analyst hides his or her role as "reader" of the discourse; in other words, the notion of "knowledge" distracts us from putting our interpretive technique on public display. Finally—and this will not be universally approved—the rules (shared knowledge, etc.) orientation, at least for those of us interested in strategic or practical *communication* theories, is just not very interesting. The issues of structure, coherence, and knowledge may have great scientific import but little relevance to practice. Even if it is grated that one could model these entities (a point I am loath to grant), these models would still not tell us how actors are getting things done in situations. Learning about these issues will not lead to better theories of practice or to theories of better practice.

I leave an issue raised earlier in this chapter unresolved. Although I questioned the definition of *communication* as concerning transmission, I have not provided any direction toward an alternative. Perhaps by applying these notions back against ourselves as we perform our theoretical discourses we could come to view the creation of an event as "communication" as the accomplishment of the interactants and analysts co-creating a "communicative" text (see Frank, 1985; McGee, 1990). The interactants behave toward one another in ways that demonstrate that they understand and feel understood; meanwhile, an observer with the proper reading strategy is there to create a text that preserves the sense of these public understandings. "Communication" becomes the result of a reading strategy encountering a text that it can read.

NOTES

1. Actually, Taylor and Cameron get ethnomethodology *wrong* in a peculiar way that allows them to include ethnomethodology in their critique of the "rules and units" approach to discourse. Properly understood, ethnomethodology does not posit either of these entities except so far as they enter members' repertoires for engaging in public (not private) acts of sense making. I will return to these matters later in this chapter, but for more on this particular misinterpretation of ethnomethodology, see Peyrot (1982) or Sharrock and Anderson (1986, particularly Chapter 7).

2. I base this on hearing him deliver two lectures.

REFERENCES

Austin, J. L. (1962). *How to do things with words*. Cambridge, MA: Harvard University Press.

Benvéniste, E. (1971). *Problems in general linguistics* (M. E. Meek, Trans.). Coral Gables, FL: University of Miami Press.

Borges, J. L. (1962). The library of Babel. In *Labyrinths: Selected stories and other writings* (pp. 51–58). New York: New Directions.

Chomsky, N. (1965). *Aspects of the theory of syntax*. Cambridge, MA: MIT Press.

Dennett, D. C. (1987). *The intentional stance*. Cambridge, MA: MIT Press.

Derrida, J. (1974). *Of grammatology* (G. C. Spivak, Trans.). Baltimore: Johns Hopkins University Press.

Derrida, J. (1988). Signature event context. In *Limited inc* (pp. 1–23). Evanston, IL: Northwestern University Press.

Fish, S. E. (1982). With the compliments of the author: Reflections on Austin and Derrida. *Critical Inquiry, 8,* 693–721.

Frank, A. W. (1985). Out of ethnomethodology. In H. J. Helle & S. N. Eisenstadt (Eds.), *Micro-sociological theory. Perspectives on socio-*

logical theory, vol. 2 (pp. 101–116). Beverly Hills, CA: Sage Publications.

Garfinkel, H. (1967). *Studies in ethnomethodology.* Englewood Cliffs, NJ: Prentice-Hall.

Goffman, E. (1959). *The presentation of self in everyday life.* New York: Doubleday Books.

Goffman, E. (1974). *Frame analysis: An essay on the organization of experience.* Boston: Northeastern University Press.

Goodwin, C. (1989). Turn construction and conversational organization. In B. Dervin, L. Grossberg, B. J. O'Keefe, & E. Wartella (Eds.), *Rethinking communication. Vol. 2. Paradigm exemplars* (pp. 88–102). Newbury Park, CA: Sage Publications.

Grice, H. P. (1975). Logic and conversation. In P. Cole & J. Morgan (Eds.), *Syntax and semantics 3: Speech acts* (pp. 41–58). New York: Academic Press.

Grice, H. P. (1978). Further notes on logic and conversation. In P. Cole (Ed.), *Syntax and semantics 9: Pragmatics* (pp. 113–128). New York: Academic Press.

Hymes, D. H. (1962). The ethnography of speaking. In T. Gladwin & W. C. Sturtevant (Eds.), *Anthropology and human behavior* (pp. 13–53). Washington, DC: Anthropological Society of Washington.

Jacobs, S., & Jackson, S. (1983). Speech act structure in conversation: Rational aspects of pragmatic coherence. In R. T. Craig & K. Tracy (Eds.), *Conversational coherence: Form, structure, and strategy* (pp. 47–66). Beverly Hills, CA: Sage Publications.

Kreckel, M. (1981). *Communicative acts and shared knowledge in natural discourse.* London: Academic Press.

Levinson, S. C. (1983). *Pragmatics.* Cambridge: Cambridge University Press.

McGee, M. C. (1990). Text, context, and the fragmentation of contemporary culture. *Western Journal of Speech Communication, 54,* 274–289.

Parsons, T. (1968). *The structure of social action.* New York: The Free Press.

Pearce, W. B. (1976). The coordinated management of meaning: A rules-based theory of interpersonal communication. In G. R. Miller (Ed.), *Explorations in interpersonal communication* (pp. 17–36). Beverly Hills, CA: Sage Publications.

Peyrot, M. (1982). Understanding ethnomethodology: A remedy for some common misconceptions. *Human Studies, 5,* 261–283.

Philipsen, G. (1989). An ethnographic approach to communication studies. In B. Dervin, L. Grossberg, B. J. O'Keefe, & E. Wartella (Eds.), *Rethinking communication.* Vol. 2. *Paradigm exemplars* (pp. 258–268). Newbury Park, CA: Sage Publications.

Potter, J., & Wetherell, M. (1987). *Discourse and social psychology: Beyond attitudes and behaviour.* London: Sage Publications.

Quine, W. V. O. (1960). *Word and object.* New York: John Wiley and Sons.

Ricoeur, P. (1971). The model of the text: Meaningful action considered as a text. *Social Research, 38,* 529–562.

Sanders, R. E. (1983). Tools for cohering discourse and their strategic utilization: Markers of structural connections and meaning relations. In R. T. Craig & K. Tracy (Eds.), *Conversational coherence: Form, structure, and strategy* (pp. 67–80). Beverly Hills, CA: Sage Publications.

Searle, J. R. (1969). *Speech acts: An essay in the philosophy of language.* Cambridge: Cambridge University Press.

Sharrock, W., & Anderson, B. (1986). *The ethnomethodologists.* Chichester: Ellis Horwood.

Skinner, B. F. (1959). *Verbal behavior.* Englewood Cliffs, NJ: Prentice-Hall.

Sperber, D., & Wilson, D. (1986). *Relevance: Communication and cognition.* Cambridge, MA: Harvard University Press.

Taylor, T. J., & Cameron, D. (1987). *Analysing conversation: Rules and units in the structure of talk.* Oxford: Pergamon Press.

Troemel-Ploetz, S. (1991). Selling the apolitical. *Discourse and Society, 2,* 489–502.

7

Listening Authentically: A Heideggerian Perspective on Interpersonal Communication

R. BRUCE HYDE

IN THIS CHAPTER, I elaborate upon the contribution of Martin Heidegger to a new model of human listening. My work builds upon that of John Stewart (1983), who termed his hermeneutic model *interpretive* listening. My own approach emphasizes the *ontological* dimension of listening. Both models share a commitment to hermeneutic phenomenology as an important source for the development of communication theory. In addition, although my concern is the entire communicative event, my emphasis upon listening is intended to reveal listening's ontological priority. All conversation lives in the listening of its participants.

With Stewart, I believe that a hermeneutic phenomenology of listening arrives at significant insights that are not reached by the dominant *empathic* approach. To distinguish his interpretive model from the empathic paradigm, Stewart proposes a contrast that has developed within the hermeneutic tradition. Hermeneutics, originally an approach to the interpretation of sacred texts, has gradually expanded the scope of its inquiry to human *understanding,* considered more broadly. Hermeneutics takes a step back to understand not only a text but also the process by which we understand that text.

One school of hermeneutics views the task of understanding as the provision of an objectively valid interpretation, one that *reproduces* the text's intended meanings. Stewart (1983) cites, as representative of this school, E. D. Hirsch's assertion that a valid interpretation must be measured against "a genuinely discriminating norm, and the only compelling normative principle that has ever been brought forward is the old-fashioned ideal of rightly understanding what the author meant" (p. 381). This type of hermeneutics, Stewart points out, may be seen as corresponding to an empathic approach to listening, because both are reproductive models. For example, *empathy* is defined in a widely used interpersonal communication textbook as "the ability to project oneself into another person's point of view, so as to experience the other's thoughts and feelings" (Adler & Towne, 1990, p. 400).[1]

On the other hand, the phenomenological hermeneutics of Heidegger and Gadamer sees human understanding as *productive*. Rather than seeing the goal of interpretation as the reproduction of the text or speaker's inner meanings, this view posits that meanings are in fact "outer," created in interaction between text and reader, or between speaker and listener. Human meanings are constructed in a shared language, a language whose already embedded meanings are drawn upon, acted upon, and modified in each instance of its use. Meaning is not something individual and internal, but is rather an event that occurs in an act of speaking and listening.

Therefore, a central characteristic of Stewart's model is *linguisticality*, and Stewart draws here upon Heidegger's (1977) statement that "Language is the house of Being" (p. 193)—which is to say that our interpretation of the world, and our *way of being* in that world, is given to us by the meanings and ontological assumptions (assumptions about the way things are) embedded in the language that we speak. In Stewart's (1983) words, "everything in the human world comes into existence in language, so that language does not 'represent' reality but *discloses* it." (p. 384). Learning a language means being initiated into a world interpretation; and we can never step outside that interpretation (i.e., outside language) to see if it corresponds to something *beyond* language. "Language is not just one of man's possessions in the world," says Gadamer (1988), "but on it depends the fact that man has a world at all" (p. 401).

An important aspect of Gadamer's view is that language is able to perform its world-disclosive function only in interactive use. According to Gadamer (1988), "language has its true being only in conversation, in the exercise of understanding between people" (p. 404). A model of communication based in hermeneutic phenomenology recognizes that, in mutually creating the meanings of the conversation, the communicators are engaged in the creation of their world. Thus the focus of such a model, says Stewart, is the *communicative event,* rather than the objectified psychological entities, the "reified selves" of the empathic paradigm.[2]

In what follows, I will first sketch briefly the rationale for an ontological approach to the study of interpersonal communication. Next,

I will present two ideas that together provide a useful context for such an approach. Finally, I will outline four key elements of Heidegger's model of human being; these elements provide the starting point for ontological inquiry into the nature of human communication.

AN ONTOLOGICAL APPROACH TO COMMUNICATION STUDY

Stewart's designation of his listening model as *interpretive* emphasizes its derivation from a hermeneutics of communication: understanding is seen as the development of a mutual reader-text or listener-speaker interpretation, rather than the re-presentation of a unilateral reality. Ontological inquiry extends Stewart's thinking in a specific direction to consider more deeply the ontological possibilities of language and communication. Such inquiry takes as its starting point Heidegger's proposal that language is ontologically determinative ("the house of Being") and thinks through the implications of that proposal for human communication. Heidegger suggests that our way of being human and the way the world is for us are given by the ontological assumptions that come along with our language. These assumptions provide the context for communication: a horizon of unspoken background meanings. Because these assumptions both generate and are regenerated in our everyday interactions, the *locus* of our way of being is the communicative event of language in use. Therefore, while an empathic, psychologically derived model focuses on the "internal" identity structure into which each of us has organized language and its accompanying ontological assumptions, an ontological model focuses instead on the interactive language processes that precede and provide the conditions for that internalization.

The central thesis of an ontological approach to listening is that interpersonal listening is a *way of being-with someone* (the hyphenated form, as I will show later, is significant in Heidegger's model). That is, our *way of listening* is generated by our *way of being*. Any attempt to enhance the effectiveness of the listening process that does not first address the ontological source and context of that process will be limited in its success.

Listening effectively to another means to be-with the other in a particular way. This particular way of being-with another may be characterized by the Heideggerian term *authentic*. Authenticity is, of course, a familiar idea to most of us: we want to be genuine, honest, "real" in our relationships with others. However, as Michael Zimmerman (1986) has pointed out, the usual understanding of *authenticity* does not quite capture the meaning it had for Heidegger. The everyday sense of the word has moral and ethical overtones, whereas, for Heidegger, "one's behavior might be morally correct, even though one might be existing inauthentically" (Zimmerman, 1986, p. xxxiv). A more precise translation of Heidegger's *Eigentlichket*, says Zimmerman, would be *"ownedness"* or "self-possessedness" (1986, p. xxxiv). Thus, authenticity is a mode of what Heidegger calls *"mineness"*; that is, one's self is always "mine to be in one way or another," and each of us has always made some decision about a particular way of being, a particular mode of mineness (Heidegger, 1962, p. 68). One mode of mineness—one way of owning one's self—is the mode that Heidegger calls *authenticity*.

But Heidegger demands that we confront a central everyday condition of life: we do *not* own ourselves in an authentic way. According to Heidegger, human beings, in their everyday way of being with one another, are *thrown* to an inauthentic mode of relationship. Authenticity is something to be achieved. Heidegger's account of human thrownness, which I will outline in the final section of this chapter, is important for an ontological inquiry into human listening. It creates the opportunity for the hermeneutic *step back,* allowing us to consider the process by which we have arrived at our present understanding of ourselves. Before we can attain the possibility of a new way of listening, we must take an honest look at the way we are listening presently; and, according to Heidegger, human beings have "a tendency to cover things up" in this area (1962, p. 359). We are oblivious to our inauthenticity. Therefore, before we can leap forward, "we must first leap onto the soil on which we really stand" (1968, p. 41). This is essential for an ontological approach to interpersonal communication: it brings us face to face with the way of being from which human interaction arises. It leads us to consider the possibility that human being is fundamentally inauthentic, and that acknowledgment of this inauthenticity is always the first authentic act.

Ontological inquiry shares with Stewart's interpretive model a recognition of the fundamentally constitutive role of language. The implications of this perspective are clearly articulated by Richard Rorty:

> What the Romantics recognized as the claim that imagination, rather than reason, is the central human faculty was the realization that *a talent for speaking differently, rather than arguing well, is the chief instrument of cultural change* [italics added]. . . . that changing languages and other social practices may produce human beings of a sort that had never before existed. . . . The method is to *redescribe lots and lots of things in new ways* [italics added], until you have created

a pattern of linguistic behavior which will tempt the rising generation to adopt it, thereby causing them to look for appropriate new forms of nonlinguistic behavior, for example, the adoption of new scientific equipment or new social institutions. (1989, pp. 7, 9)

The function of the Heideggerian perspective, then, is to provide a new ontological vocabulary by redescribing human being and human communicating. The adoption of this new pattern of linguistic behavior can, in turn, give rise to a new social institution grounded in authentic human communicative behavior.

TWO CONTEXTUALIZING IDEAS

Heidegger points out that a leap demands a "proper run" for its achievement (1959, p. 176). Therefore I will distinguish two ideas that are useful in undertaking ontological inquiry and that create a context for this step back.

First, I propose that a central element of this approach is its persistent *questioning,* as well as its insistence upon its *own* questionability. When Heidegger distinguished beings from Being—distinguished, that is, things that exist from the nature of their existence—he pointed out that most human inquiry is concerned with beings.[3] Such inquiry Heidegger called *ontical* (1962, p. 31). Inquiry into Being differs from the ontical in an important respect: it does not expect to arrive at answers. For Heidegger, the Being of human beings "is *never* an answer but essentially a question" (1959, p. 140). This is because the notion of Being is itself evasive: when interrogated, this most familiar of terms grows enigmatic, withdrawing from us even as we question it (1968, p. 9). Inquiry into Being must therefore maintain a corresponding indeterminacy. Being is in language, but it is not in words, so we can never quite capture Being itself in terminology nor contain it within concepts. One's "way of being" is less subject to precise formulation than such concepts as one's "attitude" and "identity," familiar elements of the psychological structure of understanding that we presently inhabit. Because of its elusiveness, we can talk only in such way that Being is hinted at, or perhaps evoked (Heidegger, 1971a, pp. 24–27; Johnstone, 1978, pp. 68, 75).

Heidegger's work, therefore, is not ontic argument for a particular explanation of the way we are. Rather, it articulates a vocabulary whose purpose is the evocation of a new possibility of being: a vocabulary for a being authentic based in self-ownership, so that this way of being is made available for human habitation. By thinking in the distinctions of a particular vocabulary, one comes to *dwell* in the language and in the ontological assumptions that accompany it (Heidegger, 1971b, pp. 145–161). One then begins to "come from" those assumptions into one's interpersonal communication.

Therefore I am not arguing in this chapter for the empirical validity of my perspective. Consistent with Heidegger's implications for listening, I request that this perspective be considered as if one were "trying it on." The perspective can be evaluated by standing in the questions that Heidegger raises and looking out from those questions at one's own experience—one's way of being and communicating and one's way of thinking about communication—to discover what can be observed from this horizon.

This context of questionability is essential for another reason as well. Heidegger's model is likely to provoke resistance. Being, as a topic, is not only epistemologically slippery; it may seem personally threatening. In Heidegger's words, "Existential analysis always has the character of *doing violence,* whether to the claims of the everyday interpretation, or to its complacency and its tranquillized obviousness" (1962, p. 359). Thus what Heidegger's view proposes about our way of being is likely to be uncomfortable for us to hear. It violates the commonsense verities about who we are and asks us to question the authenticity of our daily interactions. My abjural of truth claims, then, is intended to minimize this threat that Heidegger's ideas may seem to create, by freeing the dialogue from its natural tendency toward such polarizing concerns as agreement or belief. My perspective will show its validity, or it will not. A perspective that is tried on and does not fit can be taken off.

I note that, in creating this context of questionability, I do not diminish my commitment to the development of Heidegger's perspective. I have found that this perspective enables communication; its vocabulary for being human has proven liberating in my own interactions, both personal and pedagogical. Therefore, I urge students of interpersonal communication to remain open to its possibility, however tenuously that possibility must be held.

The second contextualizing idea I propose here is that a human being *is* a listening; listening is not something that human beings *do.* One is never simply an empty vessel, a passive receptor into which another pours the content of his or her speaking. Rather, each of us at every moment is always already listening in a particular way, listening from the ontological *locus* of the particular set of values and concerns that constitute our identity. Our way of being and our understanding of the world, given by these values and concerns, constitutes the listening that each of us always already is, the listening that determines the way the world occurs for us.[4]

Following any event, wide variation can inevitably be found in the perceptions of the participants or observers. A traditional way of explaining this is that each of us perceives through a different "cognitive filter." But this explanation relies upon the psychological focus of the empathic model. Stated in the vocabulary of an ontological approach to listening, each individual is a different listening for the event, and thus it occurs differently for each. By shifting the location of the perception-shaping world interpretation from one's "internal" cognitive structure to one's *listening*, we provide new access to that world interpretation: we have located it outside ourselves, in the shared communicative event, a move that I have shown to be a central aim of this approach.

As an illustration of this idea, consider the common human listening for approval. There is, I suggest, a widely shared human listening for positive assessment, for anything in a conversation that communicates that one is liked and approved of. This listening forms the unacknowledged background for much human interaction. Or consider a listening that is particularly characteristic of the academic profession: "I know" listening, a listening for whatever reinforces one's knowledge and thus one's personal identity as a scholar and educator. We tend to be most receptive to whatever is consistent with what we already know, and we tend to adjust whatever is unknown so that it reiterates and validates our knowledge. These ways of listening—listening for approval and listening to confirm that we know—affect considerably the way we hear what people say.

Consideration of the idea that one's world is constituted by one's listening inevitably focuses attention upon the deeply rooted self-interest that pervades our listening to others and shapes our interpretations of the situations that confront us. Honest self-reflection discloses a persistent underlying listening for personal reinforcement, for the validation of one's own perspective, for evidence that one is right after all. The unconcealment of this pervasive self-interest and the degree to which, in the normal course of events, we effectively conceal it from ourselves and attempt to conceal it from others is a first step in confronting human inauthenticity. In addition, it is important to recognize the paradox that attends this view: any attempt to deny or to conceal one's pervasive self-interest merely reiterates it, because the attempt is itself an act of self-interest.

On the other hand, it is essential that this inescapable self-concern should not be regarded as a deficit to be condemned and somehow corrected. The unconcealment of human self-interest should provoke neither guilt nor efforts to change. On the contrary, as I will show, it is Heidegger's view that to condemn an inauthentic way of being is ultimately to prevent its recognition: to leap to where we are we must be able to see ourselves dispassionately. This idea will be discussed more fully later; its introduction at this point is designed to prepare the ground for what follows.

THE THROWNNESS OF HUMAN BEING

In *Being and Time,* Heidegger presents his model of *Dasein*—the being of human beings—and his account of the way human possibility plays itself out in the business of everyday life. All following quotes from Heidegger, unless otherwise noted, are from *Being and Time* (1962). I will discuss four aspects of Dasein:

1. The existential priority of Being-with,
2. The disturbance of Being-with,
3. The invention of empathy as ersatz Being-with, and
4. Appropriation as the path to authenticity.

I reiterate that these ideas are not presented as answers, but as elements of a vocabulary, tools for an inquiry into the nature of human being and listening.

The Existential Priority of Being-With

Heidegger's model of the existential structure of human being turns the traditional Cartesian model on its head. In the Cartesian perspective, which is embedded everywhere in our present world-view, the "I"—the *cogito,* the individual isolated inner subject—is the prior datum. This experience of self is not merely a theory or belief arising in the situation; it is the background assumption that generates the situation and gives us our being. We *are* subjects in a world of objects, and from that ground arise our thoughts, our experiences, and our communicative practices. Heidegger points out that human interaction in a Cartesian model begins "by marking out and isolating the 'I' so that one must then seek some way of getting over to the Others from the isolated subject" (p. 154).

Heidegger challenges this view. Ontologically, he proposes, it is not that we are isolated individual beings first and then turn to a world where we encounter others. As biological entities, certainly, we "enter" the world; but as ontological entities—as human *beings*—we first come to exist *in* the world. We are not "put into" the world as a pen is put into a pocket; our relationship to the world is much more intimate than that. For Heidegger, there is *no* existence for human beings *other than* being-in-the-world:

It is not the case that man "is" and then has, by way of an extra, a relationship-of-Being towards the world—a world which he provides himself occasionally. . . . Taking up a relationship towards the world is possibly only *because* Dasein, as Being-in-the-world, is as it is. (p. 84)

Theories of identity-creation, such as symbolic interactionism, are consistent with Heidegger on this point. George Herbert Mead (1982) comments that "we do not assume there is a self to begin with. Self is not presupposed as a stuff out of which the world arises. Rather the self arises in the world" (p. 107). To arise in the world is to arise in language: our selves, like all our meanings, are created in linguistic interaction. But the world is likewise a linguistic phenomenon; thus I would modify Mead's view by suggesting that self and world arise simultaneously. As the child awakens to the meaning-function of language, he or she begins to create both a meaningful self and a meaningful world. The materials for this process are the ontological options inherited from the culture: options for world and self-interpretation contained in the culture's language. Each child's specific choices from these options are contingent upon his or her interpretations of interactions with significant others.

Thus, because we come to be in the shared medium of language and in the interactive process of world interpretation, the *kind* of being that characterizes human beings is essentially both *being-in* and *being-with*. "The world of Dasein is a *with-world*," says Heidegger, and "Being-in is *Being-with* Others" (p. 155). Or, in the words of Jean-Luc Nancy (1991): "The originary sharing of the world is the sharing of Being, and the Being of Dasein is nothing other than the Being of this sharing" (p. 103).[5] Therefore Heidegger disputes the view that being with others is simply "the summative result of the occurrence of several subjects" (p. 163). Instead, a human being is Being-with even when no others are present. Being alone, says Heidegger, is merely "a deficient mode of Being-with" (p. 157).

Because we are essentially the products of shared ontological vocabulary, self-knowledge can never be an isolated achievement; nor is knowledge of others something that must be sought through extensive "self-disclosure" of personal information. On the contrary,

because Dasein's Being is Being-with, its understanding of Being *already implies the understanding of Others* [italics added]. This understanding . . . is not an acquaintance derived from knowledge about them, but a primordially existential kind of Being, which, more than anything else, makes such knowledge and acquaintance possible. *Knowing oneself is grounded in Being-with* [italics added], which understands primordially. (p. 161)

The existential priority of Being-with gives human beings an inherent understanding of one another, an understanding that grounds even our individual self-understanding. This is not psychological understanding, based upon the acquisition of information at the level of personal identity, but ontological understanding, based in shared being. Such understanding is not an element of the Cartesian model.

The Disturbance of Being-With

Heidegger describes, in the passages I have summarized, the existential *possibility* of the human condition, the possibility of authentic human relationship. However, he next undertakes to show why, as I have suggested earlier, we are thrown to (because thrown into) a way of being that is considerably less authentic than the possibility.

The problem arises as a side-effect of our in-the-world existential structure: we run into trouble precisely *because* our "subject character" is defined "in terms of certain ways in which one may be" (p. 163). That is, human being is always being-in-the-world, and being-in-the-world is always being some particular *way*. All of these possible ways of being, says Heidegger, are modes of *concern*. In fact, a human being might accurately be characterized as a body of concerns. These everpresent concerns may take various forms: making use of something, producing something, considering or discussing something. Or, on the other hand, we may be operating in a *deficient* mode of concern, in which our concern is kept to a minimum: neglecting or renouncing something, for example, or taking a rest (p. 83). But we are always concerned; and a moment's reflection will validate Heidegger's thesis. From the moment of waking in the morning, we are always up to something, acting toward some purpose. In Heidegger's phrase, we are always acting in-order-to. Further, if we try *not* to be concerned—if we try to simply "be"—then we are being concerned for *not* being concerned. This is the trap in the injunction to "try to relax." *All* human being *is* being concerned.

One emergent product of a world full of bodies of concerns is what can be called *second-level concerns*: we start to be concerned for how we are doing in relation to all those other bodies. In Heidegger's words,

> In one's concern with what one has taken hold of, whether with, for, or against, the Others, there is *constant care as to the way one differs from them* [italics added], whether that difference is merely one that is to be evened out, whether

one's own Dasein has lagged behind the Others and wants to catch up in relationship to them, or whether one's Dasein already has some priority over them and sets out to keep them suppressed. (pp. 163–164)

Here, then, is the source of "keeping up with the Joneses," the genesis of the human preoccupation with looking good, being right, and coming out ahead: we develop a concern for the success of our concerns, those concerns that we *are* and with whose fate we identify our selves. In the Heideggerian model, this inevitable thrownness to self-concern is simply part of the existential structure of human beings; it comes with the territory of being human.

Our second-level concern creates a problem for human relationships, however, because one of the characteristics of a concern for being right and winning (which inevitably entails someone else's being wrong or losing) is an existential distance from others. Our concern gets between us and other human beings, and in so doing it breaks being-with. "The care about this distance between them," says Heidegger, "is disturbing to Being-with-one-another." This disturbance, moreover, is aggravated by our unawareness of its nature: "The more inconspicuous this kind of Being is . . . all the more stubbornly and primordially does it work itself out." Therefore the possibility, authentic Being-with, has fallen to be the everyday reality: an "inconspicuous domination by Others," others who are not so much our partners in being as our opponents in an ongoing contest of worldly concerns (p. 164).

Further, these others who dominate us become more and more impersonal and generic. They are no longer the individual others encountered in authentic Being-with; they are "not this one, not that one, not oneself, not some people, and not the sum of them all." Rather they are "the neuter, the 'they' "; and as a result of their domination, "the Self of everyday Dasein is the *they-self*":

> One belongs to the Others oneself and enhances their power. . . . This Being-with-one-another dissolves one's own Dasein completely into the kind of Being of 'the Others,' in such a way, indeed, that the Others, as distinguishable and explicit, vanish more and more. In this inconspicuousness and unascertainability, the real dictatorship of the "they" is unfolded. (p. 164)

Hubert Dreyfus (1991) has proposed that Heidegger's *Das Man*, translated here as "the 'they,' " would be more usefully understood as "the 'one' ": thus we act as we do because "one acts that way," and we are the way we are simply because "one is that way." Pressed, we cannot locate the source of these assumptions; as Dreyfus points out, we do not *know* them, we simply *are* them (p. 3). They constitute the unspoken background of our everyday existence, and are likely to be blamed on "human nature."

Thus the full possibility of being with others is displaced by a background way of being that distances us, both from each other in interaction, and from human relatedness in general. We thereby surrender the mutuality that is the very basis of our individuality. In this condition, says Heidegger, "Everyone is the other, and no one is himself" (p. 165).

Because Heidegger is describing the only way available for human beings to be-in-the-world, the judgment that we are somehow in error for being this way is inappropriate. Heidegger stresses that "the inauthenticity of Dasein does not signify any 'less' Being or any 'lower' degree of Being" (p. 68). This is difficult to grasp, because to our common sense inauthenticity certainly *seems* lower. But it is precisely this rush to judgment, this inability to look our way of being in the face, that prevents us from seeing it as it is and therefore allows it to persist in defining our interactions.

Empathy as Ersatz Being-With

In response to the inauthentic state of affairs created by the dominance of our second-level concerns, human beings invented "empathy." This invention, Heidegger says, resulted precisely from our having lost touch with the possibility of authentic relationship.

For the most part, as the preceding discussion has shown, we dwell in "the deficient or at least the Indifferent modes [of Being-with]." As examples of these deficient modes (the ways in which our domination by the "they" plays itself out) Heidegger cites passing one another by, aloofness, hiding oneself away, or putting on a disguise. As a result of our tendency to inhabit these deficient modes, we have a sense of something missing, and feel the need to compensate: "Being-with-one-another must follow special routes of its own in order to come close to Others" (p. 161).

One such "special route" was designed when psychologists, thinking from within the Cartesian paradigm that the sciences necessarily inhabit, began considering "the theoretical problematic of understanding the 'psychical life of Others.'" The phenomenon that resulted from this inquiry

> presents a way of Being with one another understandingly, but at the same time it gets taken as that which, primordially and "in the beginning," constitutes Being towards Others and makes it possible at all. This phenomenon, which is none too happily designated as *empathy*, is then supposed, as

it were, to provide the first *ontological bridge from one's own subject, which is given proximally as alone, to the other subject, which is proximally quite closed off* [italics added]. (pp. 161–162)

In other words, empathy follows from the assumptions of Cartesian dualism, a model consistent with interpersonal distance, because Cartesianism assumes the isolated subject as its primary datum. But in the Heideggerian model Being-with is prior; thus profound relatedness was always already the fundamental human condition. Empathy can never achieve human relatedness, because it reinforces, by presupposing, the separation it is designed to overcome. " 'Empathy' does not first constitute Being-with," says Heidegger; "only on the basis of Being-with does 'empathy' become possible: it gets its motivation from the unsociability of the dominant modes of Being-with" (p. 162).

Appropriation as the Path to Authenticity

Having unconcealed the ersatz nature of empathy, Heidegger proposes an alternate path to authentic interaction. Heidegger's term, for which "the event of appropriation" is the usual translation, is *Ereignis*, and it appears primarily in his later work. But some version of this idea can be found throughout his writing, and all the versions, as I read them, reverberate along a single unifying strand of thought.[6] Heidegger was aiming in all of them at the evocation of a particular ontological insight: an insight concerning our inherited way of being, and the possibility of appropriating that way of being so that we are liberated *within* the inescapable constraints it imposes upon us. This appropriative relationship is the key to authenticity. As Zimmerman (1986) puts it, "Authenticity means to be most appropriately what one already is" (p. xxiv).

The nature of the appropriative relationship is one of Heidegger's most evasive insights, one that cannot quite be cognitively subjugated, but that must be repeatedly grasped and lost as it plays at the boundary of thinkability. Such tantalizing elusiveness always characterizes ontological insight. Being loves to hide, says Heidegger (1984, p. 26). Therefore, ontological insight—the leap to where we are, the "in-turning" in-sight that recovers Being from the oblivion of its concealment—occurs as *Augenblick*, translated variously as a "lightning flash," "the glance of an eye," an "entering, flashing glance," or simply "the moment" (Dreyfus, 1991, pp. x, 321; Heidegger, 1977, p. 43). This is the way appropriation must be apprehended: it must be allowed to flash as an ontological insight, permitting us a transforming glance at our nature and possibility, and then allowed to withdraw, later, perhaps, to flash again.

Heidegger's emphasis is upon taking hold of one's self: seeing through disguises and recognizing one's Being *as* the they-self (1962, p. 167). This taking possession of one's self *as one is* constitutes authenticity. The authentic self is not one that has managed to escape the everyday thrownness of human being; rather, it is a self that has taken hold of that thrownness "in its own way." It has appropriated the everyday way of being, recognized it, allowed it, and owned it, rather than continuing to be owned *by* it. The ownedness that constitutes authenticity is thus the ownership *of* ownedness, the paradoxical and liberating taking-over of being owned.

This idea challenges the usual view that recognition of one's inauthenticity should be accompanied by an immediate attempt to correct the situation. This more traditional response is expressed by Martin Buber (1991), whose term for inauthenticity (self-concern, domination by the being of the "they") is *seeming*:

> To yield to seeming is man's essential cowardice, to resist it is his essential courage. . . . One can struggle to come to oneself—that is, to come to confidence in being. One struggles, now more successfully, now less, but never in vain, even when he thinks he is defeated. (p. 68)

Clearly, Buber's moralistic view is more familiar to us: fight the impulse to inauthenticity, he exhorts us. Struggle to *be*. But recall Heidegger's explication of our second-level concerns: any struggle to "be," translated into the human condition, is simply another concern, another in-order-to. Thus it will inevitably entail a second-level concern, a concern for how one is doing in relation to the "they," a concern for whether one is succeeding in "being," a concern, finally, for how effectively one is "seeming" to "be." "Struggling to be" is oxymoronic, like "trying to relax." Heidegger recognizes that this thrownness to in-order-to is the trap from which human beings cannot escape; therefore he proposes the possibility of freedom *within* the trap, rather than *from* it.

But acceptance of our way of being is not equivalent to surrender. To appropriate our fundamental distance from others is not to succumb to it. Critics who read Heidegger as advocating "slavish self-abnegation" to Being, as does Terry Eagleton (1983, p. 65), have stopped too soon in their consideration of this idea. They have pinned appropriation, wriggling, to a concept, rather than allowing its play to evoke the lightning flash of ontological insight. In this elusive and transforming moment of insight, made available in the event of appropriation, one attains the possibility of a relationship with one's way of being that is delicately balanced between resistance and surrender, between ownership and ownedness. It is the result, not of a struggle to be, but of a letting be that lets one be. Because it is an essentially paradoxical relationship, its balance is tenuous and easily lost. It is in maintaining oneself in this delicate balance that ontological liberation arises: the freedom to be, and to be-with.

This, then, is the design of an ontological approach to listening. It asks us to take a step back: to take a careful look at our way of being, to confront the possibility of our essential inauthenticity, and to consider Heidegger's suggestion of how this state of affairs might have come about. Heidegger proposes appropriation as a way of inhabiting our way of being and as a context for authentic interpersonal communication. Thus, Heidegger's vocabulary creates the possibility of a new ontological dwelling from which to listen.

NOTES

1. Stewart's critique of the empathic model has been challenged; see Anderson, 1984, and Bozick, 1984.

2. *Conflict*, like empathy, is ubiquitous in communication textbooks and has similar reifying tendencies. To approach a human communication problem as a conflict between opposed entities mandates a focus upon the conflicting selves; whereas if the problem is approached as, for example, a breakdown in the relational process, the focus shifts to the transaction of the communicative event.

3. Heidegger's later work moved away from the Being-being distinction and toward appropriation as the site of the Being-being relationship. In the later work, according to Joan Stambaugh, "the relation is more fundamental than what is related" (Stambaugh, Introduction to Heidegger, 1972, p. x).

4. The idea that a human being is a listening is drawn from the work of the Landmark Education Corporation, whose curriculum develops an ontological approach to human interaction. I have explored Landmark's work at length elsewhere (Hyde, 1992).

5. Nancy (1991) acknowledges that his analysis of *Being and Time* gives being-with a "privileged position" that it does not have in Heidegger's own writing: "The analytic of the being-with remains a moment, which is not returned to thematically, in a general analytic where the Dasein appears first of all and most frequently as in some way isolated, even though Heidegger himself emphasizes that there is solitude 'only *in* and *for* a being-with' " (pp. 103–104). On the other hand, Dreyfus (1991) argues that this section of *Being and Time* (entitled "The Dasein-with of Others and Everyday Being-With") is "in many ways the pivotal chapter of the book" (p. 156).

6. It is Heidegger's view (1968, p. 50; 1971b, p. 4) that a thinker thinks one thought only. I share the assessment of Graham Parkes (1987, pp. 107, 119) that the contrast between early and late Heidegger, and specifically the difference between resoluteness and releasement, is often overdrawn at the expense of the common strand that unifies Heidegger's thought.

REFERENCES

Adler, R. B., & Towne, N. (1990). *Looking out, looking in.* Fort Worth: Holt, Rinehart and Winston.

Anderson, R. (1984). Forum. *Communication Education, 33,* 195–196.

Bozick, M. (1984). Forum. *Communication Education, 33,* 196.

Buber, M. (1991). *The knowledge of man* (M. Friedman, Ed.; M. Friedman & R. G. Smith, Trans.). Atlantic Highlands, NJ: Humanities Press.

Dreyfus, H. L. (1991). *Being-in-the-World: A commentary on Heidegger's Being and time, division I.* Cambridge, MA: MIT Press.

Eagleton, T. (1983). *Literary theory: an introduction.* Minneapolis: University of Minnesota Press.

Gadamer, H. (1988). *Truth and method* (J. Weinsheimer & D. G. Marshall, Trans.). New York: Crossroad.

Heidegger, M. (1959). *An introduction to metaphysics* (R. Manheim, Trans.). New Haven, CT: Yale University Press.

Heidegger, M. (1962). *Being and time* (J. Macquarrie & E. Robinson, Trans.). New York: Harper and Row.

Heidegger, M. (1968). *What is called thinking?* (J. G. Gray, Trans.). New York: Harper and Row.

Heidegger, M. (1971a). *On the way to language* (P. D. Hertz, Trans.). New York: Harper and Row.

Heidegger, M. (1971b). *Poetry, language, thought* (A. Hofstadter, Trans.). New York: Harper and Row.

Heidegger, M. (1972). *On Time and Being* (J. Stambaugh, Trans.). New York: Harper and Row.

Heidegger, M. (1977). *Basic writings* (D. F. Krell, Ed.). New York: Harper and Row.

Heidegger, M. (1984). *Early Greek thinking* (William Lovitt, Trans.). New York: Harper and Row.

Hyde, R. B. (1992). Speaking being: Ontological rhetoric as transformational technology. Paper presented at the Speech Communication Association Convention, Chicago.

Johnstone, H. W. (1978). *Validity, rhetoric and philosophical argument.* University Park, PA: Dialogue Press of Man and World.

Mead, G. H. (1982). *The individual and the social self: Unpublished work of George Herbert Mead* (D. L. Miller, Ed.). Chicago: University of Chicago Press.

Nancy J. (1991). *The inoperative community* (Peter Connor, Ed.; Peter Connor, Lisa Garbus, Michael Holland, and Simona Sawhney, Trans.). Minneapolis: University of Minnesota Press.

Parkes, G. (1987). Thoughts on the way. In G. Parkes (Ed.), *Heidegger and Asian thought* (pp. 105–144). Honolulu: University of Hawaii Press.

Rorty, R. (1989). *Contingency, irony, and solidarity.* New York: Cambridge University Press.

Stewart, J. (1983). Interpretive listening: An alternative to empathy. *Communication Education, 32,* 379–391.

Zimmerman, M. E. (1986). *Eclipse of the self.* Athens: Ohio University Press.

8

Interpretation in Unsettled Times

DEBRA GRODIN

INTERPRETIVE APPROACHES to communication inquiry have taken a variety of forms, but they are generally distinguished by their theoretical affiliation with the social construction of human experience. There are of course a variety of ways scholars apply ideas of social construction, but typically there is an interest in how individuals make sense of their life-world and in the relationship between self, social context, and culture in the sense-making process. Due to interest in social context, interpretive researchers question the assumption of "self-contained individualism" (Sampson, 1989) that has strongly influenced the "subject" in communication research practice. Their efforts have emphasized the importance of culture and situated experience.

The world as socially constructed is not an artifact of individual imaginations operating in a vacuum, but rather the result of the common ground we both inherit from our social surroundings and create with other social actors. Through intersubjectivity human beings construct a life-world that can be shared with others. Social actors experience considerable continuity of meaning in their lives, affording a sense of personal cohesion. Most scholarship in interpersonal communication, whether interpretive or not, reflects this premise of shared understanding as both achievable and on some level requisite for communication to occur. Mutual understanding is considered a core process in communication (O'Keefe, 1992); commonality with others is considered necessary for understanding and for successful interaction.

Assumptions about intersubjectivity and commonality resulting from shared experience have been the implicit basis of much interpersonal research. In this chapter, however, I examine how the very premises of intersubjectivity that we bring to communication research may be mask-

197

ing key aspects of communication experience in the lives of those we study. Referring to my own project (Grodin, 1991) on women's use of psychological self-help books, in this chapter I discuss conditions of modernity and postmodernity that highlight the fragmentary and incoherent aspects of contemporary human experience, conditions that challenge notions of personal coherence and a high degree of commonality with others. I begin by discussing those concepts that have been the basis of interpretive work and follow this with a brief discussion of my own research. I examine some of the assumptions we may often bring to interpretive research, and why these assumptions may be limiting the scope and accuracy of our inquiry. Due to space limitations my discussion of the self-help project is restricted to selected findings that led to reevaluating the basis of my own work. Therefore, my emphasis here is not on details of my study, but on its implications for interpretive scholarship.[1]

In the second half of the chapter, I turn to the work of Anthony Giddens (1991) and Kenneth Gergen (1991) to further explore the cultural conditions that have engendered the loss of a sense of what is held in "common" in our lives. Both scholars are interested in how contemporary life amid mediated communication influences our notions of self and other. I argue that these ideas have great relevancy for inquiry in interpersonal communication and that interpretive research in our field will be well served by working toward an integration of the interpersonal and mediated communication environment.

THE CONTEXT OF
INTERPERSONAL COMMUNICATION

In interpersonal communication studies, the theme of commonality is often mentioned with regard to a larger social context, such as community or culture. For example in Trenholm and Jensen's (1988) popular text, *Interpersonal Communication*, the authors tell us that the word *communication* comes from the Latin word *munia*, connoting mutuality, exchange, and sharing among those of the *same community*. What is emphasized is the shared social and cultural basis of our interactions. In Trenholm and Jensen's words,

> Communication is collective. The relationship between human society and human communication is circular; one could not exist without the other. On the one hand what holds a society together is the ability of its members to act as a coordinated whole which would be impossible without communication. (1988, p. 7)

One difficulty in making sense of those concepts that describe contexts of communication is that levels of analysis are variable. In communication research, terms such as *culture, community,* and *society* are often used more or less interchangeably to reference a larger social entity in which members experience a sense of commonality. Although most communication scholars would probably agree that there are many "coordinated wholes" to be experienced in the larger social world, the premise of intersubjectivity as applied in our field seems to assume that a larger social world exists in which there is considerable coherence, established through shared rules of expression and understanding.

In a sense, these assumptions about coherence constitute what might generally be thought of as a "natural attitude" in our field, premises that are not often questioned. Yet, there is reason, I think, to consider how these assumptions shape our research, particularly as interpretive scholars. In light of postmodern criticism, are notions of culture as cohesive necessarily viable? Are intersubjectivity and commonality as critical to communication as we have assumed, and in the ways we have assumed? I became interested in these questions as I examined the data from my own interpretive research on women's use of psychological self-help books. My research resulted in questions about the premises of social construction, including concepts of culture, commonality, and intersubjectivity. In this chapter I explore some of these issues by discussing the phenomenal experience of individuals who participated in my interpretive study of self-help book reading.

The examination of self-help book reading is an example of research that intersects the areas of interpersonal communication and media studies. Self-help books are mass mediated texts that a reader engages with to improve relationships, self-image, even ways of communicating. Using interpretive methods, I built my research around the premise that readers make sense of mediated texts through ordinary social action, in other words through interpersonal experience. This approach elicited accounts of what participants "do" with self-help books, not simply the act of curling up with a book, but how book content becomes meaningful in the course of everyday social discourse. Accounts of self-help and social action elicited from readers, demonstrated that the women I interviewed often experience the world as fragmented, *not cohesive.* In this condition of fragmentation, cultural commonality was often illusive.

Following the work of Mead (1934), Schutz (1967), Berger and Luckman (1967), Blumer (1969), and others, my own approach to interpretive research has been based on theories of social construction and symbolic interactionism. From these perspectives, researchers are interested primarily in how people make sense of their world through the social action of everyday life. Symbolic interactionists, influenced by theories of social construction, assume that individuals are "continually adjusting what they do in the light of what others do" (Becker & McCall, 1990, p. 3). Yet, the social world is not fixed. A social constructionist perspective typically assumes that much about the social world is open, due to the ongoing, emergent nature of the world in which humans commune. This is not to say that there are no constraints on human experience, indeed social construction occurs within social contexts that circumscribe aspects of behavior. It is to say, however, that people are involved in the construction of meaning in their lives, and the interpretive researcher can examine this involvement. Like the lives of those we study, the act of conducting interpretive research is also one that transforms itself as researchers engage in social action through conversations with their participants. This chapter is in part a case study of this kind of transformation.

When applying theories of social construction to communication, researchers often underscore the way in which human beings will accept the "naturalness" or "givenness" of their perceptions of the world because, in part, "human authorship of these meanings has faded" (Rakow, 1992, p. 51). The making of meaning, however, will be altered in the face of discrepancies or other conditions that call for new interpretations. In part, self-help book readers are drawn to the genre because the *naturalness of their world has faded;* rules and ways of acting have become inaccessible or the presence of multiple and contradictory rules has made the arbitrariness of social order more apparent. Thus readers experience a loss of naturalness that shapes how they view themselves and others as social actors. It is their sense of the world as discrepant from expectations and learned social routines that makes their accounts particularly rich.

SENSITIZING CONCEPTS

Both Blumer (1969) and later Denzin (1989) describe the use of "sensitizing concepts" in interpretive research; concepts that the researcher deliberately brings to inquiry for the purpose of structuring observation. These concepts are tentatively held up to what is being studied, often drawing the researcher to aspects of the social world that are congruent to research goals. Researchers, however, may find that such concepts become problematic, perhaps by restricting observation or by affording insufficient explanatory power, as the everyday world of participants is investigated. In my own work, some of the core concepts framing the research were derived from theories of symbolic interaction and social construction and included notions of intersubjectivity, culture, commonality, and coherence. This is by no means an exhaustive list, but one that captures some of the salient ideas that influenced my research early on. I focus on several of these concepts to illustrate what they have traditionally meant for the interpretive endeavor and to explore why some of these meanings may no longer explain the range of communication experience we study.

The Concept of Intersubjectivity

Referring to the work of Alfred Schutz, communication researcher Jim Anderson (1987) describes the relationship between interpretation and intersubjective meaning. According to Schutz (1967), our experience in the world becomes meaningful to us through our acts of interpretation. Because the human mind is compelled to make sense of experience, acts of interpretation over time lead to a sense of the world as ordered and objective. What we know and understand about the world we assume others know and understand. Because we are born into a social world, these acts of interpretation are invariably influenced by those we find ourselves socially engaged with.

The intersubjective nature of meaning, in Schutz's scheme, explains why the constructed nature of human understanding is not idiosyncratic. Rather it both stems from and helps shape a store of common knowledge held by members of a society or culture. Schutz emphasizes the importance of face-to-face everyday experience and claims that with this experience we are continually "reflecting on each other's interpretations" (Anderson, 1987) thus modifying and negotiating a shared notion of reality. In Blumer's (1969) scheme, we are constantly involved in mutually adjusting and modifying our lines of action as we engage in social life.

In theory, intersubjectivity leads to the individual's experience of a common store of knowledge, what Berger would refer to as *common sense* (Wuthnow, Hunter, Bergesen, & Kurzweil, 1984). The human effort to create a world of shared meaning is taken as a sine qua non. Common sense is usually organized into myths, rituals, and sayings, forming our cultural storehouse, and is often thought of as something natural and undeniable (Geertz, 1973).

Drawing upon cultural resources enables individuals to establish a sense of coherence and order, because such resources are assumed to be symbols shared among many. Through such social activity we develop collective understandings of common situations and agreed upon ways of acting in them. "To the degree that recipe 'solutions' to 'problems' become socially shared and transmitted over time, we may speak of institutionalized culture" (Hall, 1990, p. 24). This phenomenon leads to the assumption made by many interpretive researchers that the individual is not consciously aware of the process of "common" sense making, but rather, takes for granted what he or she understands about the world as a result of their interpretive activity.

The Concept of Culture

For most interpretivists, terms such as *interactional* and *dialogic* are bound up in cultural context, for it is through such interactions that cultures are enacted, reproduced, and transformed. *Culture* is typically defined by what is held in common by social actors—"shared meanings, practices, and symbols that constitute the human world" (Rabinow & Sullivan, 1979, p. 6). Here we see the relationship between intersubjectivity and culture.

For researchers in communication,[2] culture is often construed as a local or bounded context where norms of interaction can be identified. For example, in the interpersonal area, ethnographies of communication describe discourse practices within particular contexts as key elements of social life. Hymes (1962) has looked at how interpretive activity in a speech community is ordered. The emphasis is on how cultures cohere; the implication is that cultures are cohesive.

In other interpretive work, for example the area of critical studies, researchers often view culture as a larger entity purveying dominant ideology or values that social actors must contend with. Even though dominant culture exerts influence, for some critical researchers it does so within a more fluid and diverse context where subcultures or demographic clusters of opposition can be identified. This kind of analysis illuminates realms within larger society where interpretive frameworks are not shared, potentially offering a view of cultural diversity and clash. However, even from this perspective, pockets of culture are also identified by what is held in common.

Certainly there is a way in which social actors experience a natural attitude achieved through intersubjective agreement, which then shapes a sense of shared culture. Interpersonal communication researchers in particular have also shown us that within bounded contexts, rules of interaction and conversation can be identified that circumscribe communication behavior. Yet, these examples of commonality, or high degrees of intersubjectivity reflect a bias in our work, one where we often assume that social actors generally navigate the world assuming (probably unconsciously) that an "objective" natural order exists. Work in critical studies has challenged some of these assumptions, but critical researchers also uncover an assortment of "natural attitudes" held by members who share characteristics of class, race, gender, and so forth. From these perspectives, personal confusion regarding multicultural memberships or distress over how to communicate in a culturally complex world are often elided.

In times of swift cultural change, the world of those we study may lack the sense of coherence and "naturalness" implicit in assumptions about intersubjectivity and culture. In my own research on women and self-help books (Grodin, 1991), I found that participants experienced a strong sense of incoherence regarding the cultural context of their lives. They spoke of feeling removed from what scholars describe as common sense. These experiences of research participants raise questions about the assumptions we bring to interpretive research.

There is a way in which social actors may not feel they commonly experience what has been described as intersubjective agreement. When I began the self-help book project, I was initially interested in interpretive practices held *in common* by readers I interviewed and on the intersubjective agreement that could be found among participants regarding their engagement with self-help books and the social world in general. I indeed found patterns of response that were similar across all readers in the study. Yet, the women I interviewed spoke so poignantly of their feelings of disconnection from others in their daily lives, that I was compelled to question the meaning of those shared patterns of thought and feeling that I had recognized as a researcher. Participants spoke about not understanding the rules and practices of daily life in their everyday world. In addition, many wanted to disconnect or extricate themselves from established cultural practices they associated with patriarchal power. I will expand upon these findings shortly, but in brief, the experience of those I studied included not having a common storehouse of cultural knowledge that could be taken for granted. When I began my research on women and self-help books, I had assumed the importance of cultural commonality without questioning how my participants indeed experience their world with regard to shared cultural experience. Many of my participants had an ample social life, and all worked outside the home where they were in contact with coworkers. What I learned, however, was that most participants described their interpersonal contacts as not providing them with a sense of what is shared among themselves and others. Readers' interest in self-help seemed to reflect Sherry Turkle's (1978) observation that contemporary life is characterized by difficulty in locating a shared body of knowledge and experience. In the next section I briefly expand upon these findings.

INTERPRETATION IN "UNSETTLED TIMES"[3]

In conducting a study of psychological self-help book reading, I interviewed 16 women in depth[4] for a minimum of 5 hours with each participant. Although self-help book reading is a solitary act, talking with others about the books, watching television programs featuring self-help book authors, attending therapy sessions, and so forth, all afford opportunities to socially construct the meaning of texts. Readers do not use the books as recipes, an assumption that is often made by critics of the genre who focus their analysis on texts alone (see Lerner, 1990; Schilling & Fuehrer, 1987). Instead, texts become meaningful through the reader's interpretive practices, which are in part enacted via their interpersonal relationships, whether face to face or mediated. Making sense of self-help books does not occur "alone in one's room" as the solitary act of reading might suggest, but is instead an act of social construction that draws on previously and currently experienced relationships, including the relationship that emerges through conversation with the researcher.

Throughout my interviews with women readers of self-help books, I was struck by how their own experience of everyday life departs from some of the core assumptions of interpretive research. In particular, one of the clearest patterns of response from my research participants was that of not knowing "how to act" in many situations in their lives. Culture, for them, is lacking in established ways of doing many of the things people do to get on with their lives. For example, women spoke of questions in their lives that had resulted from their interest in women's liberation. How do you have a good relationship with a man when you are changing your ideas about yourself as a woman, but find that men are not changing? How do you raise children happily when you are also interested in a career? Readers do not expect answers to these questions to be simple solutions, nor do they expect one right answer. Their questions reflect a deep uncertainty, not simply about rules of interaction (dating, for example) but about existential issues (what will the world be like 25 years from now?). Those I interviewed do not feel that they have a sufficient notion of what constitutes common sense in their social world. Obviously they do share some common store of knowledge with others and in this way are participants in what interpretive researchers describe as shared culture, but what is most important is that often *they do not feel they do,* and in many cases actually do not. In many situations and over many issues, they *do not* take the common for granted, but instead *consciously* strive to construct a sense of what constitutes the common through assorted activities, including self-help book reading.

A good example of this is the surprise and gratitude readers expressed when they learned they were not the only ones with a problem. Self-help books were viewed as providing a window onto the lives of those with similar problems. Some of these problems, like mourning the loss of a marriage, are certainly common problems in that they occur with great frequency in North American culture. Yet, the interpersonal lives of participants did not necessarily afford the kind of contact that enables a person to feel they are "not alone" with their problem. Being "not alone" means more than having someone to talk to or even knowing one person in a like circumstance. It primarily means recognizing that one is among a larger group who think, feel, and behave in similar ways.

Readers also attempt to establish a kind of general common sense, not only a connection to others who are suffering. In doing so, they are not just finding something that exists in the social world; they are also transforming their social world—because, in Rakow's (1992) words, it calls for new interpretations. It is of course not antithetical to an interpretive position that social actors use cultural resources to make sense of their world in a creative manner. On one hand, "We can understand culture as received symbols, recipes, and products that actors draw on by way of grappling in emergent meaningful ways with situational problems" (Hall, 1990, p. 23). But, particularly under condition of social transformation, acts of reinterpretation become more critical in daily life. One reader, for example, spoke passionately about how her reading in the 1950s of Norman Vincent Peale's (1952) *Power of Positive Thinking* encouraged her to question the fear tactics used by her parents in raising her. In her words, "With that very first book, religion was displayed as something that was helpful instead of something that you had to follow or terrible things were going to happen to you." This reader went on to describe the book as a strong inspiration towards women's liberation, during a time when no one was talking about feminism.

The importance of appreciating interpretive practice under contemporary social conditions became increasingly apparent as my research progressed. Women discussed their feelings of both dislocation from traditional patriarchal social practices and exhilaration as they try to function in contexts where they determined that rules and practices are unclear. What stands out in their discourse is the lack of stability in their experience of the social world and the sense of incoherence in their daily lives. I am not suggesting here that common interpretive frameworks never exist or that researchers should not look for, describe, or analyze them. Rather, I am asking whether practitioners in the field so thoroughly accept the achievement of intersubjective agreement and commonality through communication that we may be guilty of not questioning what commonality *means* in everyday experience. By emphasizing the nature of coherence in the lives of those we study we may miss the "thick description" of complexity, ambivalence, and confusion that, for many, characterizes life in contemporary America. The point is not to toss out the concept of intersubjectivity, but rather to consider the ways in which the concept may be more historically and culturally rooted than we have been willing to examine. By rethinking inter-subjectivity and other related concepts in interpretive research, we may be better able to describe the complexity of how our social and histori-cal condition engenders communication problems and realities.

Much interpretive work in interpersonal communication has aimed to discover rules and consensus among communicants, thereby not docu-menting issues of discrepancy. In many studies of interpersonal commu-nication that attempt to take culture into account, there is a tendency to focus on what Carbaugh and Hastings (1992) describe as social units for analysis and observation. These units might include situation (place or setting), norms (of interaction and interpretation), roles, and so forth. It seems the success of this approach, that has so influenced interper-sonal studies, depends upon the assumption of a rather cohesive foun-dation for a particular culture or subculture and a strong interest in how coherence is achieved among culture members. It assumes, to a large extent, that social actors take their social world for granted. In addition, there is often an emphasis on face-to-face communication within a very specific context. Yet, a salient condition of the lives of those I interviewed is that they find their interpersonal face-to-face rela-tionships to be an *inadequate source of shared meaning*. In other words, participants spoke of their difficulty in locating "like-minded" others. Participants described turning to self-help books instead of neighbors and friends for advice and information vital to their sense of well being. I underscore this point, because in interpretive work in communication and other social sciences it is assumed overall that a high degree of intersubjectivity is possible under conditions where shared meaning is reinforced by a collectivity whose members have frequent face-to-face social interaction. For example, communication researcher James Ander-son (1987) refers to a true community as a condition under which there is considerable face-to-face communication. There is ample reason to question, however, the application of some of these concepts in our contemporary world. For example, what do we mean by a true commu-nity in a world where mediated communication plays such a significant role? What interpretive work in interpersonal communication will need to work toward is the consideration of the struggles we have in manag-ing a sense of self and relationships with others in a culture that novelist Eva Hoffman (1989) describes as incompletely charted.

Particularly in the case of interpersonal communication scholarship, the limits and conditions of face-to-face communication must be acknowledged to reflect experiences of contemporary life. One issue that needs examination is how mediated communication has opened up the "conceptual limits within which people exist and that enclose and give shape to the immediate social context of everyday life" (Hewitt, 1989, p. 11). I examined these issues in trying to understand the experiences of self-help book readers and the role of reading in their lives. For the women I interviewed, their own notions of community and culture were key to appreciating their experiences of disconnection from common sense and their desires to reconnect to an order compatible with their social needs. To better understand their position and to further discuss issues relevant to interpretive research, I draw primarily on the work of Anthony Giddens and Kenneth Gergen. My coverage here is by no means exhaustive and is by necessity brief. My purpose is to emphasize the way in which mediated communication is changing our social landscape, and the implications of this change for the research we do. Differences between the former's perspective on late modernity and the latter's interest in postmodernity are also discussed.

The Mediated Context of Interpersonal Communication

One way to understand the experience of personal fragmentation among those I interviewed is to consider the distinction between premodern and modern times. Anthony Giddens (1991) describes how contemporary times are characterized by the separation of time and space. In a more traditional social order, ordinary activities of daily life would link time and space through the common denominator of place; community therefore was linked to physical location.[5] One of the contributors to the separation of time and space is mass communication and electronic communication devices, including the computer. Meyrowitz (1985) points out that television, for example, has enabled us not only to experience worlds far from our own in terms of location, but has also provided a backstage view, in Goffman's (1959) situational terms, of behaviors that we may be ordinarily shielded from in everyday face-to-face experience. Referring to the "postmodern" world, Gergen (1991) describes a condition where individuals have an unprecedented quantity and quality of social experiences, enabled by mass communication.

For Giddens as well, the "intrusion of distant events into everyday consciousness" is a key feature of mediated experience in modern times (1992, p. 27). This experience is fragmenting. We can think about fragmentation in a number of ways. It may be viewed in terms of the disintegration of a more unified traditional cultural condition, one where individuals perhaps sensed a high degree of social integration rather than discontinuity. For example, in modern life, individuals may have difficulty managing behavior and identity from social context to social context because of the plurality of life worlds they may encounter (Berger, 1974). Fragmentation may also be seen as a rupture with the past; a break with a relatively clear sense of order and authority that characterized more traditional life. Another way to look at fragmentation is a failure to achieve an integrated identity, due perhaps to the inability to construct a meaningful core in the context of social change.

According to Giddens, what these various experiences of fragmentation give rise to is a sense of not being able to take things for granted; an undermining of certainty in knowledge. Of course, this is precisely the experience reported to me by self-help book readers. In everyday life it takes the form of making the self a reflexive project that is a continuous revision of notions of self and others in response to new information or assorted experiences. Referring to the condition of late modernity, Giddens describes the challenge to personal coherence in a world where individuals must negotiate the passing of shifting social events that range from the women's movement to going through a divorce. The more change encountered in a culture, the more distanced social actors become from traditions and standards. Consequently, the process of negotiation becomes a preoccupation and necessary skill for survival. The self's ability to maintain a coherent narrative is critical. Giddens, it seems, is referring to some kind of enduring stability of self, *not* the notion of self-contained individualism or the notion of one true self. But unlike most postmodernists, he does not reject the idea that ongoing personal coherence is desirable and achievable.

Writing about the postmodern self, Gergen (1991), too, describes how the loss of certain traditions results in a life of "continuous construction and reconstruction: it is a world where anything goes that can be negotiated" (p. 7), but it is not a world where searching for personal coherence necessarily makes sense. Gergen suggests that in the contemporary West a high degree of social stimulation characterizes our lives, differing from life in more traditional social milieus. Much of this stimulation is the direct result of technologies such as television, radio, the telephone, computers, and more, that afford experiences and relationships that were not possible in previous centuries. According to Gergen, the resulting "social saturation" challenges our views of the true and the good, by dismantling "coherent circles of accord," which in more traditional times were supported by greater social homogeneity than we now experience. The average person is exposed to multiple voices and points of view that currently produce "the shocks of dislocation . . . dilemmas of identity" (p. x). Of course, a sense of dislocation is not new in the 20th century. From an early modernist perspective, however, much about this dislocation was initially cause to celebrate because it represented an unshackling from traditional constraint. Those women I interviewed indeed expressed joy about removing themselves from the restrictions of their upbringing as traditional females. However, the dislocation of our postmodern times is distinguished from the modern as we begin to question our assumptions about the coherence of culture and the self. Gergen suggests that instead of the self as contained, the self is becoming more *relational*. The self becomes less of a coherent, centered experience than a fluid experience intimately related through connections with others. Gergen concedes that a consciousness of relational selves is not widespread in Western culture, but that in academic circles, ideas such as the social construction of reality have already laid the groundwork for examining the relational aspects of identity.

Many similarities between the observations of Giddens and Gergen make it hard to distinguish the former's description of late modernity from the latter's description of postmodernity. Both scholars consider the self in contemporary times to be a reflexive project more or less conscious of its own self-construction. This consciousness, partly made apparent by the plurality of voices in the social world, engenders a sense of doubt, and the loss of a belief in one authoritative voice. On the one hand, many aspects of the traditional social order have disintegrated, but in its place we experience a world of more global dimension and unity (Giddens, 1991) and greater interdependence (Gergen, 1991), even though we simultaneously recognize human differences across the globe. Thus, for both, the ideology of self-contained individualism is rejected. For Giddens, however, this rejection does not obviate the need and achievability of personal coherence. For Gergen, the self, at least currently, is torn asunder by the "plurality of voices vying for the right to reality" (p. 7). This results in a failure of the center of self to hold and is something Gergen believes is generally problematic across the population. It is unclear whether Gergen believes that, ultimately, postmodern existence can embrace the goal of personal autonomy while experiencing a more relational self.

The ideas of both Gergen and Giddens have implications for understanding the personal confusion experienced by those who participated in the self-help book study. Participants seem to experience a tension between Giddens's description of the self's continued search for coherence, and Gergen's emphasis on a more relational self. This tension has some interesting parallels with issues of autonomy and connection in their lives. On the one hand, readers adopt a more modernist stance in their search for autonomy and disconnection from inherited traditions that disable personal power. At the same time, they partly hope for an authoritative "scientific" consensus that will help them with personal problems. On the other hand, readers read selectively and do not accept the full authority of the text. They also seek out connections with the lives of others they encounter in self-help books, adopting what Gergen seems to describe as a relational approach to identity construction. This tension may be related to the critique of some feminists, who claim that the postmodern "turn" poses unique problems. For example, some feminist authors have argued that "the subject under fire from postmodernism may be a more specifically masculine self than postmodernists have been willing to admit" (DiStefano, 1990, p. 75). In other words, there seem to be strong similarities between what feminist thinkers have long described as a more relational female self (Gilligan, 1982) and what is now being described as a postmodern self. At the same time, women who have long recognized relational aspects of self are now experimenting more with notions of autonomy and individualism, ideas that have brought much of value to women's lives. In my view what is relatively new for women as they turn to self-help is that they are establishing *abstract* connections with authors, as well as with those whose stories are told in self-help books. Women are connecting more to what Gergen calls *symbolic community*, one form of abstract community that has resulted from the deterioration of traditional communities bound in physical location. These symbolic communities lack many of the hallmarks of traditional communities that seem to form the foundation of what researchers have described as intersubjectivity. Specifically, they are not characterized by face-to-face communication, so the way meaning is negotiated with others may be more fluid, less circumscribed by cultural boundaries, in short, somewhat less coherent. Abstract communities, however, offer a new way to think about women's relational selves. Connecting to others who read self-help, for example, is not necessarily out of caring, but rather to change one's life.

"Symbolic communities are linked by the capacity of their members for symbolic exchange—of words, images, information" (Gergen, 1991, p. 214) that are mediated. Members of a symbolic community typically do not know each other, but yet experience themselves a part of a group of like minded people. Members of electronic churches such as the 700 Club are one example of such a community, albeit one that is rather cohesive. What self-help book readers connect with may be more or less cohesive than symbolic communities such as the 700 Club. For example, those who read self-help literature on codependency may actually feel they are part of a reasonably clear set of shared meanings. Those who read more widely, which characterized the reading practices of most of my participants, seem to have a more fluid relationship with the community of others surrounding the world of self-help book reading. One of my readers saw herself as a "woman who loves too much"[6] but also distanced herself from that allegiance when she discussed what she perceived as a lack of authorial support in the same book for women's desires to be dependent on men at all. Paradoxically, however, she finds her support in the lives of those women chronicled in the book, whom she views as not simply having pathologies of relating, but also as valuing caring and connection.

Writing about the postmodern self, Gergen emphasizes the relational, fluid nature of self, simply "being" rather than establishing a sense of lineal or narrative coherence. There is a fluidity of identification in the lives of those I interviewed that seems indicative of much of the relational activity that Gergen describes as characterizing our times. Yet this fluidity occurs within the context of wanting to maintain personal coherence, a notion more aligned to Giddens's view of late modernity and his ultimate objection to what he sees as postmodernism's indulgence with fragmentation. The genre of self-help seems to hold out the promise that it is possible to construct a coherent identity, and in some ways it could be argued that the more fragmented our culture becomes, the more individuals seek out books that aim to help readers pull themselves "together." The manifest content of self-help certainly reinforces desires for coherence. These texts are fundamentally *not* postmodern; indeed, they attempt to provide a totalizing narrative. But, in terms of reading practice, it is as if those I interviewed understand something about the fragmentary nature of our culture and in this recognition do not expect any one text to provide a totally synthesizing and complete allegory of experience. Significantly, no one I spoke with reads self-help books in cover-to-cover sequence, and the reading of them in fact seems to result in memories of *book fragments* that readers use therapeutically. Most self-help books are composed of a multitude of very brief stories about people's dilemmas. Few of these stories have endings or descriptions of therapeutic healing. It seems that these structural elements allow for the active development of a narrative that works for readers, not one that is formulaically presented by the author. Thus, readers seem to pick and choose what is meaningful to them, yet at the same time construct narratives of self that, like those told in the books, do not necessarily have endings. Their personal narratives are stories that they are continually "rewriting" as they continue to try to make sense of their lives. Their goal does seem to be a sense of personal coherence, but their activities seem to accept process and fluidity (a degree of incoherence) as a working part of day-to-day life. Though struggling with an incoherent social context, it might be that their conscious quest for personal coherence is something they hold strongly in common with other readers.[7]

IMPLICATIONS FOR INTERPRETIVE RESEARCH

What I have highlighted thus far are elements of fragmentation in contemporary times and how these elements manifest themselves in the world of those reading self-help books. I have emphasized that my readers experience the world in a manner that departs from traditional notions of intersubjectivity, commonality, and cultural coherence. The study of women's use of self-help illuminates a loose community of others who share a common cultural resource and who even establish a sense of common meaning around certain issues. At the same time, they find encouragement and support to reject certain traditional "common" meanings that no longer serve them. Yet, this in no way suggests that self-help book reading is the most important vehicle for connection in these women's lives or that it is even perceived by participants as enormously important. Among those I interviewed their reading played an important role in their lives, but so did other activities such as church going, therapy, the work place, and so forth. A plurality of memberships is available to most contemporary people, and the fact that some of these memberships may be with abstract communities (such as other self-help book readers) affords a sense of freedom from the constraints of a singular community circumscribed by geographic boundaries. Multiple memberships are consonant with core American values of both autonomy and connection. Indeed, as Hewitt (1989) points out, the social condition of our times enables us to make connections while also honoring our desire to be free from monolithic tradition. As communication researchers, our work will be enriched by considering how individuals sustain membership in multiple communities, and how "movement" from one community experience to the next actually occurs and is managed.

Cultural change and complexity are clearly compatible with the social constructionist view that the social world is an ongoing, emergent phenomenon, but this fluidity of experience is not an easy one for researchers to witness or describe. What communication research has generally not addressed, (whether doing traditional social science or interpretive research) is the flow of varied communication experience in the lives of those we study. One reason for the absence of this kind of account is the artificial separation between interpersonal and mediated communication experience in our scholarship, a separation that cuts off the range of communication activity characterizing daily life. In addition, this separation makes it hard to appreciate the cultural conditions shaping interpersonal communication that in part result from the influence of mediated experience. Researchers might for example consider what a day, week, or month of communication experience is like for someone, including both interpersonal and mediated experience. There is also a need to explore aspects of change and discontinuity, rule ignorance, and social confusion in the lives of those we study, and to appreciate how these experiences may connect to living in a world where mediated communication is altering our senses of self and other. In short, as communication researchers we must recognize "the realities of fragmentation in cultural process" (O'Keefe, 1992, p. 129) and direct our attention to both the "discrepant" experience and common experience in the lives of those we study. By doing so, we may describe more fully the phenomenal experience of social actors. Our descriptions may include realms of intersubjective agreement, but may also demonstrate how thin, tenuous, or elusive such agreements are. This approach may help ameliorate what Deetz (1992) has described as a tendency in interpersonal scholarship, to overlook contextual factors. According to Deetz, "it has become increasingly clear that simple interaction descriptions fail to give much guidance in response to contemporary issues" (1992, p. xvii).

Another issue interpretive communication researchers will need to address is the nature of research practice in our changing contemporary world. Interpretive research with participants has traditionally involved face to face interpersonal contact. Implicitly, with this kind of contact, researchers have a chance to experience the respondent in a naturalistic manner. However, no matter how much we hope to engender a naturalistic condition in our discourse with participants, and indeed have made claims to do so (Lindlof & Grodin, 1990), we need to recognize that aspects of our interpersonal involvement with them may represent an opportunity that is not widely available in everyday experience. For example, participants asked me if they could see research results or asked how other people I was interviewing were answering similar questions. They were clearly viewing the research situation as a unique opportunity for them to gather information. Like the authors of their self-help books, I became someone who might be able to provide them with information about the world "out there" that at times seems inaccessible. Like the self-help book authors they admired, I too had access to the stories of many people, and thus, perhaps, a sense of what might be held in common.

To enhance our understanding of the experience of those we study, we need to consider the *degree* of intersubjectivity that may be experienced in the lives of those we work with, as well as the multivarious experiences and resources that are drawn upon to develop some sense of common ground or to provide a release or separation from other areas of what might be called *dysfunctional commonality*. Participants, of course, manage the feat of communication in some manner, but we need to address the extent and ways in which participants see themselves as connected to a larger community or culture, to what extent they feel they achieve satisfying communication or understanding with others, and what role lack of understanding plays in their lives. Increased research foci on race and gender will be one fruitful way to identify experience that is discrepant.

We might also investigate the durability of individuals' notions of shared meaning. Are experiences of shared meaning in their lives experienced as a fleeting moment or to what extent do they seem enduring and stable? In Anthony Cohen's work (1985), for example, commonality within a culture or community may involve a sharing of symbols and behavioral practices, whereas meaning may vary considerably among participants. Members of a culture or community perceive that they are more like one another than like members of other cultures, but are aware of junctures and differences among social actors. This emphasis on shared "content" but variant "meaning" seems to be a useful one, at least allowing for the observation of chinks and discontinuities in our descriptions of culture and communication.

According to Stan Deetz,

> Today we live in a pluralistic society characterized by rapid change . . . such a world cannot rely on simple preexisting consensus of meaning, personal identity, or structures of roles and decision making. These must be constructed through a constant process of negotiation. (1992, p. xiii)

What we need to address in interpretive research in general, and particularly as we apply it to the interpersonal world, are issues of commonality, both its presence and absence. We need to take into account how individuals actually experience self, community, and culture from their point of view, which may include a sense of confusion, exclusion, and even exhilaration over the shifting face of the contemporary world. In other words, we must listen for the way in which participants manage their lives in unsettled times.

NOTES

1. For a detailed description of the self-help study see *The interpreting audience. The therapeutics of self-help book reading.* (Grodin, 1991).

2. I am referring here to a range of research conducted in the broad field of communication.

3. Anne Swidler (1986) uses the term *unsettled lives* to describe experience during times of cultural change.

4. I originally interviewed 11 women in depth, and later expanded the pool to 16 women. I spent approximately 5 hours with each participant.

5. For more discussion of the way in which this separation has shaped human life and sense of self, see Meyrowitz (1985) and Hewitt (1989).

6. This term is drawn from Robin Norwood's best-seller, *Women Who Love Too Much* (1985).

7. Mick Presnell pointed this out to me. He asked if indeed there are some metalevel or ideological levels of coherence operating in the lives of readers regarding the message that women *should* be able to make coherent sense of everyday life.

REFERENCES

Anderson, J. (1987). *Communication research: Issues and research methods*. New York: McGraw-Hill.

Becker, H., & McCall, M. (1990). *Symbolic interaction and cultural studies*. Chicago: University of Chicago Press.

Berger, P. (1974). *The homeless mind*. New York: Vintage Books.

Berger, P., & Luckman, T. (1967). *The social construction of reality*. Garden City, NY: Anchor Books.

Blumer, H. (1969). *Symbolic interactionism*. Engelwood Cliffs, NJ: Prentice-Hall.

Carbaugh, D., & Hastings, S. (1992). A role for communication theory in ethnography and cultural analysis. *Communication Theory, 2,* 156–164.

Cohen, A. (1985). *The symbolic construction of community*. London: Tavistock Publications.

Deetz, S. (Ed.). (1992). *Communication Yearbook 15*. Newbury Park, CA: Sage Publications.

Denzin, N. (1989). *Interpretive interactionism*. Newbury Park, CA: Sage Publications.

DiStefano, C. (1990). Dilemmas of difference: Feminism, modernity, and postmodernism. In L. Nicholson (Ed.), *Feminism/postmodernism* (pp. 63–82). New York: Routledge.

Geertz, C. (1973). *Interpretation of culture*. New York: Basic Books.

Gergen, K. (1991). *The saturated self. Dilemmas of identity in contemporary life*. New York: Basic Books.

Giddens, A. (1991). *Modernity and self-identity: Self and society in the late modern age*. Palo Alto, CA: Stanford University Press.

Gilligan, C. (1982). *In a different voice: Psychological theory and women's development*. Cambridge, MA: Harvard University Press.

Goffman, E. (1959). *The presentation of self in everyday life*. New York: Anchor Books.

Grodin, D. (1991). The interpreting audience: The therapeutics of self-help book reading. *Critical Studies in Mass Communication, 8*(4), 404–420.

Hall, J. (1990). Social interaction, culture and historical studies. In H. Becker & M. McCall (Eds.), *Symbolic interaction and cultural studies* (pp. 23–45). Chicago: University of Chicago Press.

Hewitt, J. (1989). *Dilemmas of the American self*. Philadelphia: Temple University Press.

Hoffman, E. (1989). *Lost in translation*. New York: Penguin.

Hymes, D. (1962). The ethnography of speaking. In T. Gladwin & W. C. Sturtevant (Eds.), *Anthropology and human behavior* (pp. 13–53). Washington, DC: Anthropology Society of Washington.

Lerner, H. (April, 1990). Problems for profit? *Women's Review of Books*, 15.

Lindlof, T., & Grodin, D. (1990). When media use can't be observed: Some problems and tactics of collaborative audience research. *Journal of Communication, 40*(4), 8–28.

Mead, G. (1934). *The social psychology of George Herbert Mead* (A. Strauss, Ed.). Chicago: University of Chicago Press.

Meyrowitz, J. (1985). *No sense of place*. New York: Oxford University Press.

Norwood, R. (1985). *Women who love too much*. New York: Pocket Books.

O'Keefe, B. (1992). Sense and sensitivity. *Journal of Communication, 42*(2), 123–130.

Peale, N. V. (1952). *The power of positive thinking*. New York: Prentice-Hall.

Rabinow, P., & Sullivan, M. (1979). The interpretive turn: Emergence of an approach. In P. Rabinow & M. Sullivan (Eds.), *Interpretive social science: A reader* (pp. 1–24). Berkeley: University of California Press.

Rakow, L. (1992). Some good news–bad news about a culture centered paradigm. In S. Deetz (Ed.), *Communication yearbook 15* (pp. 47–57). Newbury Park, CA: Sage Publications.

Sampson, E. (1989). The deconstruction of self. In K. Gergen & J. Shotter (Eds.), *Texts of identity. Inquiries in social construction* (pp. 1–19). Newbury Park, CA: Sage Publications.

Schilling, K., & Fuehrer, A. (1987). *The politics of women's self-help books*. Unpublished manuscript, Miami University.

Schutz, A. (1967). *The phenomenology of the social world*. (G. Walsh & F. Lehnert, Trans.). Evanston, IL: Northwestern University Press.

Starker, S. (1986). Promises and prescriptions: Self-help books in mental health and medicine. *American Journal of Health Promotion, 1,* 19–24.

Swidler, A. (1986). Culture in action: Symbols and strategies. *American Sociological Review, 51,* 273–286.

Trenholm, S., & Jensen, A. (1988). *Interpersonal communication*. Belmont, CA: Wadsworth Publishing.

Turkle, S. (1978). *Psychoanalytic politics. Freud's French revolution*. New York: Basic Books.

Wood, L. (1988, October 14). Self-help buying trends. *Publishers Weekly,* p. 33.

Wuthnow, R., Hunter, J., Bergesen, A., & Kurzweil, E. (Eds.). (1984). *Cultural Analysis: The work of Peter Berger, Mary Douglas, Michael Foucault and Jurgen Habermas*. Boston: Routledge and Kegan Paul.

9

The Ethics of Feminist Self-Disclosure

BARBARA L. BAKER AND CAROL L. BENTON

NORTH AMERICAN CULTURE increasingly advocates confessional interaction. Individuals are continually exhorted to self-disclose their most intimate secrets, often in public settings. This interest in hearing about, dramatizing, and valorizing self-disclosure may be seen in both popular media and in academic research. Interpersonal communication scholarship frequently suggests that self-disclosure, when done "appropriately," is not only a positive, but also a necessary, relational activity with emotional, social, and intellectual benefits (Alder & Towne, 1978; Phelps & DeWine, 1976; Steele, 1975). Relationships are only as meaningful as the amount of openness, intimacy, and disclosure they contain. For example, interpersonal communication textbooks such as DeVito's *The Interpersonal Communication Book* (1992) stress that the rewards of self-disclosure in developing relational trust and intimacy outweigh the potential dangers (pp. 117–118).

Women in particular are encouraged to self-disclose as part of their "feminine" nature. A societal expectation is that women maintain relational communication and freely reveal themselves to others, to nurture relationships, because women's identity is presumed to be bound up in such relationships. Indeed, many feminists consider this a strength of women's communication (Bernard, 1981; Brownmiller, 1984; Gilligan, 1982; Tannen, 1990). To elaborate, women are taught to be guardians and gatekeepers of their own and other's secrets through a variety of cultural narratives, including self-help books, romance novels, afternoon talk shows, confessionally oriented daytime dramas, and "true-life" exposes, which are primarily targeted to and consumed by women (Modleski, 1982; Radway, 1984; see also Douglas, 1977). Feminism further invites self-disclosure as a way of gaining self-knowledge and making deeper connections to other women by revealing intimate, often taboo experiences in the home (i.e., incest and other family violence). Women's self-identity is constructed in revealing self to others. However, neither interpersonal communication research nor feminist theory focus sufficient attention on the problematic ethical issues surrounding self-disclosure, especially the potential negative consequences to oneself when revealing intimate secrets.

Some of the negative consequences of self-disclosing can be seen in the public discussion of revelations by celebrity incest victims-survivors, such as Oprah Winfrey, former "Miss America" Marilyn Van DerBur, Roseanne Barr Arnold, and La Toya Jackson. These women publicly spoke the unspeakable when they disclosed the trauma of pasts filled with family incest. However, this secret breaking illustrates the tension between empowerment and violation, for whenever these women appeared angry and upset about their disclosures, they were perceived by some as vindictive, exaggerating, and unbelievable. Another example of the negative implications for women self-disclosing, in particular for breaking intimate secrets, occurred in the Thomas-Hill hearings. Hill experienced violating effects for her disclosures about sexual harassment; likewise, other women in similar situations may have also experienced a kind of violation, as the message throughout the trial clearly said, "don't tell the secret" and if you do "no one will believe you, anyway" (Morgan, 1992, p. 1). Self-disclosing can be as much victimizing as empowering. Our discussion is designed to explore the ethical dilemmas and implications of this victimizing/empowering tension, especially for women, in both studying and practicing self-disclosure.

We argue that it is difficult to know how to study and practice self-disclosure and remain ethical. Many of our communication colleagues would agree with us that the concept of self-disclosure is difficult to define and research, even by traditional methods (Bochner, 1984, pp. 601–602). Many scholars further believe that self-disclosure entails intentional, voluntary expression of information about oneself inaccessible by other means, though that definition is debated (Bochner, 1984, p. 602). There have been additional debates on apparent versus genuine self-disclosures (Miller & Steinberg, 1975). There has also been concern as to both positive and negative effects (Bochner, 1984, pp. 608–610). A vast body of research documents these conflicts.[1] These concerns, however, have been cast as either-or dichotomies, reflecting various ideological assumptions of the researcher. This dichotomizing is especially problematic for us as feminist communication scholars. In contrast, we conceive of self-disclosure as a way of constructing oneself and being constructed by others. The concepts of "authenticity," "intentionality," "coherence," and others are part of that construction between self/

other, self/self, and self/society, and they must be examined as situated interpretations rather than fixed traits.

This idea is similar to postmodern concepts, especially the importance of situated experience and the problematic self. Wood (1992) observes that postmodernism "calls attention to the situatedness of all experience and with that, the diversity of both environments and structures of belief and action to which they give rise" (pp. 356–357). Because all knowledge is situated and local, rather than based on universal truths, self-disclosure also may be viewed as situated, localized, personal, and self-defined. "Experience," says Scott (cited in Strine, 1992, p. 395), "is at once always already an interpretation and something that needs to be interpreted. What counts as experience is neither self-evident nor straightforward; it is always contested, and always therefore political." In addition, Strine (1992) observes that the self should not be seen as "an inherently unified, autonomous entity," but rather as "an evolving composite of differing, even contradictory" positions (p. 393). Self-disclosure is a highly politicized activity of self-construction, bound up in expectations for "appropriateness" that are totally dependent on the dominant power structures and the individual's relation to such structures.

Self-disclosure has not previously been treated as political and therefore has not been connected with ethical and moral implications. Following Foucault (1972), we argue that disclosures about and from one's composite self constitute a particular discursive formation created not only by the individual but also by others, sometimes without the individual's awareness. Once expressed, disclosures can operate against one as much as for one, being both reflexive and reflective. As such they participate in the discourse of power. It is a feminist truism that it is impossible to have a language that is not bound up in the language of dominance (Thorne & Henley, 1975; Thorne, Kramarae, & Henley, 1983). Likewise, our stance is that it is impossible to have a disclosure that is not bound up in issues of power and empowerment. It is a both/and phenomenon.

As the authors of this chapter, we are both women who are also researchers and not always sure how to study or how to "ethically" engage in self-disclosing.[2] We both have secrets that we have struggled with, questioning to whom, how, and when to self-disclose. One unresolved concern has been whether, by disclosing, we violate ourselves or will be trespassed upon by others. As feminists, we are not trying to discourage women from telling their secrets, but to be cognizant of the problems and ethical dilemmas that result when disclosing intimate information. As Patai (1991) stresses, there are numerous ethical issues in any feminist scholarship, therefore, we must raise questions about the ethics of our behavior in relation to those on and with whom we do our research. I also take it as a given that most women doing research on women are moved by commitments to women. Such research is *for* women, as the popular formula has it, not merely by or about them. But because "women," gender notwithstanding, are not a monolithic block, ethical questions about our actions and the implications of those actions are especially appropriate. (p. 138)

This chapter spins out the implications of appropriating a feminist stance to self-disclosure. Card (1991) observes that historically feminist ethics reflects "upon existing ethical theory by philosophers within academies, criticizing, modifying, and extending it in light of feminist appreciations of history, rejecting some views, defending others, using one's own experience as a kind of checkpoint" (p. 6). But a different perspective "comes from a politically active experience of building new relationships in the world and engaging in new social practices as an alternative to full participation in sexist society" (p. 6). Such a perspective may serve as the genesis of theorizing about the ethics of self-disclosure, with personal experiences integral, not supplemental.

Our discussion begins as a critique of the way self-disclosure has been traditionally constructed through research and application by interpersonal communication scholars. From this brief review, we continue by advocating a feminist approach to self-disclosure, but not without turning around and assessing several distinct assumptions informing this approach. We do not advocate a feminist approach blindly, nor do we suggest that applying such an approach fully solves issues related to self-disclosure. Our aim is to critique the central tension of empowerment versus violation through several feminist presuppositions exploring both theory about and the application of self-disclosure practices to people. The remainder of this chapter explicates the dialectical tensions created by these assumptions, including public and private spheres, disengaged and enmeshed boundaries, and the researcher and researched relationship.

TRADITIONAL SELF-DISCLOSURE DEFINITIONS AND RESEARCH

After Jourard (1964) introduced the idea of self-disclosure, the study of disclosure has taken its place as one of the predominant research areas within the field of interpersonal communication. Bochner (1984) stresses that, although there have been numerous theoretical and applied studies of the phenomenon of self-disclosure, there has been no consensus about how to define it conceptually or study it empirically (pp. 601–602). It is not uncommon to find *self-disclosure* defined in one instance as a linear event as "any information about himself [*sic*] which Person A communicates verbally to Person B" (Cozby, 1973, p. 73) and in another as simply information communicated about one's self (Cushman & Craig, 1976; Griffin & Patton, 1974). According to some reviewers, studying self-disclosure is complicated not only by the lack of an accepted definition (e.g., Bochner, 1984, p. 601; Chelune, 1979, pp. 2–4; Parks, 1982, pp. 79–83; Pearce & Sharp, 1973, pp. 414–415) but also because disclosure is continually presented as "particularly divorced from larger social structures and expectations" (Parks, 1982, p. 80). The power structures informing disclosure have been virtually ignored by interpersonal communication scholars.

Traditionally, self-disclosure has been examined through both positivist (e.g., Cozby, 1973; McCroskey & Daly, 1987) and humanist (e.g., Jourard, 1968, 1964/1971; Keltner, 1982) perspectives. Although both approaches draw upon different tenets and methodologies, they seemingly share an interest in several traits associated with self-disclosure. Self-disclosure is an activity that is said to be reciprocal (assuming a dyadic effect), grounded in openness (or authenticity or coherent presentation of self or transparency, etc.), and should be engaged in appropriately. Each of these traits is not only value laden but problematic to assume and endorse without reflection. Parks (1982) explicates and critiques how an "ideology of intimacy" reflects these and other embedded assumptions about disclosure woven through current scholarship and textbooks on interpersonal communication. Additionally, both perspectives share a set of masculine-based assumptions about research and application to individuals. For positivist scholarship, the impulse to quantify the experience of self-disclosure leads researchers to violate "subjects" by limiting them to nameless numbers and objects to be added up into generalizations. This way of doing research is grounded in an assumption about the necessity of focusing on universal traits rather than individual experiences. Positivist approaches rely on an assumption of objectivity or neutrality, expressed in a preference for quantitative methods (Wood & Phillips, 1984). Such assumptions have been critiqued by numerous feminists (e.g., Gregg, 1987; Harding, 1986; Keller, 1985; MacKinnon, 1982). This feminist critique argues that objectivity, when "elevated to the status of sole criterion of truth," devalues women's perceptions and experiences, reinforcing dominant hierarchical power structures (Gregg, 1987, p. 9). Those power structures are masculinist, although positivism resists making such a connection (Keller, 1985, p. 75).

In contrast, methods grounded in social humanism or humanistic psychology may seem like a solution to the problem of assumed objectivity because their focus is on the individual. Yet, we argue that such approaches are equally limiting and restrictive because they are based in a belief of communication as a way to recreate community and a positive sense of utopia. Humanist approaches privilege not what is but what ought to be. Not only are ideal "human" behaviors of self-disclosure such as openness, honesty, awareness, and empathy (Parks, 1982, pp. 80–81) still derived from male experiences and perception, but also the ideals themselves are problematic. Within this approach individuals are often encouraged to engage in high self-disclosure, prioritizing feelings at the expense of everything else including individual boundaries of privacy and secrecy. Further, a humanistic approach is equally at risk to subjectifying and exploring those researched, all in the name of understanding and authenticating the "other's" experience. In addition, Patai (1991) asserts that

> the existential or psychological dilemmas of the split between subject and object on which all research depends (even that of the most intense "participant observer") imply that objectification, the utilization of others for one's own purposes (which may or may not coincide with their own ends), and the possibility of exploitation, are built into almost all research projects with living human beings. (p. 139)

In essence, researchers have subjectified their research. Scholars have *subjected* the people they are studying to research and *otherized* them. We argue that self-disclosure is not only a construction, each instance a minefield without a set of rules or ideals, but also a process fraught with danger.

FEMINIST CONSTRUCTION OF SELF

One central belief we hold is that both gender and self-disclosure may be viewed as socially constructed realities. The argument for treating gender as constructed has been made by many feminists (e.g., Alcoff, 1988; De Lauretis, 1986, 1987; Showalter, 1989). We do not see gender as a signifier of some type of essential essence. Instead, gender "is an on-going accomplishment . . . gender does not cause communication practices; gender *is* a communication practice" (Rakow, 1987, p. 80). We also agree with Showalter's (1989) assertion that

> gender is not only a question of *difference*, which assumes that the sexes are separate and equal; but of *power*, since in

looking at the history of gender relations, we find sexual asymmetry, inequality, and male dominance in every known society (p. 4).

Gender operates as "a posit or construct, formalizable in a nonarbitrary way through a matrix of habits, practices, and discourses" (Alcoff, 1988, p. 431). Gender is seen as a political position, with the identity of an individual woman "the product of her own interpretation and reconstruction of her history, as mediated through the cultural discursive context to which she has access" (pp. 433–434). Alcoff's concept of positionality permits a subjectivity, or self-identity, that is neither essentialized nor erased, constructed through both social practices and discourse. This cultural context is informed by personal experiences and perceptions, with disclosures about the self influencing perceptions of one's (gendered) identity.

For many feminists, such disclosures about self are automatically empowering, a counter to the hegemonic positioning of woman as a silent "other." When kept within the private sphere, women's discourse is often devalued, even silenced (Foss & Foss, 1991, p. 14). Speaking out about oneself becomes a way to gain a voice to reconstruct, or reposition, a sense of the female self. In this way, the personal becomes political. Langellier and Hall (1989) point out that such a stance "raises particular ontological questions about what it means to be a woman and to be treated as a woman" (p. 179). Feminism valorizes the need of women to speak aloud, to name themselves. For Morgan (1992),

> it is the surfacing of the depths onto the shore, of the private into the public, of the hidden and despised into the light. It is momentum against inertia. It is the energy of action. It is the earth erupting. It is the people speaking. *It is us.* (p. 1)

Yet self-disclosure is also an act of violence, of deconstructing oneself so as to re-create–co-create oneself. Every time one speaks, there is a potential gain in self-other knowledge, but there is also a potential loss of self. Some secret piece of identity is made public and therefore vulnerable to erasure, dismissal, or reinterpretation. This potential for violence became apparent in a public lecture by poet-author Maya Angelou, when she shared with a large university audience the story how she chose not to speak after a childhood rape.[3] Not telling was one way to gain control over her identity, though intimately this self-silencing became too restrictive. She regained her voice to "render" herself;[4] yet, even as she repeated this story, she became visibly vulnerable.

Although we advocate a feminist approach to self-disclosure, we are concerned with how individual women can unwittingly lose themselves in the struggle to gain a voice. In freeing up the voice, might we violate ourselves? Might we become enmeshed with another? Is telling secrets detrimental? If so, in what ways is it detrimental? Are there times when this detriment is worth it because of something we gain? In addition, we are concerned with the process of researching self-disclosure, using other women's stories. How do we conduct our work as women in a male-dominated society? How do we stay ethical to our subjects and ourselves? Patai (1991) argues that

> even "feminist" research too easily tends to reproduce the very inequalities and hierarchies it seeks to reveal and transform. The researcher departs with the data, and the researched stay behind, no better off than before. The common observations that "they" got something out of it too—the opportunity to tell their stories, the entry into history, the recuperation of their own memories, perhaps the chance to exercise some editorial control over the project or even its products, etc.— even when perfectly accurate, do not challenge the inequalities on which the entire process rests. Neither does a sisterly posture of mutual learning and genuine dialogue. For we continue to function in an overdetermined universe in which our respective roles ensure that *other* people are always the subject of *our* research, almost never the reverse. (p. 149)

Rakow (1987) urges feminists not to forget that

> we are what we study. We bring to our research our own subjectivities, based in large part on our genders. We also bring race, class, and other sensibilities, all part of our socially constructed identity. We need to be aware of how these parts of us act upon our research. (p. 81)

We agree that there are tensions between naming and silence; yet we are concerned about how self-disclosure is both empowering and violating. Ideally, a feminist approach to self-disclosure would work to make the "subject" a coresearcher in constructing disclosing behavior, with the presumed "objective-subjective" split reconceptualized as interdependent modes of knowing (Spitzack & Carter, 1989, p. 34). Such a reconceptualization implies that "the researcher and the researched cannot be separated; they are both enmeshed in the sociocultural world" (p. 35). As Langellier and Hall (1989) argue, we must understand "the researched not as objects to do research *on*, but as participants in a dialogue" (p. 201). Such an approach to self-disclosure is not a panacea to traditional methods, but can yield insights so long as feminists continue to be self-reflexive. Foss and Foss (1989) believe that a strength of a feminist approach is "its grounding in vulnerability and self-questioning," which mitigates against the assumptions of being "right" (p. 80). This tendency in feminist theory toward self-critique further justifies it as a constructive approach for examining self-disclosure, one that seeks to put the focus back on the woman–the person.

SELF-DISCLOSURE AS EMPOWERMENT AND VIOLATION

The ethical dilemmas of feminist research are crystallized in the central, yet largely ignored, experience of self-disclosure as both powerful and violating, spun out in such assumptions as valuing the move from private to public and political; prioritizing methods grounded in women's everyday lives; and working toward reciprocity, intersubjectivity, and the cocreation of a voice for both the researcher and her "subject." Embedded in these assumptions are ethical tensions and implications. The remainder of this chapter explores the dialectical tensions that accompany such assumptions, especially when applied to several narrative dilemmas.

In developing our arguments about the ethical implications of the tension between empowerment and violation, we rely on two essays from *Women's Words: The Feminist Practice or Oral History* (1991), both of which develop a feminist critique of oral history. Judith Stacey's "Can There be a Feminist Ethnography?" and Daphne Patai's "U.S. Academics and Third World Women: Is Ethical Research Possible?" pose serious dilemmas regarding the possibility of engaging in feminist research and the resultant tensions of such an endeavor. Stacey's essay examines the issues of research as both a process and its product. Patai explicates several goals and procedures of feminism as she questions the ethics of feminist research. She warns that "[n]either purity nor safety resides in calling one's research 'feminist' " (p. 150).

Like Stacey and Patai, we are not specifically analyzing discourse; instead we propose some standards for both practicing and researching self-disclosure. We intend to speak not only to researchers, but also to all of us as disclosing individuals, both promoting *and* cautioning self-disclosive behavior. It is essential to explore the tensions that erupt when critiquing both the research and practice of a feminist approach to self-disclosure.

To move from the internal or private to the external or public involves a recalibration of self-identity. Although the current trend in mediated discourse, interpersonal theory, and feminist theory is toward valorizing public display, the revelation of one's inner secrets without thinking about the results, the deconstructing/reconstructing of the self for an external audience, especially when making taboo private disclosures (such as family violence, incest, rape, etc.), has ethical ramifications. Potential disclosers must confront at least three ethical issues, including (1) the decision and motivations informing whether to reveal the information; (2) how to perform and reveal the information; and (3) the potential fallout (personally and professionally) from the revelation. Current feminist thinking in communication has not sufficiently addressed these concerns. And, although interpersonal textbooks do address some of these issues, they avoid the political implications of their assumptions and implicit ideologies.

Decisions and Motivations

The dialectical tension between self-disclosure as both empowerment and violation has rarely been discussed in terms of the questions and issues that motivate individuals to make the decision to self-disclose. In fact, guidelines for "appropriate" self-disclosure seem to revolve around how to avoid burdening the other with the self-disclosure. But what of the burdens to the self? If an individual is pressured into revealing, is the deep discomfort of an intimate disclosure worth the risk? From a feminist perspective, women may feel impelled to make the decision to self-disclose because they have been told they ought to, due to both social expectations of femininity and "feminist policy" that make the personal and private into the political and public.

Self-disclosure can be used as a way to manipulate relationships and as a way an individual might violate the self. There also is an assumption by feminists that it is more violating not to reveal hidden information, with not revealing viewed less as an issue of privacy and more as a kind of lying (Rich,1979). In this context, a liar might be an individual who allows the other person to disclose more than she does, because she may feel safer and less threatened facilitating the other's disclosure. For Rich, this is clearly an act of manipulation. Honesty, then, becomes a feminist strategy. Rich observes that we need "a new ethics; as women, a new morality" to "understand the terrible negative power of the lie in relationships between women" and ask "how do we make it possible for another to break her silence?" (p. 185). A woman who is a liar "lives in fear of losing control" and "cannot even desire a relationship without manipulation, since to be vulnerable to another person means for her the loss of control" (p. 187). The reverse of this issue is not addressed, which is a woman who tells the "truth" and loses control. Self-disclosing does not automatically result in empowering the speaker, infusing the relationship with open honesty and ethical integrity, or facilitating deeper intimacy between participants. There may be occasions when disclosing is a manipulation of the relationship or the participants therein. Although Rich argues against wanting "the kind of power that can be obtained through lying" (p. 190), we remain convinced that power is often obtained by not examining the motivations informing an intimate disclosure.

Finally, some women may feel that they ought to talk about intimate secrets even when they do not want to and feel uncomfortable revealing such information. In general, feminism has not addressed the pressure it puts onto women to self-disclosure intimate concerns. The line of thinking that embraces unfettered self-disclosure as necessary feminist behavior is a dangerous one and ethically problematic. The following narrative dilemma explicates some of the concerns and tensions underpinning the motivations behind the decision to self-disclose.

> NARRATIVE DILEMMA 1   I am currently facilitating a support group for women who were sexually abused and incested. I have been working very hard to show that I am a participant more than a leader. I don't want to be perceived as expert. Everyone in the group is taking an equal stance, but I have an enormous secret that I have been going back and forth on whether to reveal to the group. I feel this secret may be important (to the abuse work) especially to who I am based upon my past; however, I am afraid it is going to slant the discussion and dynamics of the group. Still, if this is a group that deals with incest, you cannot get around the fact that you probably have some issues with sexuality.
>
> The whole dilemma is whether or not I should tell them I am a lesbian. I have gone around and around but cannot seem to make a decision because I am not sure of my motivations. I am interested in how I would tell them and the potential consequences, but am really wondering why I would tell and whether telling is so noble. Am I self-disclosing this for me; in essence saying, this is what a lesbian can look like and it is not such a bad thing (educational mode)? Would I become a lesbian spokesperson and feel an obligation to expose the stereotypes and myths they might have? Would it be a validation of myself? Or is it because my lesbianism is an essential part of myself? Even so, by telling I allow them to reconstruct me into a deviant. I am not sure which is more violating—telling or not telling. I am a participant in the group, active and emotionally available in every area except my sexual orientation. The group is supposed to be dealing with sexuality, yet when all the other women are talking about their husbands (all but one are married), I

don't talk. I have issues with my own intimate relationships, but I either avoid disclosing or monitor the pronouns used to disclose. Am I keeping hidden for me or for them? I do not want anyone to feel that my lesbianism is a result of being incested. Besides, Blume (1990) makes the case that sexual orientation is not an aftereffect of incest.

Also, it seems like there is some sort of woman thing going on. It is almost as though I see the group as my mother. Transference. I want to get understanding, acceptance, or approval from them. That is what my mother has not done. Actually, she has not accepted that I was incested or that I am a lesbian. Maybe I want to tell them only so that I can get the emotional acceptance my mother has withheld. While such transference might be part of the healing process of therapy, a support group is not therapy. My group members do not have the abilities a counselor has in working though traumatic issues. It is unethical to expect them to be my mother?

All of this is about the decision that I have been unable to make because I am unclear about my motivations. Even though there might be consequences to letting them know my sexual orientation, that is less of a concern. Maybe none of them would actually judge me (in a therapeutic situation, because the group bonds, it has a larger reason for being an entity; in the group the women say things they would not tell their husbands). This is not about whether I would be "out" or that one of them would call up somebody and say anything. It is about whether I should tell them and why am I doing this. I am not clear about it.[5]

In examining the preceding narrative, we are confronted with a morass of interpersonal and intrapersonal concerns as well as feminist and woman-centered issues. Most of these concerns are related to why the speaker is unable to make the decision to self-disclose her lesbianism to the women in her incest support group. If one believes that self-disclosure (openness about oneself) is more ethical, it is easy to see how this speaker might feel unethical and deceptive by not openly and honestly revealing her lesbianism. After all, she does know more about her group members than they know about her, which violates expectations of reciprocity. Equally compelling is the fact that such a disclosure could result in more negative than positive benefits. She might actually be rejected, gossiped about, or treated as a deviant.

Much of the speaker's dilemma reveals a confusion regarding the underlying motivations and justifications about disclosing this intimate information. She is not sure of all the issues that inform her desire to reveal her lesbianism. She seems equally uncomfortable allowing the group to validate or reconstruct her sexual identity. Moreover, both incest and lesbianism are taboo subjects, our society's "dirty little secrets." Either decision, whether she discloses or not, results in some type of an alteration of self-identity. The dilemma is particularly problematic because any choice involves a recalibration of identity by the self or others. Does the speaker usurp herself by "telling on herself" while concomitantly beating herself up for not being honest and "telling the truth" of her life experience? The crux of this narrative dilemma may come down to whether the decision to disclose taboo information is an act for or against the speaker. Unfortunately, it is difficult to apprehend any noticeable difference in the locus of the violation for this speaker; it is a both/and situation. Both decisions suggest a reframing of the self. This reframing might be creative and affirming or destructive and violating or both. By not being able to make a decision, by remaining paralyzed, the speaker constructs herself behind the unspoken secret of her sexuality. She is unable to decide whether or not to tell her secret. The speaker needs to take all motivational nuances into account before making a decision for or against disclosure of taboo narratives. Rather than provide artificial solutions to this dilemma, we believe it is more useful to list emergent questions suggested by the narrative that might be regarded by the individual. The following probes reflect relatively standard concerns raised in traditional discussions of self disclosure as well as more politically motivated ethical issues:

1. What are the burdens upon the self if I do or do not self-disclose?
2. Are these burdens for the self worth possible risks?
3. How am I defining burdens?
4. How am I defining risks?
5. Why do I want or not want to tell this information?
6. What associations do I have with keeping or sharing secrets?
7. What do I hope to gain interpersonally or intrapersonally from telling?
8. What am I afraid I might lose interpersonally or intrapersonally from telling?
9. What are my motives and reasons for telling or not telling?
10. What are the possible burdens upon the other if I do or do not self-disclose?
11. Are these burdens for the other worth possible risks?
12. What do I get or lose, emotionally, by keeping myself confused about this self-disclosure?
13. Am I being more ethical when I tell or not tell, or is there any difference?
14. How am I defining *ethical*?

There are no right and wrong to these questions. Rather, they are intended as probes for an individual to enter into dialogue with one's self to examine what, why, and how one may self-disclose. The following discussion on performance and fallout provides additional questions that examine the tensions between self-disclosure as empowerment and violation.

Performance

In describing a performance of self-disclosure behavior we are most interested in examining how a person reveals and enacts information to others, in particular how identity is recalibrated for the benefit of the self or the other. Bauman (1992) observes that performance, as communicative behavior, "is situated, enacted, and rendered meaningful within socially defined situational contexts" (p. 46). The performance of self-disclosure is equally situated in the speaker's experience of being a self relating to others, involving choices, which may not always be apparent to the speaker. Some questions raised include: What is the speaker's relationship to the audience when constructing an intimate self-disclosure? How does a potential discloser enact her text? And, to what extent does the production affect the performance of the disclosure?

When it comes to performing self-disclosure, the central tension is how a woman can stage the disclosure and still be true to her sense of self and her experiences. Trebilcot (1991), in discussing the process of trying to be honest as feminists, wonders if we can break free of patriarchal word choices to "make authentic accounts for ourselves" in our stories to others. She asks,

> [d]o I remember all that happened or is some of it too painful? Am I trying to prove that I made a choice in order to be freer when in fact I was forced? Am I giving false reasons for what I did choose in order to appear more acceptable to myself or to others? Am I omitting parts of my story because I am embarrassed? And so on. (p. 48)

Trebilcot's questions point to the recognition that our stories can be performed in such a way as to create distance between persons, rather than create or enhance interpersonal bonds. It may be possible to violate the relational boundary as well as an individual's own boundaries through the performance of intimate experiences. Further, although the "inauthentic" presentation of self is usually deplored as deceptive, as wearing a mask, it may very well be that what people believe to be "authentic" self-disclosure is just another way to keep hidden, a way of conjuring up our feelings about our experiences so as to keep in control. The following narrative dilemma illustrates some of these tensions.

NARRATIVE DILEMMA 2   I saw this call for personal stories about sexual harassment in the university, to serve as the data for a potential article, and I immediately felt I had to respond about my experiences, though the prospect seemed scary to me. Very few people had ever heard about any of my experiences, though I'd been revealing more since Anita Hill went public. I felt an obligation to be part of the study, though I also worried about both my motives and the possible negative effects of such a disclosure. I let other matters take priority as a way of handling the dilemma, until I received a flyer in the mail making a second request for the stories. I then committed myself to writing up my stories.

One problem was that I had very little time, approximately one weekend, to construct these stories, since I received the flyer after the official deadline. I was told to fax my stories to one of the persons involved in collecting them. The idea of faxing the material to unknown recipients at the other end, without even being able to place the stories in an envelope marked "confidential," created additional anxieties. I finally resolved part of it by using a cover letter, but, as I watched the pages feed into the fax machine, I felt uneasy. Certainly the recipient of my fax will know I was a victim/survivor of sexual abuse, and there was the possibility that a lot more could figure it out. Nor did I want to wind up as some type of spokesperson for sexual harassment. I was less worried about the potential fallout, though, than I was in trying to decide how to expose myself, how to reveal my experiences and stay true to them.

I struggled with several issues surrounding the basic construction of my stories. How would I write them up? What words and phrases would I choose? I was confronted with the need to be fairly explicit versus the desire to remained anonymous. Such anonymity could be violating to, yet also protective of, my experience. In addition, I was faced with the reality that although anonymity might protect me, the recipients of the stories would still construct an image of who I was, reconstructing me in ways beyond my control, then conveying that reconstruction to others. Should I pretend that the stories were not mine—that I was relating the experiences of others? Hiding my identity in that way could be a type of lying. I also faced the decision of naming persons and places, wrestling with the appropriateness of such naming, since several of the men involved no longer worked in a university setting. I wondered about framing these stories for the researchers, a group who included people I know as acquaintances, and those I don't know. I questioned how the stories were to be used in the final article—Would I want people to be able to figure out that I was the source? Would I write them so that the harassers could recognize themselves? That could create problems, especially since a lot of the research on sexual harassment suggests that offenders do not perceive themselves as such. Yet, would it be truly authentic to delete their names?

I had to decide how to portray myself—as a victim, or as a survivor. The label, *victim*, has a lot of negative connotations, yet that is how I felt when I realized I'd been sexually abused, and I felt like it would be a self-betrayal not to recognize this and somehow convey it in the stories. I was unclear on how to do that. I have a lot of self-blame and shame surrounding these experiences, and I'm not sure how to tell them truthfully, since I went through a lot of denial about each one, and then a lot of anger, which has lead to current difficulties in trusting male colleagues. I didn't want to write the stories in any way that seemed self-serving, as some type of catharsis (though I am not sure if catharsis is a bad thing, or that I could avoid it); yet, I wasn't clear how to circumvent that problem.

Complicating the matter was the three-page limit. I could not give very much detail in so few pages. While some incidents were limited to verbal harassment and inappropriate flirting, at least four of them involved blatant sexual coercion and assault. I struggled with how much I should include, whether to limit it to the most violating story, though that would be the most painful to discuss, or to share all four, or even to include some of the other, more minor, experiences. Would such detail trivialize my experiences in a way I hadn't intended? Perhaps the sheer volume of including all stories carried more weight, since one of the goals of the researchers was to document the extent of such harassment in academe.[6]

A number of important issues are in this narrative. Although certainly concerned with both her motivation and the possible negative consequences of disclosing her experiences with sexual harassment, the primary dilemma for the speaker revolves around the need to be true to her experience in an contrived circumstance. Throughout this narrative, the speaker struggles with the task of creating and performing an accurate account of herself and her experiences so that the researchers can construct a reasonably valid picture of her to use in their study. Yet the problem remains that, in doing so, she ultimately violates herself or permits others to do so. No matter how she chooses to present her information, as hers or someone else's, openly or anonymously, she faces the same possibilities that her self-image will be altered (by herself and others), and the reality of her experiences will be distorted, possibly to the extent of underplaying their importance to her sense of self.

Because the stories are part of a written text, designed primarily for anonymous analysis (to be then reported as part of the data in a study), she is able to be somewhat freer in the way she frames her disclosures. The fact that the narratives will be used as part of a group of stories provides safety for the speaker, a way to ensure privacy and maintain boundaries. The speaker wonders if she should recount her experiences as occurring to some other woman. Such a strategy could further preserve her self-integrity and privacy; yet, it could conversely sever her connection with her own experience, creating a new type of denial, a distancing not only from the recipients, but also from herself. By hiding the truth, she could be trespassing on her own identity as much as any outsider. Further, as a type of lying, such a strategy might demonstrate a lack of trust in the researchers.

To claim the stories as her own, but to remain anonymous, both about who she is and who the perpetrators are, may not be a better solution, as it is more exposed, less private, without being completely truthful. Yet if she reveals herself and names the men who abused her, she runs the risk of becoming known as a "victim," which is often socially constructed as a very powerless position, a type of loser (Rabinowitz, 1990, pp. 107–108). Her hesitation to be known as a victim illustrates how problematic it is to be labeled by ourselves and others, since such labeling alters our ideas about ourselves, deconstructing and reconstructing identity. An additional trespass might occur in the use of the stories, for the researchers will, in essence, "poach" from each narrative, reframing them so as to create their study. No matter how careful, the researchers will invariably encroach upon the speaker's self-boundaries, combining her stories with those of others. The speaker must take all these issues into account in the performance of her intimate revelations.

Again, rather than provide artificial solutions to this dilemma, we have listed possible questions derived from, or implied by, the narrative, which individuals might use in considering how to perform self-disclosure:

1. How do I name myself and my experience?
2. How is the self-disclosure crafted? What words do I choose?

3. How should the self-disclosure be staged? What nonverbal behaviors do I choose?
4. Does the self-disclosure conceal as much as reveal?
5. How much feeling should I show in my performance?
6. How can I keep my boundaries when revealing secrets?
7. How is the self-disclosure different with different "audiences"—strangers versus friends, large versus small, and so on?
8. How is the self-disclosure different in different settings—public versus private, written versus oral, and so on?
9. Can I become trapped in a particular setting or in the role of spokesperson?
10. Will I become too exposed through telling my story?
11. How can I provide safeguards from overexposing myself?
12. How can I provide safeguards from overburdening others?
13. What conditions might make it appropriate to frame my story as someone else's or as hypothetical?

Once more, there are no right or wrong answers; the questions act as probes to aid the person in the presentation of her self-disclosures. The final section on fallout continues to explore the tensions between empowerment and violation in revealing ourselves to others.

Fallout

The fallout from self-disclosures may include the effects on oneself, both personally and professionally, and on others. More than either of the previous two categories, interpersonal practitioners have concerned themselves with the implications and consequences of self-disclosing. The following briefly touches on some issues cogent to understanding potential fallout with taboo revelations. Such issues are dramatized and foregrounded by several examples of public disclosures of sexual abuse—taboo secrets, such as the story of Anita Hill. Initially Hill was reluctant to reveal her secret and hoped to keep it within the Senate Judiciary Committee. After the story was leaked to the press, however, she came forward to explicitly testify that Judge Clarence Thomas had sexually harassed her. For her public disclosures, Hill was denigrated, demonized, disbelieved, and generally violated, not just by the Senate, but also by many in the media and the nation. In writing about this case and others, Morgan (1992) observes how women who speak out about sexual abuse are often accused of "setting up" the man:

> if she has a pristine history, she is a prude; if the accused is less powerful than her, she is classist; if he is richer, she is a gold digger; if she is a woman of color accusing a white man, she is crazy; if she is a white woman accusing a man of color,

she is a racist; if she and the accused are both persons of color, she is a traitor to her race; if she and the accused are both white, she provoked him; if he is powerful, she is an opportunist, or a pawn of his enemies. (p. 1)

Trebilcot (1991) observes that

even if I am able to relate a story fully and without self-deception, there may be good reasons for not doing so. What if my mother reads this? My partner? My friends? The people I work with? My employer? Sometimes concern about the reactions of others is exaggerated: . . . in other cases, though, there is danger in honesty. (p. 48)

This danger is magnified in situations where taboo secrets, such as sexual abuse, are revealed. Hill (1992) herself notes that such abuse "is treated like a woman's 'dirty secret'," and that telling about it often leads to detrimental results, such as job loss and emotional devastation (p. 32). Yet Hill also says that the response to her testimony "has been at once heartwarming and heartwrenching" (p. 32). She has discovered that she is not alone.

Potential fallout need not be externally imposed, it can come from one's internal reactions. One example of such reactions came from the speaker of Narrative Dilemma 2 after her story had been anonymously published ("Our Stories," 1992) as a part of a group of other stories on sexual harassment:

I expected to feel some anxiety upon the publication of my story, mostly related to whether or not readers could determine which was mine. I also expected to feel a cathartic effect from having the story out in print—not only would others be able to learn from my story, but also I would be able to put the memory of the harassment behind me. This was not exactly what happened. I was unprepared for the variety of mixed emotions I had when I saw my story. I felt some fear that I'd given too many clues to my identity, but I felt even more uncomfortable that I *had not* identified myself. It was disconcerting to see myself identified with a number, especially in the articles analyzing the stories. Having my narrative in print was not as cathartic as I'd expected; I felt all the shame and guilt all over again, coupled with an intense anger. This was magnified when I read that the stories had been shared with a group of graduate students who had argued about the 'naivete' of the narrators, and whether they shared some of the blame for the harassment (Taylor & Conrad, 1992, p.

407). Once more I felt violated—how could those people know about my level of sophistication or the degree of coercion involved? I feared that others saw me as a pitiable victim, an identity greatly at odds with my self-identity as a successful professional woman. Yet, I also believe that it was important to share my story. I tried to resolve some of the dissonance I felt by reading my story to a women's studies class. My students generally reacted with shock and support, and some were moved to share their own stories with me. I felt a deeper connection with these students and more powerful than I had felt when I had initially seen the stories.[7]

The speaker's reaction to the publication of her secret shows that even when one tries to predict the potential consequences of revealing oneself to others, one cannot know how these consequences will have an impact upon and alter self-identity. In the preceding example, the speaker feels that her self-identification is ruptured, not only by others, but also by herself as she responds to seeing herself cast as "naive" and a "victim". She is surprised by the extent of her shame and anger, and the lack of relief. As Wood (1992) observes, recalling harassment "is typically accompanied by a painful return to a subjective position of dependency and powerlessness" (p. 360). This older identity clashes with the speaker's current construction of identity.

Again, there is no easy resolution to such issues. We believe that the following questions ought to be considered by the individual who is concerned with the consequences of her self-disclosure:

1. How might others use or misuse this disclosure?
2. Can I afford to reveal this disclosure?
3. What do I actually lose personally or professionally by disclosing this information?
4. What do I actually gain personally or professionally by disclosing this information?
5. What are the external consequences during and after the disclosure (in the short and long term)?
6. What are the internal consequences during and after the disclosure is made (both in the short and long term)?
7. Can I accurately predict the fallout?
8. Is this fallout worth it?
9. How will revealing this bring me closer to or drive me apart from others?
10. How will my relationship(s) accommodate this disclosure?

Probes such as these may provide continued assistance for the individual facilitating her intimate self-disclosures. The next section turns from personal situated experience to questions of scholarship, with a brief examination of the ways in which the tension of violation and empowerment shape and strain the relationship between researcher and method.

INTERPRETATIVE APPROACH: THREATS AND OPPORTUNITIES

Wood (1992) argues that interpretative scholarship is not concerned with discovering generalizable abstractions presumably applicable to all people. Instead, such a position recognizes "that validity is variable and contingent on contexts, including mediated and symbolic representations that constitute meanings," thereby exploding views of the self (p. 358). When scholars strive to enact interpretative approaches to the area of interpersonal communication, several unique tensions must be addressed, including how and why participants become co-researchers and the implications for researcher and the researched. Feminist research, although advocating more equality between researcher and researched, has not fully discussed the impact of the research on either. Yet we, as authors, also are particularly sensitive to the potential problems posed by scholarship in which the researchers use themselves as primary sources of data. The following addresses some of the threats posed and opportunities available when engaging in an interpretative approach to self-disclosure.

The scholarly voice we privilege here is that of neither Barbara nor Carol but a hybrid of both. We are coauthors constructing a third voice to foreground our stance as co-researchers. This coauthor, co-researcher position is different from traditional academic guidelines that restrict the use of the (subjective) self as data. An interpretative approach accommodates our roles as both researcher and researched and facilitates the dialogue between us. Our numerous dialogues explored feelings and discomfort about the process and product of our inquiry, an inquiry critiquing women's disclosure of taboo topics.

The use of ourselves as text and the struggle of doing self-disclosure on each other and our implied audience is integral to our approach. Our subjective experiences are used to construct a self-identity not mired in the expectations of others. Although we have anchored our method to our experiences, we are interested in the implications of our scholarly breaking of secrets, particularly how using ourselves as primary sources affects the production of scholarship. We cannot avoid a critique of our own choice to privilege anonymous secret breaking. By presenting our own narrative dilemmas we have tilted the imaginary scale in favor of engaging in intimate revelations. Perhaps there is a slant in our whole approach toward valorizing self-disclosure. There is a hierarchy of secrets, is there also a hierarchy of self-disclosure?

Our readers may note that we do not indicate who authored the dilemmas, whether ourselves, different persons, one or both of us. We avoid labeling in favor of asking questions, foregrounding decisions, performance, and fallout. It matters to us that we choose these intimate secrets as illustrative of breaking the hierarchy of secrets, both publicly, but also anonymously. The writing of this chapter has entailed enormous risks of how and what to tell to each other, how the narratives would be presented, and how we as academics might be reconstructed by our colleagues. The actual speaker of each narrative is less crucial in some respects than the subject addressed because the ethical issues raised are important for scholars and practitioners of self-disclosure. This strategy keeps topics highlighted while also protecting the speaker. Still, we rely upon a self-reflexive way of engaging in and talking about self-disclosure, about researching and practicing disclosive relationships. We trade off extensive public presentation of the self in favor of analyzing the manner in which taboo experiences are articulated.

As we review and assess the present perspective to self-disclosure we carefully interrogate whether we are usurping ourselves or giving ourselves voice. The critique continues by struggling with concerns for theory, research, and practice not routinely raised by either feminists or interpersonal communication scholars. Questions raised by this approach include

1. How and why will we do this research?
2. Can we keep from privileging ourselves as researchers?
3. How do we empower ourselves as subjects?
4. How do we violate ourselves, either as subjects or researchers? Is this violation worth it?
5. How can we use self-disclosure to co-create texts of our self identity?
6. How do we know that our choices result in ethical, morally responsible scholarship?

We continue to ask these and other questions, knowing there will never be smooth, clear-cut answers. Just because we rarely have the answers does not mean we should neglect asking the questions. The struggle, this self-disclosive dance, is imperative.

SUMMARY

How can our feminist research and practice in self-disclosure be made more ethical? How can we keep from "otherizing" not only the women we study, if they are different from us, but also ourselves as we self-disclose to others? Maybe it is impossible to be completely ethical, to not "otherize," but we must start confronting the implications of our communication behavior and our scholarship. Foss and Foss, in *Women Speak: The Eloquence of Women's Lives* (1991), suggest one way to do so. They urge that feminists collaborate, arguing that

> [t]o focus on one individual as the creator of a text often is inaccurate in that it ignores the contributions of those around the communicator to its creation. More accurate, we believe, in women's lives, is a view of "author-ity" [*sic*] as process of collaboration that emerges in interactions with others (p. 112).

As just detailed, we have grappled with the collaborative process of co-authoring and co-researching through the creation of this text.

In the end, we have few real answers to the complex dilemmas created by self-disclosure of intimate narratives, feminist approaches to self-disclosure, or collaboration. Ultimately, we want the questions to be asked, struggled with, and temporarily managed. Humans may be most ethical when they join in the dialogue and wrestle with their deepest fears, beliefs, and values.

NOTES

1. The research on self-disclosure has been extensive. Rather than repeat it, we refer the reader to the detailed reviews in A. P. Bochner (1984) and M. R. Parks (1982).

2. This chapter was created in an unusual manner. At first we were concerned with making both voices heard, not stepping on each other's boundaries, and examining how we were constructing the writing of this chapter. During February and March 1992 we engaged in a series of discussions that were audiotaped. These tapes were transcribed, without identifying who said what, and used as the rough draft of this chapter. We both felt pleased with the results of our joint effort. We create very similarly, though describe differently in written language. One of us is adept at elaboration whereas the other excels at summarizing. We constructed a third "person" who is the one writing this. This conceit took away some of the tension, if not the responsibility, in collaborating, meshing our voices together. The actual creation of the chapter, then, became both narrative and performative. We grappled with performance issues surrounding the creation of this study, especially in disclosing ourselves to each other within the confines of a collaborative academic relationship.

3. Maya Angelou lecture, Central Missouri State University, November 21, 1991.

4. Angelou's use of the word *render*, and her discussion about that use, reflects her own awareness of how speaking out could be an act of violence. She repeated over and over how the verb carried multiple meanings. Although the first definition of *to render* is "to recite," it can also refer to a process of melting down, extracting, and clarifying, or to the act of yielding and surrendering something to another (*Webster's third new international dictionary of the English language, unabridged* (1961) p. 1992).

5. This narrative was derived from a taped conversation between the authors, March 1992.

6. From taped conversations between the authors, March 1992.

7. From a conversation between the authors, December 1992.

REFERENCES

Alder, R. B., & Towne, N. (1978). *Looking out/looking in* (2nd ed.). New York: Holt, Rinehart and Winston.

Alcoff, L. (1988). Cultural feminism versus post-structuralism: The identity crisis in feminist theory. *Signs: A Journal of Women in Culture and Society, 13*, 405–436.

Bauman, R. (1992). Performance. In R. Bauman (Ed.), *Folklore, cultural performances, and popular entertainments* (pp. 41–49). New York: Oxford University Press.

Bernard, J. (1981). *The female world*. New York: Free Press.

Blume, E. (1990). *Secret survivors: Uncovering incest and its aftereffects in women*. New York: John Wiley.

Bochner, A. (1984). The functions of human communication in intepersonal bonding. In C. Arnold & J. Bowers (Eds.), *Handbook of rhetorical and communication theory* (pp. 544–621). Boston: Allyn and Bacon.

Brownmiller, S. (1984). *Femininity*. New York: Fawcett Columbine.

Card, C. (1991). The feistiness of feminism. In C. Card (Ed.), *Feminist ethics* (pp. 3–31). Lawrence: University Press of Kansas.

Chelune, G. (1979). Measuring openness in interpersonal communication. In G. Chelune (Ed.), *Self-disclosure* (pp. 1–27). San Francisco: Jossey-Bass.

Cozby, P. (1973). Self-disclosure: A literature review. *Psychological Bulletin, 79*, 73–91.

Cushman, D., & Craig, R. (1976). Communication systems: Interpersonal implications. In G. Miller (Ed.), *Explorations in interpersonal communication* (pp. 37–58). Beverly Hills, CA: Sage Publications.

De Lauretis, T. (Ed.). (1986) *Feminist studies/critical studies.* Bloomington: Indiana University Press.

De Lauretis, T. (1987). *Technologies of gender: Essays in theory, film, and fiction.* Bloomington: Indiana University Press.

DeVito, J. (1990). *The interpersonal communication book* (6th ed.). New York: HarperCollins.

Douglas, A. (1977). *The feminization of American culture.* New York: Avon Books.

Foss, K. A., & Foss, S. K. (1989). Incorporating the feminist perspective in communication scholarship: A research commentary. In K. Carter & C. Spitzack (Eds.), *Doing research on women's communication: Perspectives on theory and method* (pp. 65–91). Norwood, NJ: Ablex.

Foss, K. A., & Foss, S. K. (1991). *Women speak: The eloquence of women's lives.* Prospect Heights, IL: Waveland Press.

Foucault, M. (1972). *The archeology of knowledge* (A. M. Sheridan Smith, Trans.). New York: Pantheon Books (original work published 1971).

Gilligan, C. (1982). *In a different voice: Psychological theory and women's development.* Cambridge, MA: Harvard University Press.

Gregg, N. (1987). Reflections on the feminist critique of objectivity. *Journal of Communication Inquiry, 11* (1), 8–18.

Griffin, K., & Patton, B. R. (1974). *Personal communication in human relations.* Columbus, OH: Charles E. Merrill.

Harding, S. (1986). *The science question in feminism.* Ithaca, NY: Cornell University Press.

Hill, A. (1992, January–February). The nature of the beast. *MS.,* 32–33.

Jourard, S. (1964/1971). *The transparent self* (rev. ed.). New York: Van Nostrand Reinhold.

Jourard, S. (1968). *Disclosing man to himself.* New York: Van Norstrand Reinhold.

Keller, E. F. (1985). *Reflections on gender and science.* New Haven, CT: Yale University Press.

Keltner, J. (1982, November). *Speech communication, sensitivity training, experimental learning, or "touchy-feely" revisited.* Paper presented at the meeting of the Speech Communication Association, Louisville, KY.

Langellier, K. M., & Hall, D. L. (1989). Interviewing women: A phenomenological approach to feminist communication research. In K. Carter & C. Spitzack (Eds.), *Doing research on women's communication: Perspectives on theory and method* (pp. 193–200). Norwood, NJ: Ablex.

MacKinnon, C. (1982). Feminism, Marxism, method, and the state: An agenda for theory. In N. O. Keohane, M. A. Rosaldo, & B. C. Gelpi (Eds.), *Feminist theory: A critique of ideology* (pp. 1–30). Chicago: University of Chicago Press.

McCroskey, J. C., & Daly, J. (1987). *Personality and interpersonal communication.* Newbury Park, CA: Sage Publications.

Miller, G. R., & Steinberg, M. (1975). *Between people: A new analysis of interpersonal communication.* Chicago: Science Research Associates.

Modleski, T. (1982). *Loving with a vengeance: Mass-produced fantasies for women.* London: Methune Press.

Morgan, R. (1992, January–February). Editorial: Bearing witness. *MS.,* 1.

"Our stories": Communication professional's narratives of sexual harassment. (1992). *Journal of Applied Communication Research, 20,* 365–390.

Parks, M. (1982). Ideology in interpersonal communication: Off the couch and into the world. In M. Burgoon (Ed.), *Communication yearbook 5* (pp. 79–107). New Brunswick, NJ.: International Communication Association.

Patai, D. (1991). U. S. academics and third world women: Is ethical research possible? In S. B. Gluck & D. Patai (Eds.), *Women's words: The feminist practice of oral history* (pp. 137–154). New York and London: Routledge.

Pearce, W. B., & Sharp, S. M. (1973). Self-disclosing communication. *The Journal of Communication, 23,* 409–425.

Phelps, L., & Dewine, S. (1976). *Interpersonal communication journal.* St. Paul, MN: West Publishing Company.

Rabinowitz, V. C. (1990). Coping with sexual harassment. In M. A. Paludi (Ed.), *Ivory power: Sexual harassment on campus* (pp. 103–118). Albany: State University of New York Press.

Radway, J. (1984). *Reading the romance: Women, patriarchy and popular literature.* Chapel Hill: University of North Carolina Press.

Rakow, L. F. (1987). Looking to the future: Five questions for gender research. *Women's Studies in Communication, 10,* 79–86.

Rich, A. (1979). *On lies, secrets, and silence: Selected prose, 1966–1978.* New York: W. W. Norton.

Showalter, E. (Ed.). (1989). *Speaking of gender.* New York: Routledge.

Spitzack, C., & Carter, K. (1989). Research on women's communication: The politics of theory and method. In K. Carter & C. Spitzack (Eds.), *Doing research on women's communication: Perspectives on theory and method* (pp. 11–39). Norwood, NJ: Ablex.

Stacey, J. (1991). Can there by a feminist ethnography? In S. B. Gluck & D. Patai (Eds.), *Women's words: The faminist practice of oral history* (pp. 111–120). New York and London: Routledge.

Steele, F. (1975). *The open organization.* Reading, MA.: Addison-Wesley.

Strine, M. (1992). Understanding "how things work": Sexual harassment and academic culture. *Journal of Applied Communication Research, 20,* 391–400.

Tannen, D. (1990). *You just don't understand: Women and men in conversation.* New York: Ballantine Books.

Taylor, B., & Conrad, C. (1992). Narratives of sexual harassment: Organization dimensions. *Journal of Applied Communication Research, 20,* 401–418.

Thorne, B., & Henley, N. (Eds.). (1975). *Language and sex: Difference and dominance.* Rowley, MA.: Newbury House.

Thorne, B., Kramarae, C., & Henley, N. (Eds.). (1983). *Language, gender, and society.* Rowley, MA.: Newbury House.

Trebilcot, J. (1991). Ethics of method: Greasing the machine and telling stories. In C. Card (Ed.), *Feminist ethics* (pp. 45–51). Lawrence: University Press of Kansas.

Wood, J. (1992). Telling our stories: Narratives as a basis for theorizing sexual harassment. *Journal of Applied Communication Research, 20,* 349–362.

Wood, J., & Phillips, G. M. (1984). Rethinking research on gender and communication: An introduction to the issues. *Women's Studies in Communication, 7,* 59–60.

10

A Phenomenological Inquiry
into the Relationship
Between Perceived Coolness and
Communication Competence

LEDA M. COOKS AND DAVID DESCUTNER

THE VAST LITERATURE on communication competence has been criticized for, among other problems, its inattention to cultural issues of change and diversity and for its neglect of political issues pertaining to class, race, and power. Finding fault with a scholarly literature by identifying that which it excludes is one legitimate critical approach. Our chapter shares the aim of encouraging scholars to consider cultural and political issues related to communication research, but it takes the different approach of working critically from inside the competence literature to highlight its limitations and promote a broader range of inquiry.

Our study centers on the communicative practice of using *cool* to describe favorably the actions of others during interaction. The original source for our interest in the ascription of "coolness" lay in our observations of the frequency of the practice in daily interaction. We subsequently found that this practice, notwithstanding its regular occurrence, has been overlooked by interpersonal scholars and moreover raises doubts about the adequacy of the standard measurement and resulting understanding of communication competence. As we began to plan our study, we discovered that this ignored practice afforded us the opportunity not only to conduct inquiry from a postmodern framework seldom adopted by interpersonal scholars, but also to use that framework's reconfigured concepts of self and communication.

RATIONALE FOR THE STUDY

The characteristics of the competent communicator have been the focus of an abundance of research. Communication competence has been shown to be an important variable in establishing one's self-esteem (Steffen, Greenwald & Langmeyer, 1979), academic success (Hurt, Scott & McCroskey, 1978), loneliness (Spitzberg & Canary, 1985), and to play a part in successful and satisfying relationships (Duran & Zakahi, 1987), in the classroom (Rubin & Graham, 1988) and among married couples (Gottman & Porterfield, 1981). The wealth of empirical evidence on the subject underscores its importance in academic, social, and occupational contexts (Spitzberg & Hurt, 1987). Underlying this research is the assumption that competent communicators behave in ways perceived to be appropriate and effective. Trenholm and Rose (1981) report, for example, that "in order to act and speak appropriately, individuals must recognize that different situations give rise to different sets of rules; compliance and noncompliance separate those who 'belong' from those who do not 'fit in' " (cited in Spitzberg & Cupach, 1984, p. 101). Effective communication, in turn, has been conceptualized as the instrument achievement of conversational and relational goals in the interaction (Spitzberg & Cupach, 1984). The phenomenon of coolness presents one anomaly for this conventional understanding of competence.

Despite a large number of measures designed to assess both cognitive and behavioral approaches to competence (see, for example, Spitzberg & Hurt, 1987), the ability to communicate in a competent manner is a skill that both defines and defies research in interpersonal communication. Of 132 competence instruments, Spitzberg and Hurt (1987) identified only 5 scales designed specifically to assess behavioral deficits. Of those measures found to be related to interpersonal communication, few attempted to generalize beyond interaction specific to the research context. Relational and communication competence are constructs often used to describe an individual's ability to interact appropriately and effectively within the context of the relationship or interaction. Although appropriate and effective behaviors are no doubt desirable in interaction, research employing the competence construct has tended to view competence as subsuming other desirable or effective communication behaviors. Yet, the competence variable fails to explain or "cover" ascriptions of desirable and effective interaction behaviors such as "cool." The nature of "coolness" seems to transcend the boundaries of appropriate and effective behaviors—perhaps because the competence construct is itself mediated by influential factors that the dominant (research) culture considers important.

The judgment of what constitutes a construct's validity is a judgment about truth and the nature of an empirical reality. Social science research, although empirical in nature, establishes truth claims on the basis of objective knowledge about the nature of a construct. As Lather (1991) notes, the subjective (tacit) knowledge about experience is equally valid in social scientific understandings of human behavior. Subjective understanding in the human sciences is recognized as an attempt to be "*strong* in our orientation to the object of study *in a unique and personal way*—while avoiding the danger of becoming weak, self-indulgent or of getting captivated and carried away by our unreflected preconceptions" (van Manen, 1990, p. 20). Thus, inquiry into the nature of coolness can be seen as an attempt to engage reflectively in a dialogue with the variable-analytic research in the area of interpersonal competence.

In the same vein, inquiry into the "lived experience" of coolness may also be seen as an effort to extend understandings of communication competence through revealing ways in which a priori theory is somehow changed by the logic of the data (i.e., the lived situation in which perceptions of "coolness" occur). Whereas Cronbach and Meehl (1955) observe that *construct validity* must be dealt with in ways that recognize its roots in theory construction, traditional social science research has attempted to isolate and reduce differences or contradictions in theory to error terms. Validity in this instance addresses the building of theory through "ceaseless confrontation with and respect for the experiences of people in their daily lives to guard against theoretical imposition" (Lather, 1991, p. 67). Approaching validity in this manner means trading traditional means of verifying the truth of a construct with an "interactive dialogic logic" (Reason & Rowan, 1981) that enlists techniques such as triangulation and reflexivity (Guba & Lincoln, 1981) by talking through research conclusions with respondents.

Further, although the person perceived to be cool might well be effective, her or his effectiveness may not necessarily be seen as advancing instrumental goals of interaction. Neither would the person perceived to be cool always act appropriately in the manner in which appropriateness is defined previously. "Fitting in" does not seem to be a primary concern of the persons judged to be cool by the participants in our study; in fact, holding strongly to one's sense of self against the pressure to conform appears to be one mark of the cool person. Our participants, for instance, described the cool person as "highly individual," a "risk taker," a "non-conformist" who "does not care what other people think." What this might mean is that, although being perceived as cool is an important and desirable attribute, it does not seem to depend on mainstream (appropriate and effective) behavior in all contexts.

Indeed, the ability to identify with a subculture and still remain competent in the mainstream culture seems to be a chief characteristic of those perceived to be cool. The tension between persons perceived to be cool and the norms of the mainstream culture is less important than how those persons express their stance. The ambivalent, playful, occasionally mocking, and even contradictory manner in which these persons "speak to and against dominant social codes" is, as Pollock and Cox (1991) contend, the "challenge of the postmodern" (p. 175). Furthermore, despite their stance against conformity, cool persons seldom seem to alienate themselves from the mainstream. According to Fox (1987), the peripheral members of a subculture "serve as conduits between central members of a subculture and conventional society" (p. 366). Those members who remain on the margin may be more likely to be perceived as risk takers, even though they remain within the limits of culturally approved behavior. In other words, those persons who can function within the dominant culture and still cross over the boundaries to identify with the subculture seem more likely to be perceived as cool.

CULTURAL AND EPISTEMOLOGICAL FRAMEWORK OF THE STUDY

Given the preceding discussion of dominant culture, subcultures, and the boundaries that seem to divide them, it should not be surprising that cultural issues and concepts figure in our study. Such issues and concepts, which largely define our study's framework, represent a break with the traditional ways of doing interpersonal communication research and of thinking about epistemological matters tied up with such research.

Implicit in most interpersonal communication research, especially that which employs variable analytic methods, is a set of assumptions rooted in what Harvey (1989) calls *modernism*. Research of this sort assumes the possibility of discovering theories with the requisite formal elements that function as "metanarratives." It likewise assumes that the task is to draw fairly strict boundaries to divide realms of inquiry according to specific types of communication; these types are assumed to be composed of mainly consistent traits and actions that can be determined with a reasonable degree of precision. Communication itself is assumed to be a strategic, purposeful activity enacted by design. Taken for granted as well by this research, and specifically the measurement techniques it employs, is a binary logic that assumes a person either is or is not a competent communicator.

Our inquiry proceeds from a different set of assumptions, rooted in what Harvey (1989) and others call *postmodernism*. From the start of our study it was plain that its focus—the ascription of coolness—could not be examined fruitfully from a modernist perspective. The variety of accounts our participants gave of coolness and cool others, many of which contradicted each other and some of which were self-contradictory, made the goals of formal theory building irrelevant. Similarly, our discovery that coolness was understood differently in different contexts and could not be distilled into specific types of actions also called into question the modernist perspective. We also found questionable both the modernist conception of communication as successful only when it is strategic, as well as that conception's variable analytic view of communicative competence as an either-or phenomenon.

Communication scholars have recently begun to discuss the implications that postmodernism holds for their field's research. McGee (1990) avers that "it is time to stop whining about the so-called postmodern condition and to develop realistic strategies to cope with it . . . "(p. 278). One such coping strategy, according to Conquergood (1991), is to integrate the assumptions of a "critical, cultural politics" into the design and execution of communication inquiry. Our study attempts such an integration by assuming with Conquergood (1991) that genres, borders, and categories are indistinct and porous, and that the modernist notion of the unified self deserves to be supplanted by the postmodern notion of the self as "a polysemic site of articulation for multiple identities and voices" (p. 185).

Denzin (1991) supplies a conceptual guide to postmodern communication inquiry, beginning with the proposition that "the postmodern scene is a series of cultural formations which impinge upon, shape, and define contemporary human group life" (p. x). Such formations are evident in "institutional sites" that individuals inescapably encounter in everyday life, including those of education, politics, business, media, and popular culture. Denzin (1991) maintains that "in these sites interacting individuals come in contact with postmodernism, which, like the air we breathe, is everywhere around us" (p. x).

Consequences of this "contact with postmodernism" abound, including the widespread recognition that much of what we experience is "undefinable," and even what we can define is subject to plural and often contradictory interpretations. Another such consequence is the emergence of what Denzin (1991) calls the *postmodern self*, which accepts the inevitability of individual and cultural differences and thereby embodies the plural, contradictory character of postmodern culture. One significant feature of the "postmodern self" is that it is, particularly when engaged in interaction, preoccupied with the "visible" as manifested in surface effects or signs.

Modernist social theory and research, for the reasons specified previously, cannot adequately take account of how communication operates in the postmodern scene. Denzin (1991) points to the "blindness" of modernism when it comes to understanding postmodern culture and its accompanying communicative practices, and he contends that "new ways of inscribing and reading the social must be found" (p. ix). Semiotic phenomenology is one of these "new ways" because it does not rely "on abstract terms divorced from the worlds of lived experience" and also disavows the modernist view that a researcher inhabits "the privileged position of the absolute spectator" (p. xi). Further, semiotic phenomenology shares with postmodern inquiry a commitment to set aside the quest for grand theories in favor of microstudies that intensively explore local circumstances and practices. Finally, Denzin's (1991) claim that researchers working from a postmodern perspective must recognize and address how they are "grafted into every action and situation" (p. xii) they study accords well with Lanigan's (1988) claim that the "phenomenologist is directly concerned to account for the researcher in the activity of doing research" (p. 338).

INTERVIEWING APPROACH AND FORMAT

Interviews can illuminate the experience of interpersonal communication, but they do so in different ways and serve different ends. Traditional interviewing methods are careful to separate the knower from that which is known, and their purpose usually is to extract information from "subjects" (Langellier & Peterson, 1987). A hierarchical relationship is created whereby the interviewer and the interviewees are clearly unequal and norms of reciprocity do not apply. This sort of asymmetrical relationship is fully compatible with the assumptions and procedures of conventional, modernist social science (Denzin, 1989; Patton, 1980).

Although most traditional interviews seek to minimize or reduce the conversation to isolated units of communication for measurement of a fixed and defined concept, the phenomenological interviewer looks for ways to explicate a phenomenon by gathering descriptions of the structures of meaning that make up lived-experience (Langellier & Hall, 1989; Oakley, 1981). The goal of phenomenological interviewing is to promote a nonhierarchical relationship between the researcher and those who participate in the research. In phenomenological interviewing, the interviewer and the interviewees are considered "coresearchers" who are equally committed to gaining a better understanding of lived-experience (Nelson, 1989a). The interactional model for phenomenological interviewing is that of a dialogue. The interview protocol is designed to elicit descriptions of experiences; in our case, this meant the details of everyday life that structure the meanings and values that our coresearchers hold about the practice of ascribing coolness to others.

Patton (1980) and other methodologists (e.g., Langellier & Hall, 1989; Lanigan, 1984; Mies, 1983) have suggested the combined use of individual and group interviews as complementary sources of data for phenomenological studies. The aim of group interviews, as Patton (1980) indicates, is to "get high quality data in a social context where people can consider their own views in the context of the views of others" (p. 335). Langellier and Peterson (1987) amplify Patton's point with their claim that the group interview has the advantage of making "present what is absent in an interview: the social context of meaning" (p. 7). If a nonhierarchical relationship is to be realized in group interviews, then researchers must follow Mies's (1983) recommendation to establish mutuality and reciprocity with the coresearchers. Phenomenological researchers must also heed Langellier and Peterson's (1987) advice to avoid situating themselves outside the group during interviews in the dubious stance of "absolute spectators." Having outlined phenomenological interviewing and made a brief argument for group interviews, we now clarify the format we used in our study.

The individual and group interviews were loosely structured around the coresearchers' experience of observing others in social settings while engaged in dyadic and group interactions. Based on Patton's (1980) guidelines for doing qualitative research, we asked the coresearchers for descriptions of their understanding of coolness and about what enters into their ascriptions of cool to others. Specifically, we asked about their view of what it means to be cool, about the general attributes of coolness, about how and why they perceive another person as cool, about their personal exemplars of coolness, about what has influenced their understanding of coolness (media, race, class), and about how group membership affects their view of coolness. In keeping with the requirements of phenomenological interviewing, we supplied the coresearchers with information about ourselves and volunteered our own thoughts and examples about the topics under discussion. In these ways we tried to establish a dialogue with the coresearchers in which the norms of mutuality and reciprocity would be in effect.

INTERVIEW STAGES

To explore what the ascription of coolness might mean we first identified a mixed population (males, females, Anglo Americans, African Americans, Asian Americans) of varying ages. All of the 75 participants were asked to write a detailed description of a person they perceived to be cool; they were also asked to describe how that cool person would perform during interaction and where they would locate themselves relative to either a subculture or the dominant culture. After identifying several themes in this first stage, we then selected 10 individuals (apart from the first sample) to become coresearchers and interviewed them at length.

The individual interviews proved to be disappointing, as the coresearchers were unwilling to supply the "thicker" kind of descriptions we sought, even though we made a concerted effort to establish a dialogue with them. Coresearchers gave fairly simple answers and were reluctant to elaborate on their answers when asked. Consistent with a postmodern conception of coolness, the coresearchers seemed to be fairly comfortable with not being able to identify the characteristics of cool; yet they claimed knowledge of coolness as a phenomenon. Still, examples were difficult to obtain from the coresearchers, as were richer answers to the more complex questions having to do with cultural influences, race, and class. Varying strategies and protocols were used, but with no discernible change in the coresearchers' responsiveness. At best the individual interviews yielded some clues and insights that allowed us to construct better protocols for the group interviews, which fortunately were much more productive.

Lanigan (1988) claims that "Merleau-Ponty's existential method of phenomenology . . . constitutes a unique semiotic phenomenology when applied to the analysis of conscious experience as manifest in discourse and action" (p. 174). Applying semiotic phenomenology requires accomplishing the three steps of description, reduction, and interpretation. Lanigan (1988) notes that "each step follows upon the other in a dialectic progression from description to reduction to interpretation, and yet each step is part of the others in a systemic completeness of reflective intentionality" (p. 173). The "systemic" character of this method whereby, as Lanigan (1988) argues, "each step is entailed in every other step" (p. 337) is what helps establish the theoretical requirements of validity in phenomenological inquiry.

The step of description began by our listening several times to the interview tapes before transcribing them; we then read them twice before starting any analysis. We were careful not to impose hierarchical ordering on the coresearchers' statements (Nelson, 1989a). We also sought to identify the widest possible number of what Nelson (1989a) calls *thematic topics* and *thematic descriptions* (p. 232). We tried to avoid equating our interview protocol with the thematic topics and thematic descriptions, and we were at least partly successful because they turned out to be distinct. It was plain, as Lanigan (1988) observes, that description, reduction, and interpretation are all involved in the primary step of description. The process of listing practices for describing themes requires a structuring and organization of the coresearcher's ideas. In this manner, the "lived experience" of the group interview cannot be described without first reducing that experience to written form and then privileging some of those forms of expression over others.

The reduction step attempts to extract from the coresearchers' discourse those "words and phrases that function as existential signifiers— that is, as 'revelatory phrases' " (Lanigan, 1988, p. 147). Thematizing the discourse is the principal activity of the reduction step, and its aim is to articulate, by way of reflection, a "pattern of experience" expressed through the essential elements of the phenomenon under investigation. Here and elsewhere we endeavored to meet the semiotic phenomenological obligation to remain situated within the discourse even as we engaged in reflection about it. We listened again to the recorded group interviews as we read through the transcriptions and attempted to grasp the essential themes of coolness that emerged for each group.

Phenomenological interpretation, sometimes called the *hermeneutic step,* involves two moves. First, we critically reviewed the revelatory phrases derived from the reduction step to find the two that ultimately we selected as the "signified in the discourse" (Lanigan, 1988, p. 147). Second, we found a statement in the discourse that effectively rendered explicit the meaning that formerly was only implicit in the discourse. That statement, in ways we later show, is "revelatory of the lived-meaning" embodied in the discourse. Revealing-disclosing meaning in this way is a hermeneutic phase of the methodology of semiotic phenomenology. Moreover, by now it was obvious that the three steps of semiotic phenomenology constitute a hermeneutic circle: the whole, partially identified in the description step, is reduced to its constitutive themes, which are then recombined and reexamined in the interpretation step to reveal a richer understanding of the description. This hermeneutic process occurs within each step as well. With this explication of our method completed, we now turn directly to the task of analyzing the group interviews with the three steps of semiotic phenomenology.

DESCRIBING COOLNESS

Lanigan (1988) urges researchers working on the description step to attend to the connotative level of meaning as revealed in the signs concretely present in coresearchers' discourse that indicate their "awareness of what a phenomenon is" (p. 337). Our coresearchers clearly displayed their awareness of the phenomenal practice of ascribing coolness to others, even though their statements disclose the extent to which their understandings of the practice are complex, differentiated, and even contradictory.

Our coresearchers routinely disagreed on large and small matters pertaining to the practice. For example, speaking of the practice, one coresearcher said that "it's not used too much," only to be immediately challenged by another coresearcher saying that "I think it is used too much." The lack of agreement evident within and across groups turned out to be an advantage because the coresearchers, in arguing for their individual views, ended up providing the kind of rich descriptions without which interpretive inquiry cannot proceed. Our reflection on their statements and the discourse generally led to the emergence of four thematic topics: the difficulty of specifying coolness, the attributes and actions of cool persons, the conditions of coolness, and exemplars of coolness.

Difficulty of Specifying Coolness

Coresearchers' statements illustrate that it was difficult for them to specify either what coolness is or how they decide to ascribe it to others. Some equate coolness with an "image" and others claim "it is a style thing." Some coresearchers stated they judge another to be cool "within the first 30 seconds," but others maintain such a judgment is a "developed opinion" for them. Sometimes coolness is related to attractiveness, but other times the judgment is differentiated: "I can say someone looks cool, but I'm not saying that they are cool." Sometimes those perceived to be cool inspire admiration ("Everyone kind of looks up to them because they are kind of different or special"), and other times they are not perceived as admirable. On this latter point, one coresearcher stated: "I don't necessarily look up to someone who I think is cool. I may find qualities I like about them, but I don't know if I'd really admire them."

That quite different people can be perceived as cool was reported by many of the coresearchers. For example, consider this statement: "All my friends are so different from each other, and each is cool." Many also reinforced the view expressed by one coresearcher, who said that "everybody's different in what they think is cool or not."

Attributes and Actions of Cool Persons

In many of the coresearchers' statements the attributes and actions of persons perceived to be cool figured prominently. Those perceived to be cool were thought to be neither "followers" nor "leaders," neither "whiners" nor "geeks," both "serious" and "witty," "dominant" and "laid back," "conventional" and "rebellious," "traditional" and "progressive." Cool persons are perceived to be "risk takers" who display "poise" and "control," but they also are likely to be "extreme" and "outrageous" (as manifested in "eyelid piercing") and to violate "social rules."

Such actions of cool persons are appealing, as one coresearcher said, because "someone willing to be an asshole deserves respect." Cool others, furthermore, seem singularly able to transgress norms "and get away with it."

A related thematic topic here was the role of context in connection with the actions of the cool person. In dyadic interaction the cool person was described as "compassionate," "sensitive," and a "good listener and communicator." A person perceived to be cool is likely, in dyadic interaction, to "really be interested and to really care," and is always willing to "make time for friends. Always. Above all." Those same cool persons, when viewed in a group or social setting, were perceived to act differently. They maintain "distance" and appear "reserved." They are less likely to conform to situational rules and more likely to present themselves as "unconventional" and even "impersonal." In such settings, the cool person both "stands out and blends in with the group." The "individualistic," nonconforming side of the cool person, then, is more likely to be presented in such settings.

Conditions of Coolness

How others earn the perception of coolness was a topic that surfaced in all the groups. Many comments showed an awareness of how different social classes, ethnic and racial groups, and university organizations have their own conceptions of coolness. One coresearcher spoke of the "hicks" in his town and how their sense of being cool diverges from that of "kids" like himself from a different social class. Another recalled how his rural upbringing made him uncomfortable with urban "culture" and "city people" in particular: "I mean we grew up working on the farm with the cows and horses and crops and everything, and everybody else was from the city and it was a totally different culture. We didn't hang out together, obviously, because we had different ideas of what was cool." Another co-researcher made the more general point implicit in these statements: "There are so many different groups under which each person can be classified, so many different groups of people. And each group has their own ideal of coolness."

Although there was wide recognition that groups have fairly specific understandings of what being cool means for them, the coresearchers also commented on how "crossing over" and between groups often leads to being perceived as cool. Those persons who "can basically go in between" groups—belonging and simultaneously "standing apart" and getting noticed—are likely to be perceived as cool. Those who "can go in both directions" and still maintain "balance" and group affiliation probably will be perceived as cool, as will those "who do things you would like to do but feel you can't because of certain restrictions."

A related thematic topic here was that persons who strive to be perceived as cool are unlikely to have their efforts rewarded. A person who seeks "to portray an image" of being cool or "tries so hard to be cool" probably will not be perceived as she or he wishes. One co-researcher evokes well this idea: "It's funny because the people I look at that think they're cool are the people I look at and think, 'Who are these people?' "

Similarly, someone who "dresses straight out of a magzine" or according to "the media's version of style" also is unlikely to be seen as cool. Coresearchers here mentioned GQ, J. Crew, "Beverly Hills 90210," and certain styles of dress ("preppie") and grooming ("shaved sides") as examples of the kinds of influences a truly cool person rejects. The cool person is not susceptible to "fads" started by the media, and indeed the key to being perceived as cool is "to remain constant over the fads." The coresearchers stated that although "the media have a big influence on what is considered cool," they themselves had resisted such suasion and instead had formed their own sense of coolness.

Exemplars of Coolness

Within and across groups there was a great deal of discussion on the topic of whom the coresearchers see as exemplars of coolness. Sean Connery, Clint Eastwood, David Letterman, Dennis Miller, and Bart Simpson were regularly identified as such exemplars. Distinctions within this group of exemplars were drawn along the lines of who is seen as an authentic cool person and who is seen as a manufactured cool person. Letterman is perceived as "real" because he "says what a lot people think but what a lot people won't say—and that's what's cool." Letterman has the additional coolness credential of "not following traditional television formats" and of openly ridiculing General Electric (the company that owns the network that carries his show). In contrast, Bart Simpson has been "sold" to the "kids" as a cool person, and the coresearchers were not convinced he was anything more than a "fad."

Individual coresearchers called attention to the fact that their own exemplars of coolness were often contradictory choices. One coresearcher named as his exemplars a "football player who's a stud with long, blonde hair and blue eyes" and Harry Connick, Jr. Conceding that these exemplars are "distinctly different people that I think are cool," this coresearcher noted that "even within myself I have different ideas about what *cool* means." He added, however, that he was sure that "inner qualities" had little to do with the exemplars he selected.

Phenomenological Reduction

What these thematic topics represent are the clusters of the coresearchers' expressions (signs) of their connotative understandings of coolness. With the reduction step our task is to find revelatory phrases and patterns of experience within the discourse that "nominate what the discourse is about as conscious experience (Lanigan, 1988, p. 147). Put simply, our aim with this step, following Nelson (1989a), is to transform the coresearchers' descriptions into "more general, concise expressions" (p. 235). Our analysis yielded these expressions: the difference(s) of coolness, the individuality-conformity relations, and the visibility of coolness.

The Difference(s) of Coolness

Coresearchers were aware of the multiple and contradictory ways in which they both understand coolness and ascribe it to others. One coresearcher's observation that "things that are different are cool" qualifies as a revelatory phrase that apprehends the coresearchers' consciousness of both coolness and the ascription of coolness. Indeed, the varying senses of "difference" and "different" run throughout the discourse. For instance, to be perceived as cool a person must be seen as different or distinctive in some manner, which in effect makes the person an "other" unlike the coresearchers themselves. No unifying characteristics or univocal accounts were given of cool persons other than that they were different. A summary of this expression might be that coolness and those perceived as cool are not definable but infinitely describable in their difference.

The Individuality-Conformity Relation

That coolness and cool persons are undefinable is the bridge to our next reduction, which denotes the coresearchers' awareness of the individuality-conformity relation as it pertains to the consciousness of coolness. Speaking of how cool persons transcend conformity, one coresearcher offered an apt revelatory phrase: "Only dead fish go with the flow." With that phrase the coresearcher encapsulates many statements by other coresearchers about how cool persons evade conformity ("going with the flow"), at least in most contexts, and thereby avoid being perceived as "dead fish."

Not only do cool persons escape the social conformity imposed on them by institutions and media, they somehow manage also to escape the penalties that "uncool" others invariably suffer for not conforming. Worth noting here is that the coresearchers report being subject to such penalties when they do not conform, which entitles the inference that the coresearchers do not think of themselves as cool. As one coresearcher admitted: "My idea of cool is that someone who is like that. That's not who I am." Cool persons, then, stand as the "other" to our coresearchers, provoking mystery ("I'm not sure how they get away with it") even as they resist definition.

The Visibility of Coolness

That our coresearchers found it difficult to define coolness and yet could describe cool persons in seemingly endless detail and distinguish between group cool and dyadic cool leads to the third reduction concerning the visibility of coolness. The perception of a person as cool seems seldom to have anything to do with her or his "inner qualities," except as those are displayed after the original perception that she or he is cool. Moreover, the perception of coolness, according to the coresearchers, is not reducible simply to "good looks," "personality," or a "sense of humor." However, coresearchers did claim to be able to identify an "uncool" person solely on the basis of one action or attribute.

Much as people report that they know obscenity when they see it, so too did the coresearchers report knowing coolness when it enters their perceptual field. A revelatory phrase that concisely expresses this intuitive grasp of coolness came from one coresearcher who, in speaking about how she recognizes another person as cool, simply said: "You just know."

Another way of representing this reduction is to say that the ascription of coolness depends on the perception of image as constituted by the surface, material features of the person. Although coolness itself may be irreducible, particularly after an ascription has been made, the materiality of its presence is affirmed throughout the coresearchers' discourse. Likewise affirmed is the fluidity of perceived coolness, as coresearchers made it clear that they are aware that it changes according to class, group membership, and type of setting and interaction. At once material and fluid, perceived coolness as described in the discourse epitomizes a "both-and" phenomenon. Reducible phenomena in theory admit of either-or explication, but perceived coolness cannot be so reduced. Its very capacity to sustain so many different relationships in dialectical tension—group versus dyadic, individuality-conformity, contrasting exemplars—is what obstructs simple, straightforward attempts to account for it.

PHENOMENOLOGICAL INTERPRETATION

In taking the final step of interpretation we were looking for, as Lanigan (1988) recommends, the "sign of self in consciousness as part of the plane of reflection" (p. 174). We specifically were interested in the lived meaning embodied in the coresearchers' consciousness of both coolness and their own practice of ascribing it to others. Toward that end we sought and found a revelatory phrase from the reduction step that we think stands as "the signified in the discourse." We then located a statement in the discourse that made explicit the lived meaning that formerly had been only implicit in the discourse. Finally, we place our interpretation within the framework of postmodernism.

Consciousness of Coolness

The coresearchers did not seem to carry around anything approximating firm or "a priori" definitions of coolness. They were content to identify particular signs of coolness and, having done so, to offer "ad hoc" statements of what coolness means to them as the discussions ranged over a variety of topics. There seemed to be no fixed understanding of what constitutes coolness, only that it varies according to the persons being perceived, the groups to which they belong, and the attributes and actions they exhibit. As one coresearcher observed of the problems his group was encountering in trying to define coolness: "We're going in circles."

The criteria for coolness, in other words, appear to the coresearchers in the act of perceiving a person. Asked retrospectively how they account for their perception that someone is cool, their statements were marked by circular definitions that stressed the visible and changing characteristics of the cool person. The coresearchers seemed to negotiate for themselves what coolness means in the course of observing or interacting with another person, and often their accounts of coolness are multifarious and contradictory because they rely on "ad hoc" grounds.

Their descriptions of their own practice of ascribing coolness to others had the same fluid, mutable character they ascribe to coolness itself. Their acknowledgment of difference and differences, their recognition that it is a highly personal judgment, and their repeated admissions of uncertainty all resemble their accounts of coolness per se. Because the coresearchers reflexively asserted the tautological, contradictory nature of their own definition of coolness, these characteristics seem to be valid "essential features" of the phenomenon under study.

The statement that we claim makes the lived meaning of the coresearchers' experience of both coolness and their practice of ascribing it to others explicit is as follows: "If you're talking about a person's personality maybe it's just one way of grouping a bunch of likeable characteristics about a person under one heading—as cool." Note that the characteristics of the cool person collectively are treated as an aggregate, which means there is no hint of systemic interrelationships or assumptions of coherence. Ascribing coolness is not, as this same coresearcher insisted, an "in-depth" judgment by any means. It seems instead to be a "shorthand" term for a favorable perception of a person based on surface, visible features that often are contradictory and therefore resist distillation and encompassing definitions.

Postmodern Traces and the Postmodern Self

Reading between the lines of the coresearchers' statements, we found traces of the influence of postmodernism and the postmodern self in particular. The modernist notion of a consciousness centered on certain core values and practices that focus motivation to create a determinate life-world bears little relation to what emerges from the discourse. What did emerge is a postmodern consciousness marked by dispersal and fragmentation. Asked to reflect on coolness and their practice of ascribing it, coresearchers offered statements based on no firmly held principles or commitments. If such principles or commitments were mentioned, they were adopted and dropped according to the interactional demands of the scene. Writing of the ephemerality of self-knowledge and truth, Gergen (1991) noted a similar tendency of postmodern consciousness:

> As we absorb multiple voices, we find that each "truth" is relativized by our simultaneous consciousness of compelling alternative. We come to be aware that each truth about ourselves is a construction of the moment, true only for a given time and within certain relationships. (p. 16)

Coresearchers' own reflections pointed to an understanding of coolness with no grounding save for fragmentary characteristics lacking coherence or anything resembling systemic organization. Their accounts of coolness, then, did not refer to any definitive characteristics or an interrelated set of characteristics, but instead were expressed through the postmodern metaphor of dispersal that disavows the modernist sense of a centered, unified consciousness (Harvey, 1989, pp. 43–45). Conquergood (1991) and Lannamann (1992) independently have urged communication scholars both to recognize the ideological underpinnings of the modernist conception of the self and to embrace the postmodern conception of self advanced by Denzin (1991), Gergen (1991), and others.

Another trace of postmodernism was evident in the coresearchers' preference for the "idiolect," or individualized expression-action, as against the master code of normative action. (Connor, 1989, pp. 112–114). Whereas modernist social theory privileges master codes in both its study and explanation of social practices, postmodernism instead privileges individual practice that flouts the master code. Coresearchers intimated their preference for the idiolect in two ways: in their recognition of differences among each other on the question of what coolness is and who is cool, thereby suggesting their own accounts be viewed under the sign of the idiolect; and in their descriptions of cool persons where they make reference to those persons' distinctive, idiosyncratic practices as unconstrained by norms associated with the master code.

A third trace of postmodernism surfaced in the apparent ease with which coresearchers acknowledged the indeterminacy of both coolness and their own understanding of coolness. Modernist social theory assumes that the impulse to reduce uncertainties is strongly felt because humans are uncomfortable with ambiguity. Our coresearchers reflexively remarked on this supposed impulse (e.g., "I realize I should know what coolness is") but downplayed its force by regularly calling attention to how uncertain they were and how ambiguously they were describing coolness and cool others. Postmodernism takes such indeterminacy as a given in contemporary culture, so it should not be surprising that the coresearchers admitted their own uncertainty without seeming to be unduly defensive or concerned.

Postmodernism furthermore disputes the modernist proposition that individual and social types can be found that represent-define classes of persons and groups. The modernist metaphor of "type" is supplanted in postmodernism with the metaphor of "mutant" (Harvey, 1989, pp. 44–46). The "mutant" is a phenomenon difficult to define or classify because it changes continually and is not uniform in its meaning or univocal in its expression. Its hallmarks are not unity but dysfunction, no coherence but juxtaposition. Significant for our study is that coolness seems to be such a "mutant" phenomenon, at least according to how it is described by our coresearchers. By extension, those persons our coresearchers report perceiving as cool also qualify as "mutant" phenomena. Nowhere is the status of cool persons as mutants better seen than in their ability to be perceived as competent communicators in one context even as they are acting at variance with the conventional view of communicative competence.

All these traces of postmodernism lead us to conclude that the modernist conception of self does not fit with our coresearcher's discourse and therefore should be replaced with Denzin's (1991) idea of the postmodern self. Specifically, in the interstices of the coresearchers' discourse are clues of a new kind of self, content to operate solely on the level of the visible and feeling no need to give "depth" accounts of phenomena. This new self is similarly content with indeterminacy, difference, and contradiction. It recognizes itself in its own fragmentary reflection and accepts the inevitability of ambiguity. The postmodern self valorizes equivocation by claiming to understand others very well, but concedes that it understands itself not very well at all. In this same spirit of equivocation, the postmodern self grants the sweeping influence of the media, but represents itself as unswayed by such influence. It makes judgments about matters such as communicative competence in ways that are neither uniform nor consistent. In talking about all these matters, the postmodern self evidences little interest in trans-contextual criteria, preferring instead to rely on localized, context-specific judgments.

IMPLICATIONS AND CONCLUSIONS

Our inquiry demonstrates that the practice of ascribing coolness to others would be difficult to analyze, much less explicate, from a modernist perspective. Support for an overarching theory accounting for the practice is limited; nor is there evidence in the discourse for claiming that the actions of those to whom coolness is ascribed can be typified. The discourse also suggests that persons who by design seek the ascription of coolness are unlikely to succeed through such calculated efforts. Also emerging from the discourse is the discovery that, contrary to the modernist perspective, coolness cannot be measured or understood in binary terms.

What our inquiry does suggest is the utility of examining coolness and the ascription of it from a postmodern perspective. Coolness seems to be a perceived quality best understood in light of what postmodernists (e.g., Fiske, 1989; Geertz, 1983; Nicholson, 1990) call *local inquiry.* Even in such particular circumstances it remains difficult to define *coolness*; in postmodern terms, then, coolness remains indeterminate. Unable to be easily typified, coolness appears to be, again in postmodern terms, a "mutant" phenomenon constituted by conflicting attributes and actions that vary according to context. Coolness represents, in brief, a dispersal of such attributes and actions that resists definition. Coolness seems, at bottom, to have a "both-and" property in which contrasting elements are not reconciled but instead left in tension with one another.

The implications these findings hold for the standard view of communication competence are significant. When describing persons they perceive as cool in dyadic contexts, the coresearchers gave accounts that correspond to accepted aspects of competence: the perceived cool person, when engaged in one-to-one interaction, exhibits exceptional communication skills, including sensitivity, empathy, active listening, and respect for dyadic norms. That same person is perceived to act differently in a social or group interaction, but nevertheless is perceived as highly competent. Such a cool person maintains a considerable distance and reserve and usually is unconcerned with norms or conformity. This ironic distance enacted by the cool person earns respect but not necessarily admiration; it allows the cool person to violate norms without consequence and still be perceived as competent and effective.

Finally, our study ideally adds to the recent conversations among scholars about which directions interpersonal research should take. These conversations originated in what Leeds-Hurwitz (1992) calls an intensive interest across the field in "social approaches to interpersonal communication" (p. 131). Postmodernism and its bearing on culture and communication, questions of identity and expression, the requirements of reflexivity, the moral and practical complexities of studying interaction, and the possibilities of "performance-centered" studies that concentrate on specific and naturally occurring communication phenomena are all topics that both recur in this fieldwide conversation and figure centrally in our project. In particular, our purpose was to encourage interpersonal scholars to broaden their understanding of communication competence and to rethink their views of empirical research and validity. How well we realized our purpose is arguable, but the need to ask such questions and to encourage such rethinking is now well beyond argument.

REFERENCES

Connor, S. (1989). *Postmodern culture.* Cambridge, MA: Basil Blackwell.

Conquergood, D. (1991). Rethinking ethnography: Toward a critical cultural politics. *Communication Monographs, 58,* 178–194.

Cronbach, L., & Meehl, P. (1955). Construct validity in psychological tests. *Psychological Bulletin, 52,* 281–302.

Denzin, N. (1989). *Interpretive interactionism.* Newbury Park, CA: Sage Publications.

Denzin, N. (1991). *Images of postmodern society.* Newbury Park, CA: Sage Publications.

Duran, R. & Zakahi, W. (1987). Communication performance and communication satisfaction: What do we teach our students? *Communication Education, 36,* 13–22.

Fiske, J. (1989). *Understanding popular culture.* Boston: Unwin Hyman Press.

Fox, K. (1987). Real punks and pretenders. *Journal of Contemporary Ethnography, 16,* 344–369.

Geertz, C. (1983). *Local knowledge.* New York: Basic Books.

Gergen, K. J. (1991). *The saturated self.* New York: Basic Books.

Gottman, J., & Porterfield, A. (1981). Communication competence in the nonverbal behavior of married couples. *Journal of Marriage and the Family, 43,* 817–824.

Guba, E., & Lincoln, Y. (1981). *Effective evaluation.* San Francisco: Jossey-Bass.

Harvey, D. (1989). *The condition of postmodernity.* Cambridge, MA: Basil Blackwell.

Hurt, H. T. (1984). Communication competencies for teachers: Avoiding aporia. In R. Bostrom (Ed.), *Competence in communication: A multidisciplinary approach* (pp. 129–150). Beverly Hills, CA: Sage Publications.

Hurt, H. T., Scott, M. D., & McCroskey, J. C. (1978). *Communication in the classroom.* Reading, MA: Addison-Wesley.

Lannamann, J. (1992). Deconstructing the person and changing the subject of interpersonal studies. *Communication Theory, 2*(2), 139–147.

Langellier, K., & Hall, D. (1989). Interviewing women: A phenomenological approach to feminist communication. In K. Carter & C. Spitzack (Eds.), *Doing research on women's communication* (pp. 193–220). Norwood, NJ: Ablex.

Langellier, K., & Peterson, E. (1987). *An alternative to the individual interview in feminist communication research.* Paper presented at the annual convention of the Speech Communication Association, Boston.

Lanigan, R. (1984). *Semiotic phenomenology of rhetoric: Eidetic practice in Henry Grattan's discourse on tolerance.* Washington, DC: Center for Advanced Research in Phenomenology and University Press of America.

Lanigan, R. (1988). *Phenomenology of communication: Merleau-Ponty's thematics in communicology and semiology.* Pittsburgh: Duquesne University Press.

Lather, P. (1991). *Getting smart: Feminist research and pedagogy with/in the postmodern.* New York: Routledge.

Leeds-Huritz, W. (1992). Forum introduction: Social approaches to interpersonal communication. *Communication Theory, 2*(2), 131–138.

van Manen, M. (1990). *Researching lived experience: Human science for an action sensitive pedagogy.* London, Ontario: State University of New York Press.

McGee, M. C. (1990). Text, context and the fragmentation of contemporary culture. *Western Journal of Speech Communication, 54,* 274–289.

Mies, M. (1983). Toward a methodology for feminist research. In G. Bowles & R. Duelli Klein (Eds.), *Theories of women's studies* (pp. 117–139). London: Routledge and Kegan Paul.

Nelson, J. (1989a). Phenomenology as feminist methodology: Explicating interviews. In K. Carter & C. Spitzack (Eds.), *Doing Research on women's communication* (pp. 221–241). Norwood, NJ: Ablex.

Nelson, J. (1989b). Eyes out of your head: On televisual experience. *Critical Studies in Mass Communication, 6,* 387–404.

Nicholson, L. J. (1990). *Feminism/postmodernism.* New York: Routledge.

Oakley, A. (1981). Interviewing women: A contradiction in terms. In J. Roberts (Ed.), *Doing feminist research* (pp. 30–61). London: Routledge and Kegan Paul.

Patton, M. (1980). *Qualitative evaluation methods.* Beverly Hills, CA: Sage Publications.

Pollock, D., & Cox, J. R. (1991). Historicizing "reason": Critical theory, practice, and postmodernity. *Communication Monographs, 58,* 170–179.

Reason, P., & Rowan, J. (1981). Issues of validity in new paradigm research. In P. Reason & J. Rowan (Eds.), *Human inquiry* (pp. 239–252). New York: John Wiley.

Rubin, R., & Graham, E. (1988). Communication correlates of college success: An exploratory investigation. *Communication Education, 37,* 14–27.

Spitzberg, B. (1988). Communication competence: Measures of perceived effectiveness. In C. Tardy (Ed.), *A handbook for the study of human communication* (pp. 67–103). Norwood, NJ: Ablex.

Spitzberg, B., & Canary, D. (1985). Loneliness and the relationally competent communication. *Journal of Social and Personal Relationships, 2,* 387–402.

Spitzberg, B., & Cupach, W. (1984). *Interpersonal communication competence.* Beverly Hills, CA: Sage Publications.

Spitzberg, B., & Hurt, H. (1987). The measurement of interpersonal skills in instructional contexts. *Communication Education, 36,* 28–45.

Steffen, J., Greenwald, D., & Langmeyer, D. (1979). A factor analytic study of social competence in women. *Social Behavior and Personality, 7,* 17–27.

Trenholm, S., & Rose, T. (1981). The compliant communicator: Teacher perceptions of classroom behavior. *Western Journal of Speech Communication, 45,* 13–26.

Index